IMAGES
of America

SMITHTOWN

ISBN 978-0-7385-6453-1

Published by Arcadia Publishing
Charleston, South Carolina

Printed in the United States of America

Library of Congress Control Number: 2008938754

For all general information contact Arcadia Publishing at:
Telephone 843-853-2070
Fax 843-853-0044
E-mail sales@arcadiapublishing.com
For customer service and orders:
Toll-Free 1-888-313-2665

Visit us on the Internet at www.arcadiapublishing.com

Contents

ACKNOWLEDGMENTS

Since the Smithtown Historical Society was founded in 1955, thousands of photographs and documents have been filed away for future generations to study, reflect upon, and gain knowledge from. Hundreds of people have been involved in this ongoing effort, and it is impossible for us to thank each and every one of them, but without their dedication, this book would have been inconceivable. Unless otherwise noted, the photographs are in the collection of the Smithtown Historical Society.

The authors would also like to thank our editor at Arcadia Publishing, Rebekah Collinsworth, for clearing and smoothing the path to a relatively painless publication process. A special thank-you goes to Cathy Ball and Caren Zatyk, the wonder duo of selfless, brilliant, and hardworking librarians for the Richard H. Handley Collection of Long Island Americana at the Smithtown Library, who supplied many fine photographs and a great deal of the research material that forms the foundation of this book. We would also like to thank Lee Corbani, Earl Scott, and Diane Michels Henze for agreeing to lend their pictures for this book.

Noel Gish and Louise Hall provided their expertise and cogent advice, dropping everything to review this manuscript. Along the way, additional help came from Dahlia O'Hara, Elizabeth Jenks, Kris Melvin-Denenberg, Gail Hessel, Carol Shybunko, and Joan Rockwell Gifford. Smithtown's history extends beyond the walls of the society and library and is chatted about over stacks of pancakes at the Country Kitchen, in classrooms at the Smithtown Elementary School, and even in line at the checkout counter of Waldbaums Grocery Store, where some of the photographs in this book are enlarged and mounted on the walls. We are truly grateful to produce this for a community that cares deeply about its history and sees the past as prologue to its future development.

INTRODUCTION

At one of the busiest intersections on Long Island where routes 25A, 25, and 111 meet in Smithtown, one expects to be stuck in traffic for five minutes or more these days. As people stop and start, inching their cars forward, perhaps their eyes wander over the landscape and fix on several early-19th-century buildings that seem out of place amid the asphalt jungle. The tall, stately, white clapboard Smithtown Presbyterian Church, which dates from 1827, sits on one corner of this intersection. Across the street stands the Caleb Smith House, a handsome early Federal structure that dates from 1819. In the very heart of a bustling community, these two historic structures are at once reassuring reminders of preservation and also indicative of just how much Smithtown has changed.

The town of Smithtown, located in the middle of Long Island's north shore in western Suffolk County, is 50 miles east of New York City. Looking beyond its long spans of pavement, strip malls, and modern commercial enterprises, Smithtown is still characterized by a diversity of natural resources. The Nissequogue River, some 30 miles of shoreline along the Long Island Sound, and many woodlands, hills, and dales, are still enjoyed by its residents. Tall oak trees that date from the American Revolution still line the highway just west of Hauppauge's Methodist Church. Indeed, the quality of Smithtown's land and scenic vistas has always made it an attractive place to live.

Its first residents were part of the extensive network of Algonquin groups that lived across the region. Although little is known of the Nesaquakes and the other Native Americans who lived here, there is much evidence that they hunted, fished, and farmed an abundantly rich land along the riverbanks and the Long Island Sound. The arrival of English settlers in the 1650s and 1660s brought deadly disease and outright theft of their land, spelling a tragic downward spiral to this indigenous community. Today many of Smithtown's place names, including Nissequogue, Commack, Hauppauge, Nesconset, and Sherrewogue, are the only reminders of the area's first inhabitants.

The name of Smithtown, however, comes from its founder, Richard Smythe, who left his Yorkshire home at the age of 22 in 1635, bound for the West Indies. Smythe (the surname Smith was used in succeeding generations) eventually migrated to the Massachusetts Bay Colony in 1637 and arrived in Southampton, Long Island, sometime after 1640. Banished from this community for unknown reasons in 1656, Smythe resettled on the north shore of Long Island and was conveyed the first portion of land that eventually encompassed Smithtown in 1663. Over the following 14 years, Smythe secured the boundaries of present-day Smithtown through a series of legal actions.

A far more colorful and mythical tale explains the community's origins through the ride of a pet bull, known as Whisper. In this well-embroidered story, Native Americans granted Smythe the total sum of land he could cover in one day on the sturdy back of Whisper. There are several variations of this yarn that first appeared in early-19th-century writings, and the story is certainly an easier explanation than the complex reality of legal proceedings and the pilfering of Native American land that was the true story of Smithtown's beginnings. Today the legend lives on in Smithtown's official seal, its high school mascot, an annual five-kilometer race known as the Running of the Bulls, and especially the anatomically correct five-ton bronze statue of a bull that sits at the junction of Jericho Turnpike and Route 25A.

Despite the founding myth, leisurely bull rides probably were part of the early life of Smithtown. The town's early growth was relatively slow, and the agrarian area was somewhat isolated from its island neighbors. By the start of the American Revolution in 1776, just 97 families made their homes in Smithtown, with a total population of 716 (this figure includes 161 slaves). The town's population was widely scattered, although close to 30 of the families were clustered in homes at Head of the River and in Smithtown Branch. During the war, Smithtown was firmly behind the patriot cause, with 103 men signing the Articles of Association and only 18 sympathizers of the crown declining to sign. Like the rest of Long Island, Smithtown was occupied territory during the struggle for independence and suffered dearly for its patriotism.

In the years directly following the American Revolution, Smithtown's largest social change came with the gradual end of slavery. Manumission appears to have gained speed after 1788, when Thomas Tredwell, one of Smithtown's largest slave owners, released his 26-year-old slave Charles "in consideration of [his] fidelity and past services." By the time the terrible institution was officially abolished by New York State in 1827, most slave owners in Smithtown had already freed their slaves. While some African Americans remained in the community, engaged as coachmen, stable boys, and domestic servants, the black population of Smithtown continued to plummet throughout the 19th and 20th centuries. Today the black population of Smithtown stands at less than 1 percent.

Formalized schooling arrived at Smithtown with the opening of a one-room schoolhouse that was located on property between the Presbyterian church and Epenetus Smith's tavern. This little school may have been built as early as 1790 to house a private institution, but it became a tax-supported public school in 1816. The school served ages 5 to 16 at Smithtown Branch for the next 50 years and included the poet Walt Whitman among its schoolmasters. The original one-room schoolhouse is still standing on Singer Lane and looks much like it did on its original site.

While the local economy revolved around farming, there was also brisk activity along the Nissequogue River. Commercial trade that began in Head of the River with the construction of a dam in 1721 and the subsequent development of the Philips Mills that churned out cloth, lumber, and flour was greatly expanded in 1798 when another dam was built across the headwaters of the river at Bushy Neck. The new dam backed up a huge body of water and created Stump Pond. The water rushing through the dam's sluices was used to drive yet another gristmill, fulling mill, and sawmill. Even a tannery was established at this new industrial complex known as New Mills.

With so many goods being produced, the mill owners began to search for markets, and this led to a demand for ships. The Nissequogue River provided the avenue to the Long Island Sound, and cargo sloops and schooners began to make regular runs to a rapidly growing New York City, bringing cordwood, lumber, cloth, and agricultural products to the city to be exchanged for factory goods, horse manure, and wood ashes. Along the river, docks and landings were created where vessels could load and unload cargo. Shipbuilding yards turned out ships to be used in the coastal trade. The Nissequogue River became the focal point of commercial activity in Smithtown.

In the years following the Civil War, Smithtown continued to grow with the arrival of the railroad in 1872. Farmers could now rely on the train to ship dairy products, poultry, and market crop vegetables to New York City. Tourists began to arrive in Smithtown, encouraged by the arrival of new stores, boardinghouses, and hotels. At the same time, the railroad sounded the death knell for sloops and schooners involved in the coastal trade—they could not compete with the train's ability to move goods cheaper and faster.

The railroad also transformed Kings Park, first settled as St. Johnland in 1865 and later renamed for the Kings County Mental Asylum that arrived in 1885. Seeking employees, the hospital brought the area's largest influx of Irish and Jewish immigrants to date and provided the impetus for a new Main Street district. Meanwhile, Smithtown Branch was evolving into a bustling town that supported the arrival of a new bank, library, and town hall by 1912. Encouraged by this growth, immigrant newcomers from Europe, including Germans, Austrians, Italians, Greeks, Swedes, Poles, and Russians, found their way to Smithtown Branch. Many Italians settled in San Remo west of the Nissequogue River, while groups from Norway, Sweden, and Denmark came to St. James.

New and old residents alike relied on dramatic transportation improvements. Modernization came to the town through automobiles and new home construction. The stock market crash of 1929 and the Depression that followed it slowed the pace of further development in the 1930s and 1940s. Some improvements went forward anyway, such as the arrival of a brand-new movie theater in Smithtown Branch in 1933 just across from the Bank of Smithtown. To the west of the theater, Glamore Ford opened a new showroom, and the Blue Jay Market opened up a new self-service grocery store complete with cash registers.

After World War II, a flood of newcomers arrived in Smithtown and changes came at a feverish pace. In just 20 years between 1950 and 1970, the population exploded by 400 percent from 20,993 people to 114,657. New housing developments were laid out; shopping centers emerged in the middle of town; new stores, restaurants, and businesses opened up; and today's Smithtown emerged. Today a new generation of immigrants from El Salvador, China, India, and elsewhere is dramatically enriching Smithtown's cultural and demographic landscape.

While many of these changes were a breath of fresh air, there was a downside. With increased development, old landmarks faced the wrecking ball and a new generation of residents was pressed to the task of saving the town's history. The Caleb Smith House, built in 1819, was located on Jericho Turnpike in Commack until 1955. Threatened by development, local residents rescued and moved it nearly five miles to its present site. It "barely escaped the woodpile," according to eyewitnesses but survived to become the firm foundation of the Smithtown Historical Society. Today it is repository to the society's collection of over 9,000 artifacts and archival materials. In 1957, the Smithtown Library opened its Richard H. Handley Collection of Long Island Americana to the public, a treasure trove of books, maps, photographs, and rare documents.

These days, the historical society and the library share more than just a parking lot. They also bond through a firm commitment to preserving tangible traces of the community's history. The photographs and illustrations within this volume are just a small selection of what is available for researchers looking to gain rich, new insights on Smithtown's past and present.

One

Bullish Boundaries

Smithtown's boundaries are the unique product of one man's perseverance and vision; that man was Englishman Richard Smythe. It took Smythe 12 years of protracted struggle with his Huntington neighbors to secure the land, but in the end, he prevailed and staked a claim to 55 square miles of territory that became Smithtown. It indeed was "Smythe's town" during his lifetime. During the course of his life, he ruled over his domain as a father over his children, because many of the people who settled in his town *were* his children, grandchildren, and great-grandchildren. As the family patriarch, he doled out the land to his kin and gave them property to settle and call their own. But the lands he owned were so extensive that it was not until 1736, 44 years after his death, that his grandsons and granddaughters assembled and divided up the lands of Smithtown. There was so much land to settle that the Smiths all tended to remain in the community, and as a result, there are thousands of Smith family descendants living in Smithtown today.

Smythe left Smithtown an incredible legacy. Yet Smythe, the man, the "Bull Rider," remains an elusive historical figure. While certain interesting items are known, such as his involvement with Quakerism, the facts of his birth are not really known, and his parentage, background, and education are only guessed at. It is also unknown why he came to America, when he married, what his wife's maiden name was, or how he managed to obtain one of the largest proprietary land grants in the New York colony. Even his burial site remains a mystery.

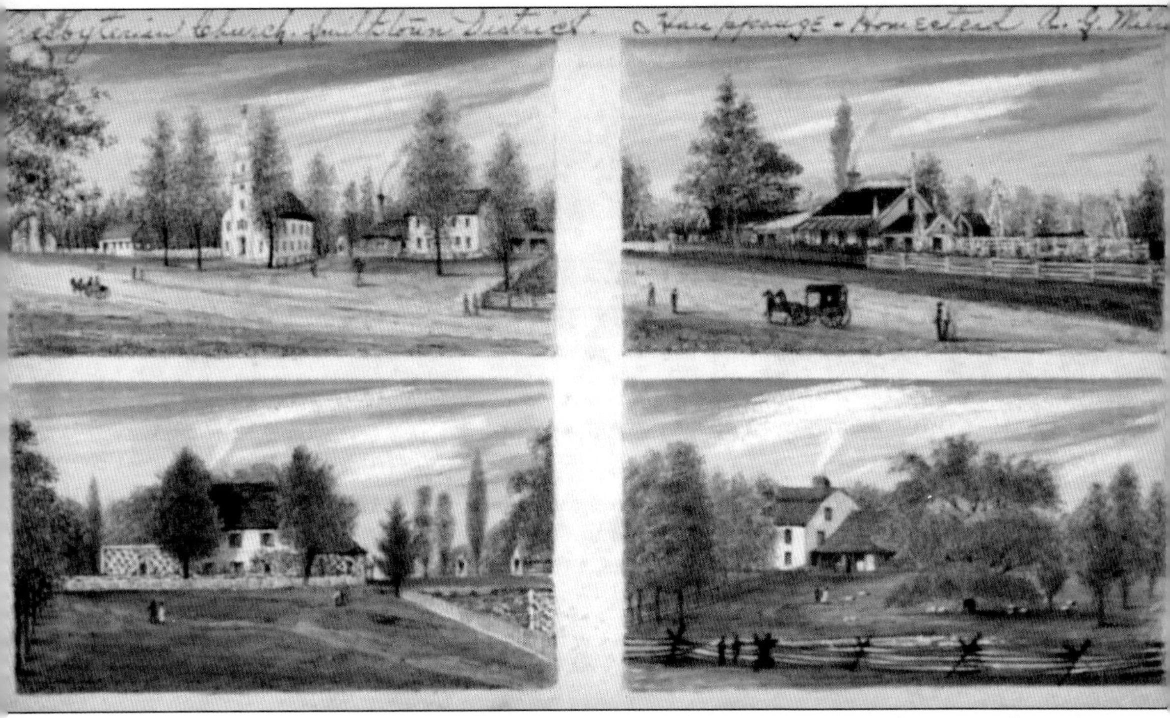

MINIATURE WATERCOLORS OF SMITHTOWN AREA, C. 1850. These scenes by artist Alexander Milne are among the earliest views of the community, characterized at the time by charming rural simplicity. Smithtown in 1850 was a town of just 1,972 people scattered over nearly 55 square miles. Most of the residents at this time descended from families that had been among the area's earliest settlers, including the Smiths, the Mills, the Hallocks, the Blydenburghs, the Arthurs, and the Newtons. The stately Presbyterian church seen in the top left corner became the community's focal point.

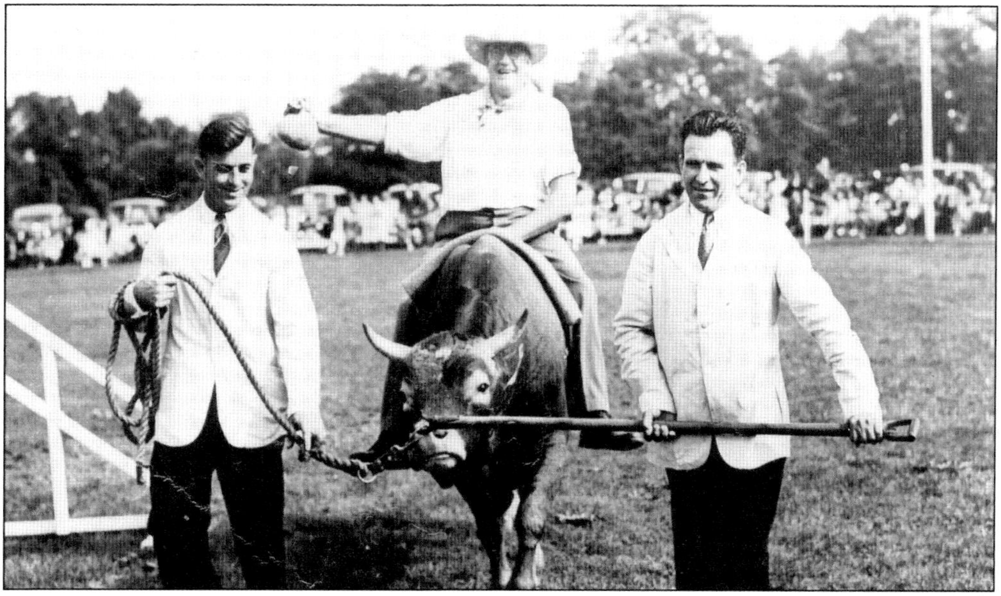

COMMEMORATING RICHARD SMYTHE'S RIDE, C. 1936. Since the early 1800s, the Smiths and their descendants have spread the tale of how Smythe acquired the land that became Smithtown. One version of the legend posits that he arranged a deal with the local Nesaquake Indians to claim all the territory he could cover from sunrise to sunset on the back of a bull. Having chosen the longest day of the year, June 21, and having trained his bull ahead of his ride, Richard Smythe rode around an area that turned out to be 55 square miles in size.

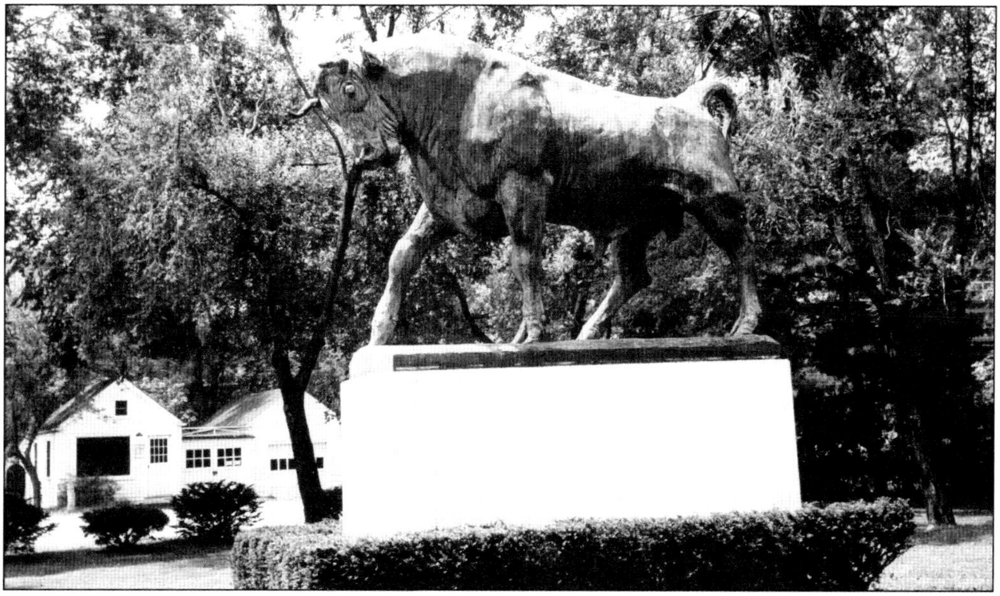

STATUE OF RICHARD SMYTHE'S BULL. Cast in bronze, this huge statue is 9 feet tall, 14 feet long, weighs five tons, and has been in Smithtown since 1941. This bull has done a lot of striding since he was first conceived at the School of Fine Arts in Paris in 1908 by sculptor Charles Cary Rumsey. Designed in France, cast in Brooklyn, put on display in front of the Brooklyn Museum from 1929 to 1932, consigned to a Long Island City warehouse, and finally brought by train to Smithtown in 1941, the bull proudly holds his head up, having finally made it here.

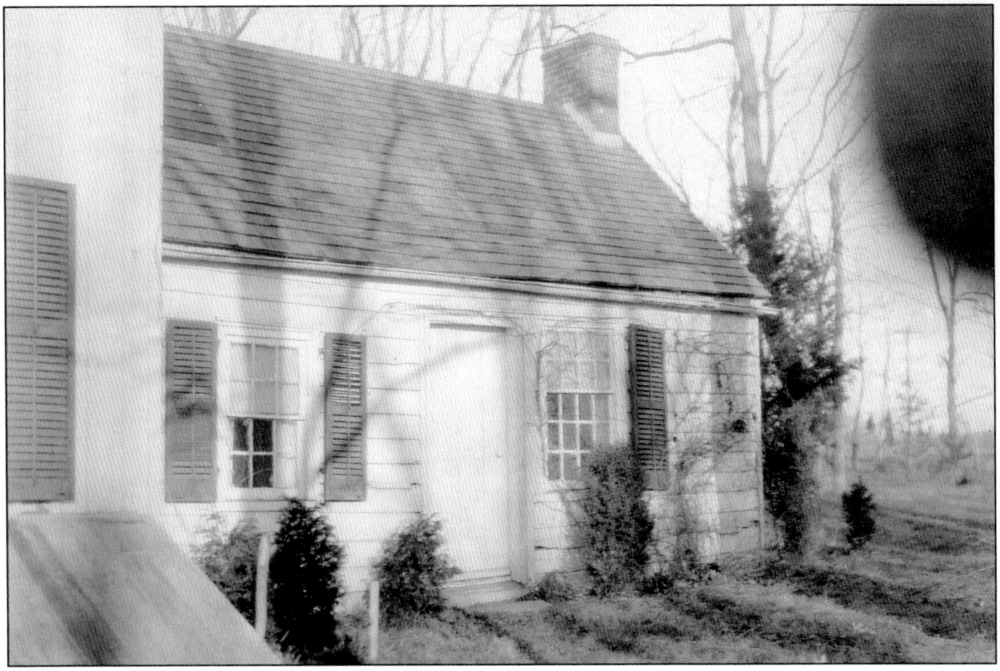

RICHARD SMYTHE'S KITCHEN, C. 1955. Smythe chose a site for his home near the Nissequogue River in an area where a Native American village once existed and where River Road and Moriches Road meet today. The kitchen wing of his structure may still exist as an attachment to Jonathan Smith's former home that once stood on the northeast corner of Moriches Road and Long Beach Road.

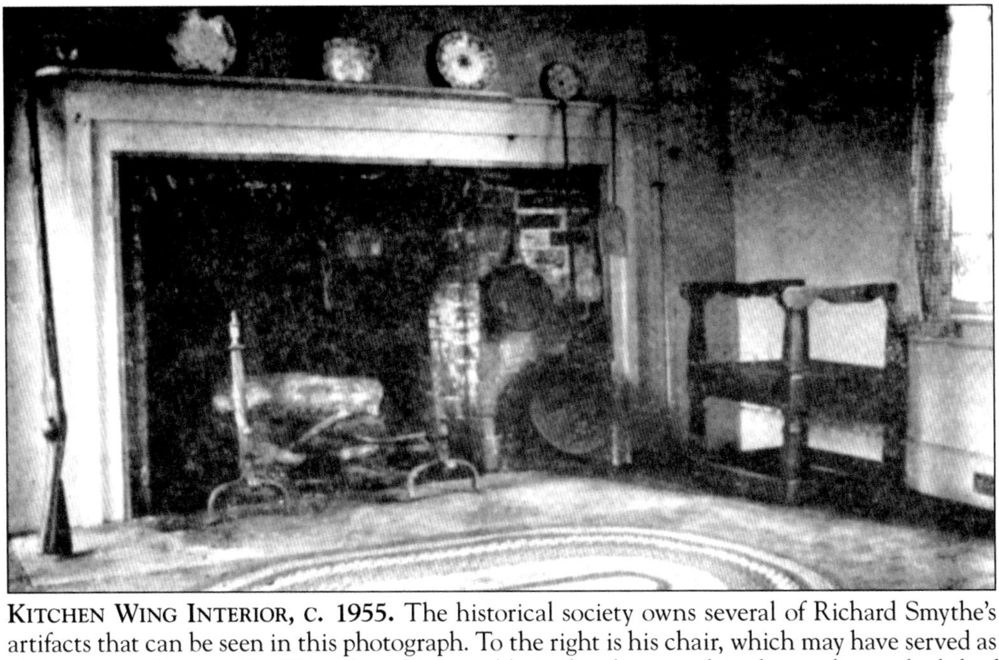

KITCHEN WING INTERIOR, C. 1955. The historical society owns several of Richard Smythe's artifacts that can be seen in this photograph. To the right is his chair, which may have served as the base to a tilt-top table. The other object visible in the photograph is the musket to the left of the fireplace, known as "Old Crib," and said to have belonged to Smythe.

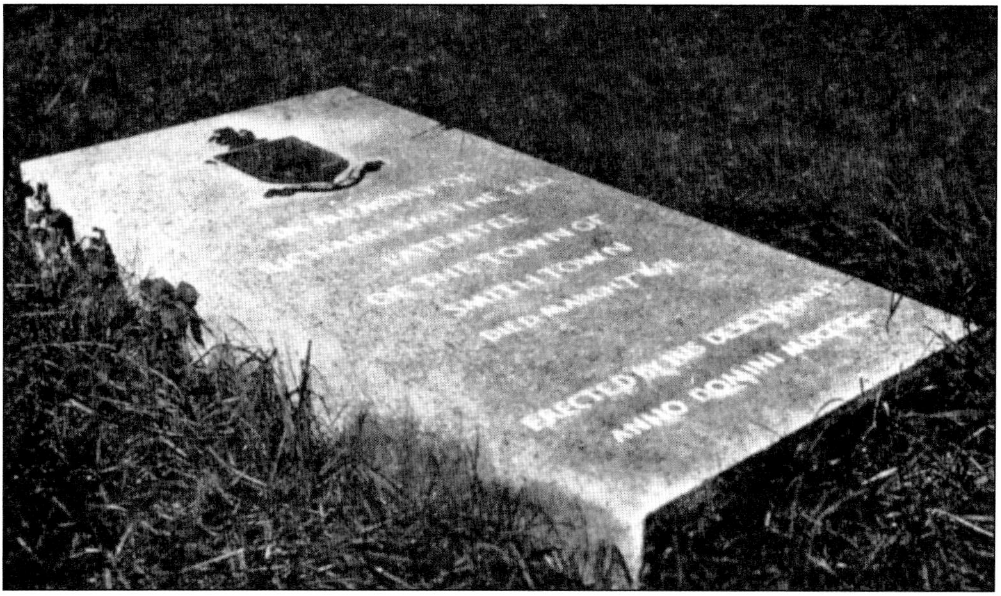

COMMEMORATIVE STONE FOR RICHARD SMYTHE. This stone was placed in the Smith family graveyard by descendants of Smythe at the dawn of the 20th century. The stone bears the crest of Smythe, commemorates his role as "the Patentee of the Town of Smithtown," and states that he died on March 7, 1692. Smythe's age at the time of his death and his actual burial site are unknown.

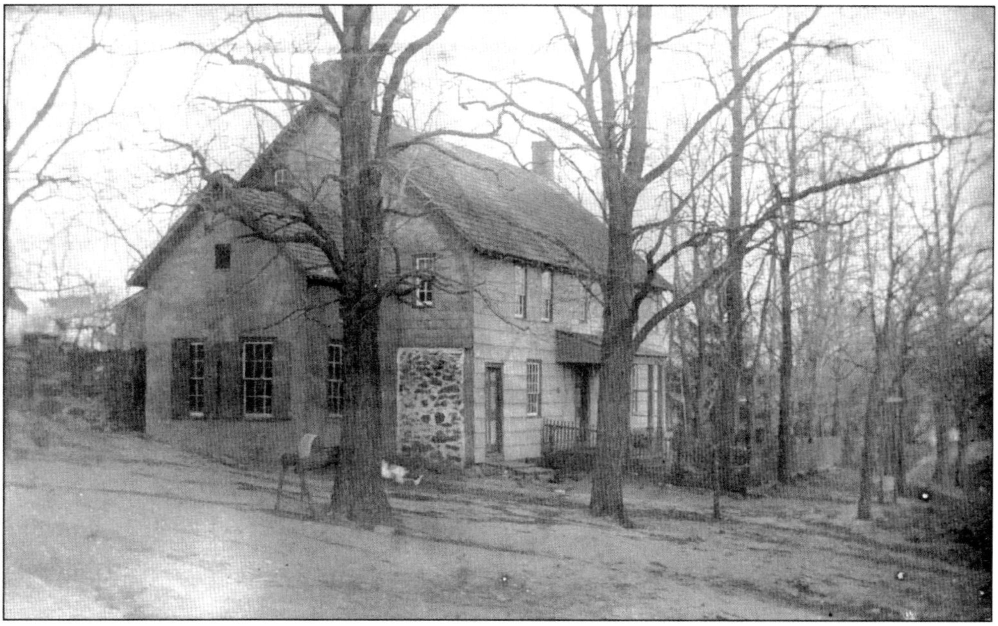

OBADIAH SMITH HOUSE, C. 1880. This is the earliest known photograph of the Obadiah Smith House, a remarkable structure that sits on the west bank of the Nissequogue River off St. Johnland Road in San Remo. Smith, a grandson of Richard Smythe, built it early in the 1700s. The house was carefully preserved by the Smithtown Historical Society in the 1960s and 1970s.

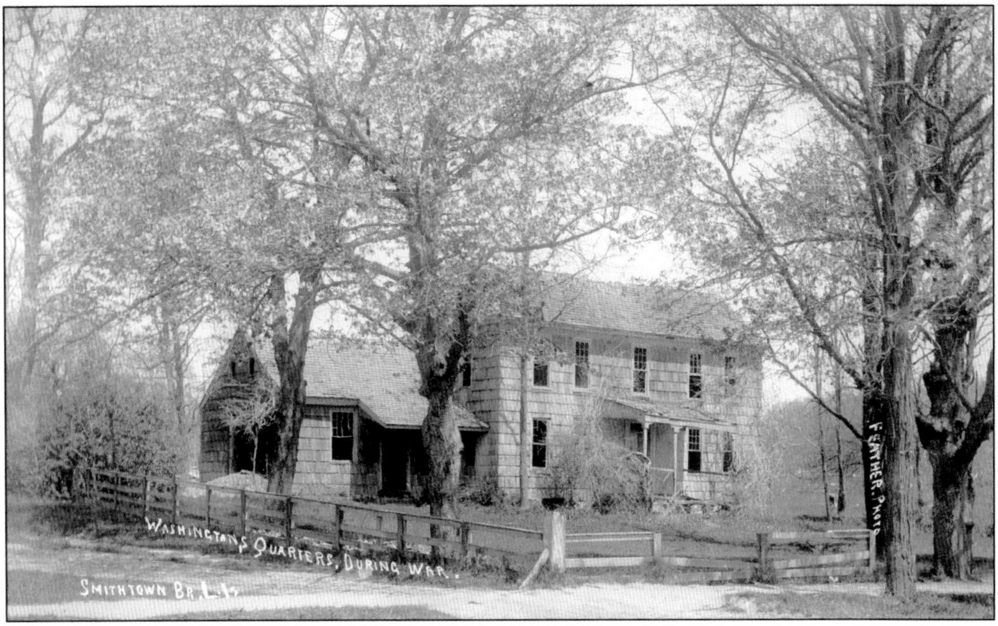

WIDOW BLYDENBURGH'S TAVERN, C. 1890. This structure was built sometime around 1720 and was located on the northeast corner of Middle Country Road and North Country Road where the Smithtown Library sits today. In 1790, Pres. George Washington stopped briefly at "Widow" Ruth Blydenburgh's tavern to "bait his horses" during his tour of Long Island. The building was torn down in the late 1930s after years of neglect.

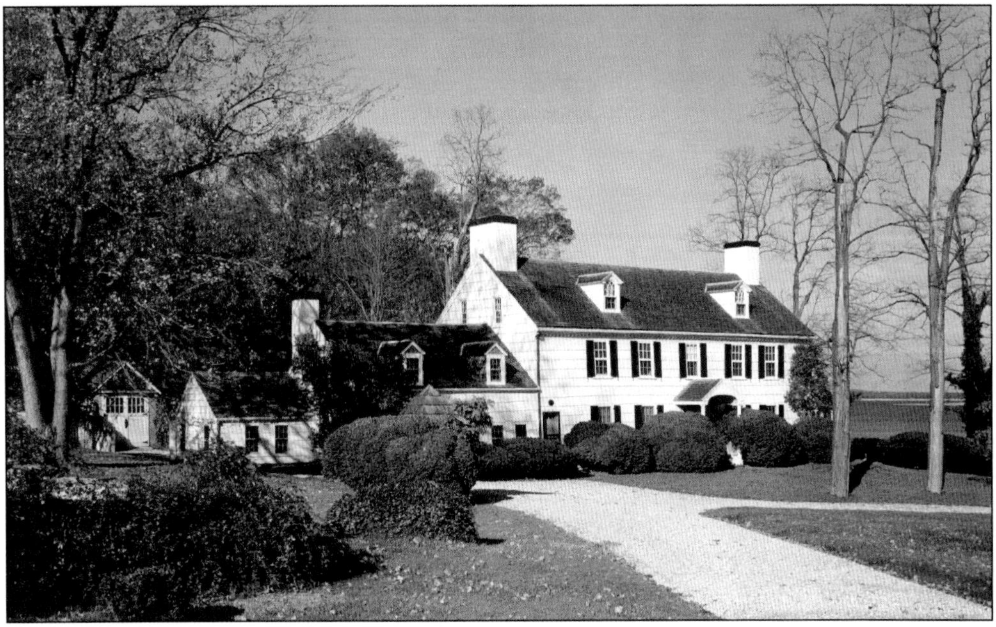

EBENEZER SMITH'S HOMESTEAD, C. 1950. This photograph was taken at the end of Smith Lane in Nissequogue overlooking Stony Brook Harbor. In 1736, when the lands of Richard Smythe were divided among his descendants, Ebenezer Smith (1712–1747) received this house and 150 acres of land on the west side of Stony Brook Harbor. The house remained in the Smith family through five generations.

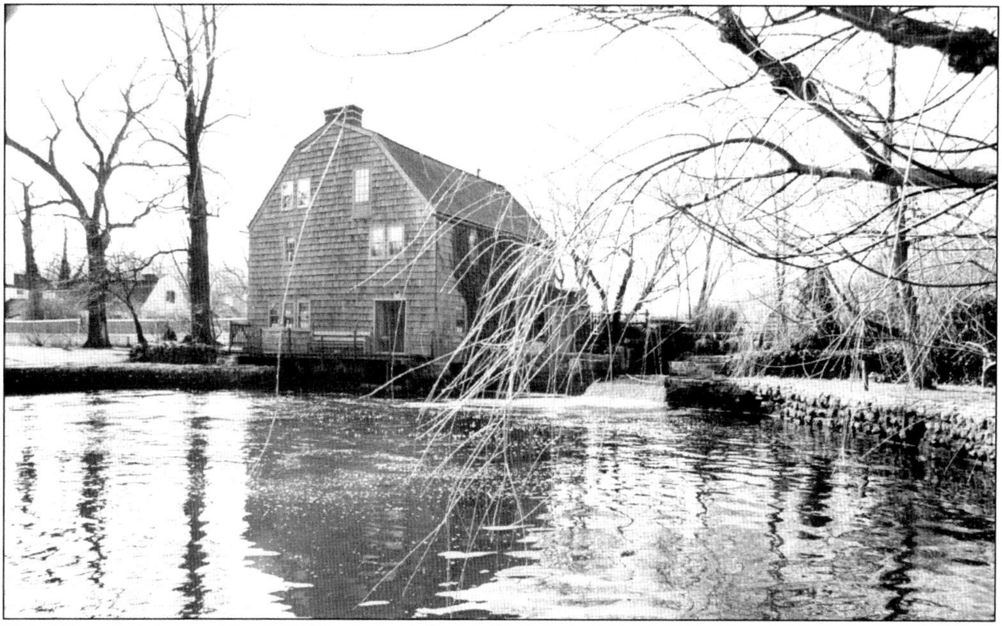

THE OLD MILL, C. 1930. The gristmill was built sometime after 1725. The mill wheel was horizontal beneath the house and was turned by the water running through the sluice. The miller's house dates from the same time period and can be seen to the left of the gristmill. This mill was important to the local farmers, and grain was ground here until the mill was abandoned in 1909.

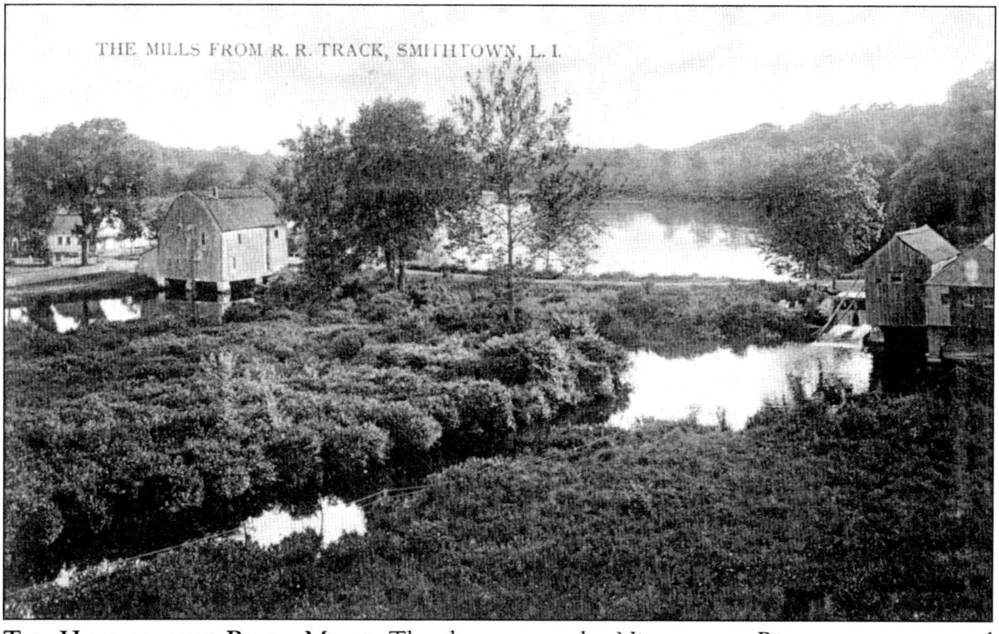

THE HEAD OF THE RIVER MILLS. The dam across the Nissequogue River was constructed around 1725 when Amos Willets, Richard Willets, Daniel Smith, and Richard Smith worked together to build it. The four men then built a sawmill. Then a fulling mill, built to process raw wool, was added, and that was followed by a gristmill. This complex of mills at Head of the River became the commercial and industrial heart of Smithtown for the next 200 years.

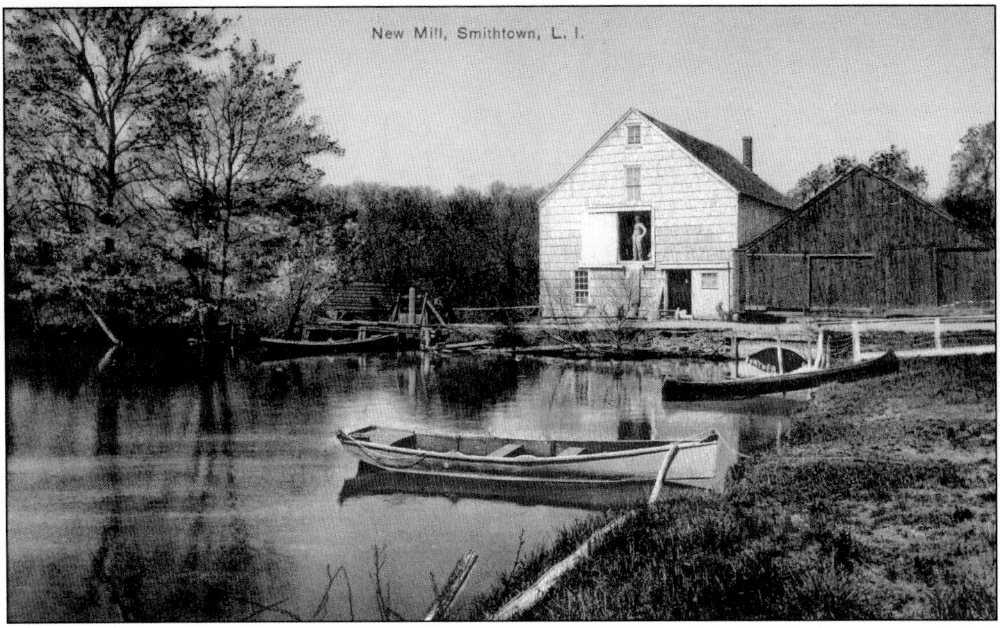

THE NEW MILLS, C. 1900. An agreement made in 1798 between two Smith cousins, Caleb Smith II and Joshua Smith II, and Isaac Blydenburgh, the youngest son of Ruth Blydenburgh, led to the construction of a dam across streams that fed the Nissequogue River, and Stump Pond was created. Water flowing out of the dam was used to power a gristmill and a sawmill that were built on the dam.

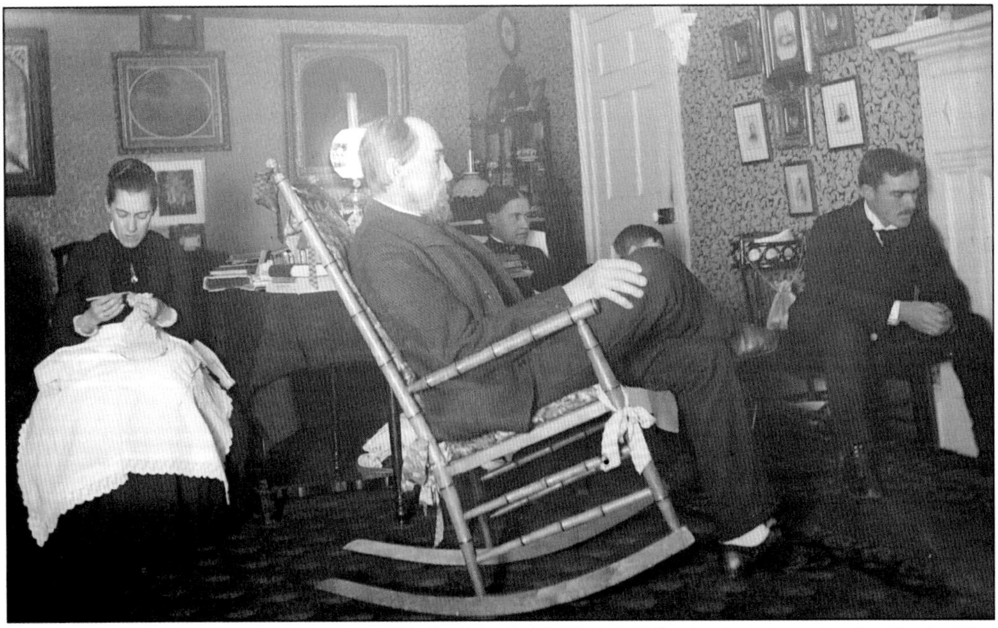

ISAAC BLYDENBURGH'S HOUSE. Isaac Blydenburgh (1775–1858) built a house on Bushy Neck. The mills prospered, and in 1821, he could afford to build a grand house there. This photograph shows the fancy parlor of the house with framed portraits and patterned wallpaper. The carved mantels in this house were reputedly made by George Curtis, the same man who built the Smithtown Presbyterian Church. Five generations of Blydenburghs lived in this house until 1941.

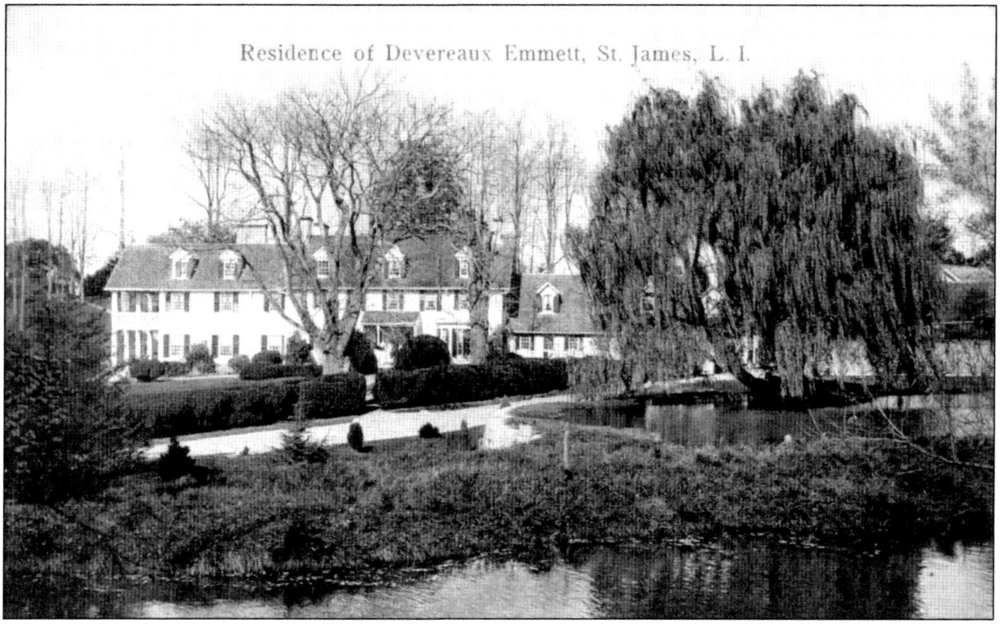

SHERREWOGUE, C. 1900. Adam Smith, a son of Richard Smythe, built the original house (to the right in the photograph) sometime around 1688. The larger two-and-a-half-story center section is thought to predate the American Revolution, and the wing to the left was later added. Smith's lands extended to the brook where he built the dam and original gristmill in Stony Brook. Sherrewogue remained in the family until 1943.

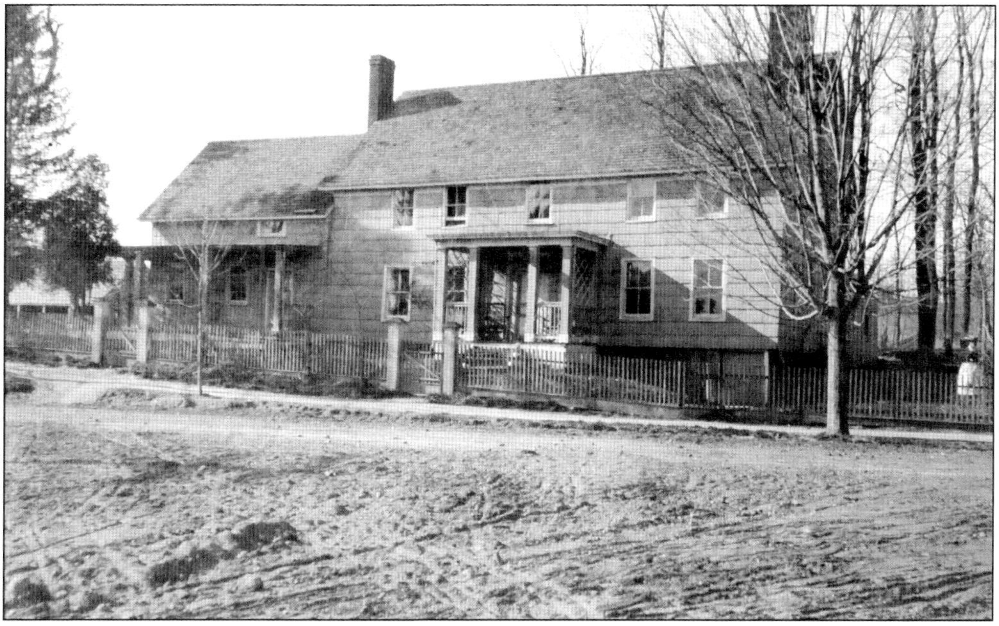

EPENETUS SMITH TAVERN, C. 1900. One of the most historically significant buildings in Smithtown, this tavern has occupied four different sites in town and now sits on the Smithtown Historical Society's property on Middle Country Road. The interior framing of the little saltbox wing of this house suggests that it was built around 1690. The two-story main block of the tavern was added about 1740 when Epenetus Smith acquired it.

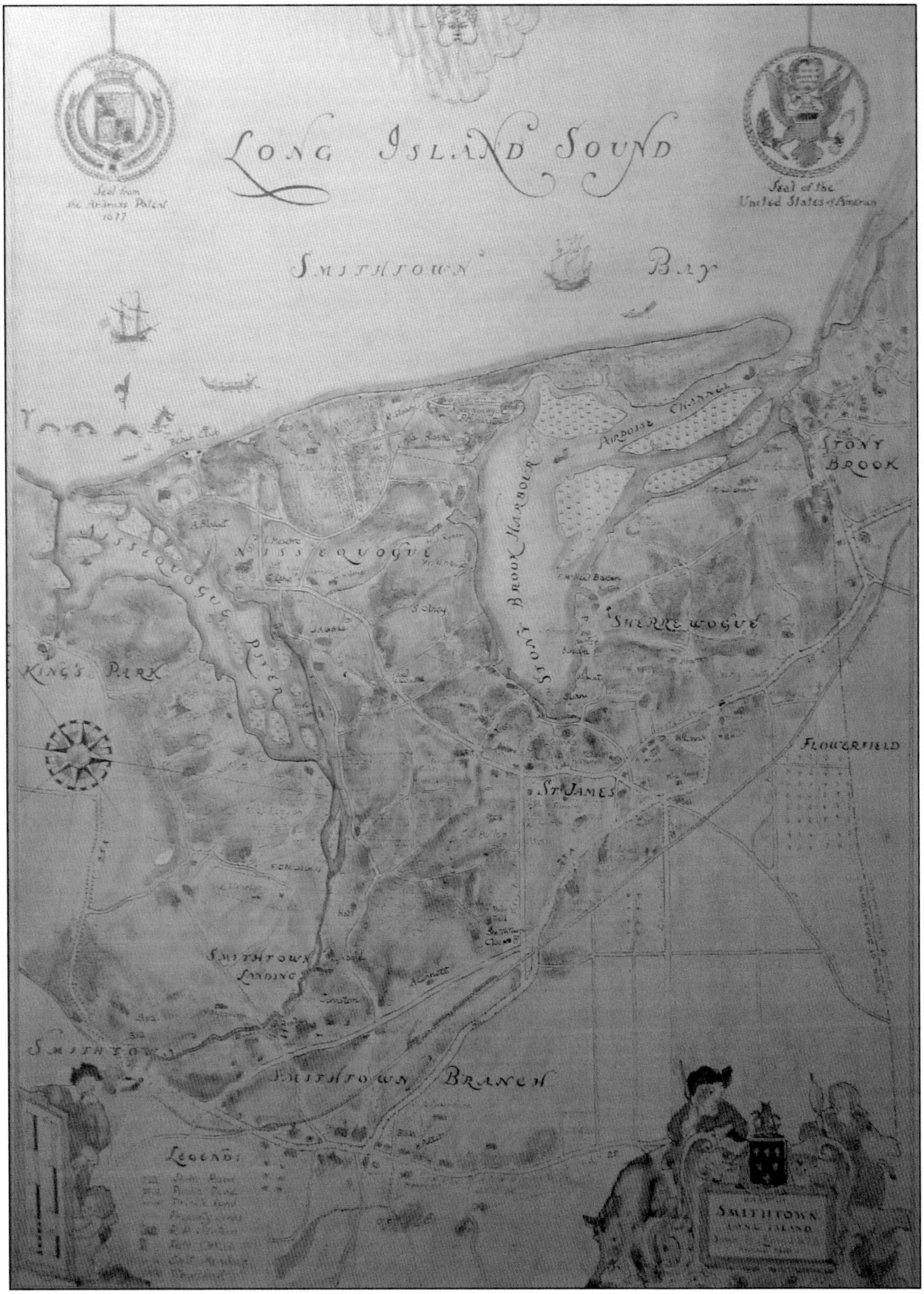

WATERCOLOR MAP OF SMITHTOWN, 1946. Lawrence Grant White, the son of architect Stanford White and a prominent architect himself, executed this beautiful view of Smithtown just before the enormous changes of the post–World War II years. The map depicts a rural calm of meadows, forests, and water channels, with no reference to the modernization that Smithtown was starting to undergo.

Two

The People of Smithtown

Reading the census rolls of early Smithtown feels a bit like reading the guest list for a wedding rehearsal. Several last names tend to predominate. The Mills, Blydenburghs, Wheelers, Darlings, and especially the Smiths formed a large percentage of the population of 1,413 in 1800. Over the course of the 19th century, the town's growth was incremental despite several small influxes of immigrants. Residents of all walks of life, from blacksmiths and farmhands to prominent architects and writers, chose to make their homes here, creating a fascinating social history. In 1884, architect Stanford White married Bessie Springs Smith and soon moved into a Colonial farmhouse in St. James that he extensively renovated beginning in 1891—the wildly eclectic, wonderfully creative Box Hill. Other prominent local residents eventually followed, including the vaudevillian Willie Collier, the accomplished photographer Toni Frissell, and the talented writer Cornelia Otis Skinner, to name just a few.

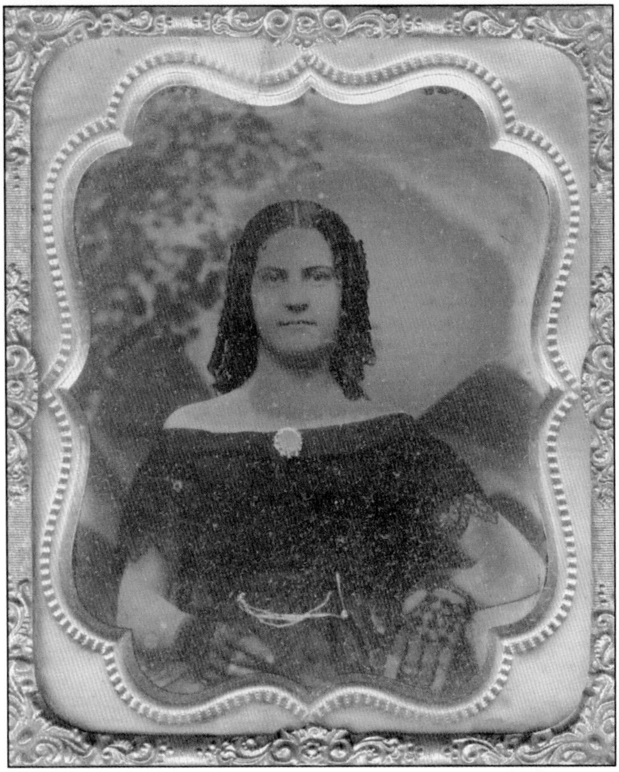

MARY KATE WICKS, c. 1861. In elegant attire on the eve of the Civil War, Mary Kate Wicks (1839–1866) sat for this local portrait. Her wedding on March 21, 1861, to Smithtown dentist James Otis Smith (1837–1923) at the Congregational church in Commack took place just three weeks prior to the start of the war. The young couple settled in Smithtown and had two daughters before Mary Kate's untimely death in 1866.

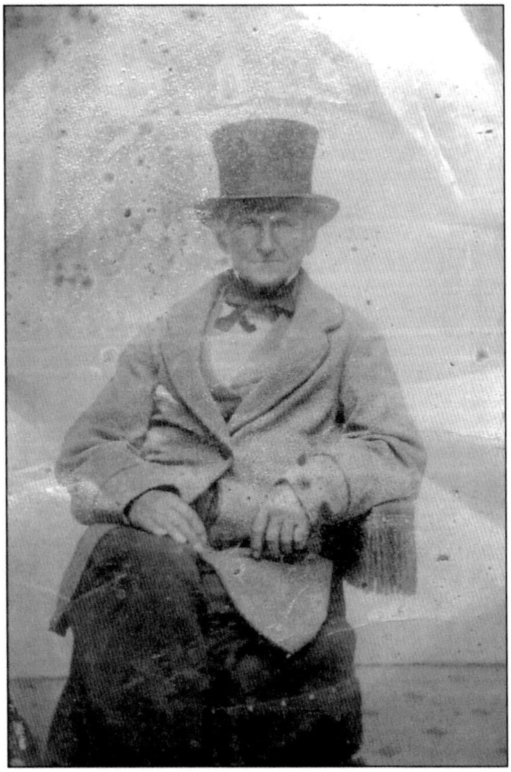

EBENEZER SMITH, 1860. Sixty-five-year-old Ebenezer Smith (1795–1879) peers intently at the lens, posing for this portrait in his stylish top hat. The son of a judge and state senator, he married his second cousin Sarah, the daughter of Caleb Smith. The couple's marriage lasted nearly 60 years until they passed away within five days of one another in 1879. (Smithtown Library.)

SMITH DAUGHTERS, C. 1866. This portrait of two of the Smith daughters was painted by Shepard Alonzo Mount (1804–1868), brother of the famous American genre artist William Sidney Mount (1807–1868). Bessie (left) and Ella (right) were the children of Judge John Lawrence Smith, a Suffolk County judge, and nieces of wealthy New York City department store baron A. T. Stewart. Both inherited part of Stewart's fortune in 1876 and went on to marry important people, becoming extremely involved in social and philanthropic pursuits.

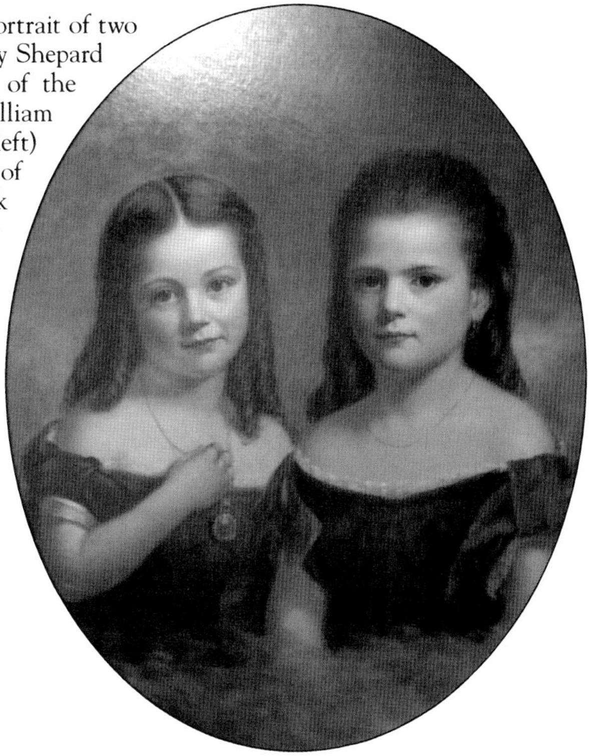

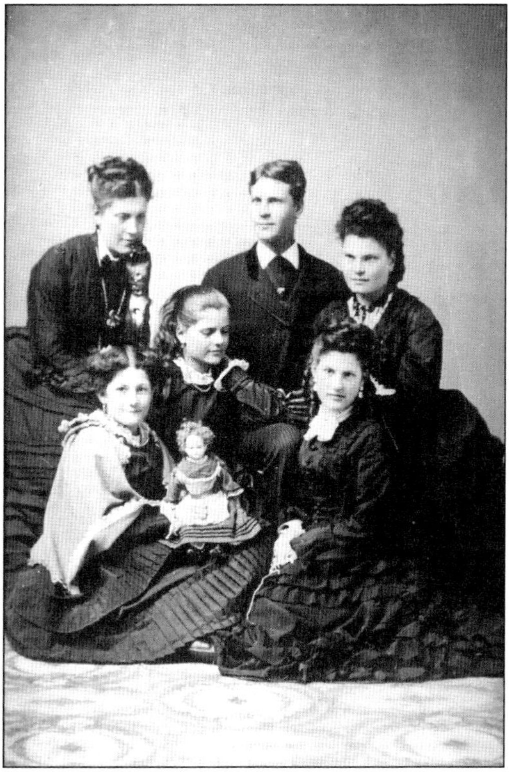

CHILDREN OF JUDGE JOHN LAWRENCE SMITH, C. 1870. Judge John Lawrence Smith's children are pictured here. From left to right are (first row) Bessie Smith (holding doll) and Kate Smith; (second row) Ella Batavia Smith; (third row) Cornelia Smith, James Clinch Smith, and Louise Smith. This photograph was taken not long after the children's other brother, Lawrence Woodhull, died at West Point Academy on April 21, 1870.

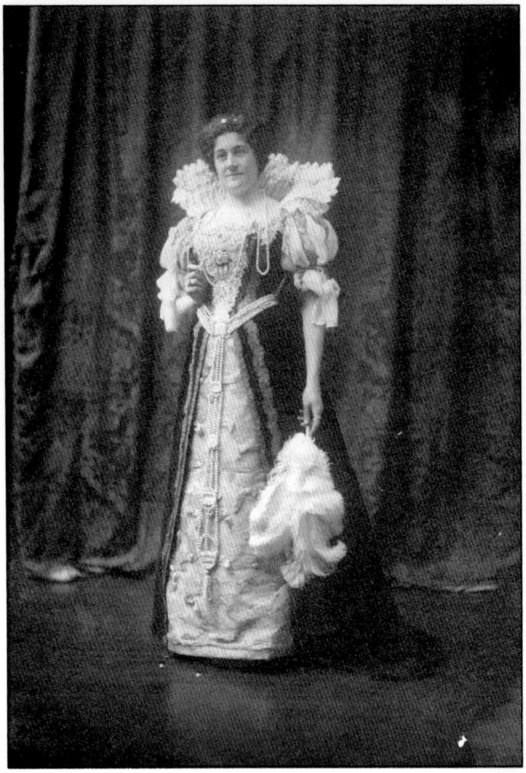

BESSIE SMITH, C. 1890. Bessie Smith's future husband, the famously talented architect Stanford White (1853–1906), and her own connections kept her in the Gilded Age mainstream of New York's upper class. In the early 1880s, she was immortalized in several bas-relief portraits by American sculptor Augustus Saint-Gaudens. The Whites lived in a pebblestone-and-stucco-facade house on Moriches Road in St. James called Box Hill, an enlarged and converted farmhouse designed by Stanford White.

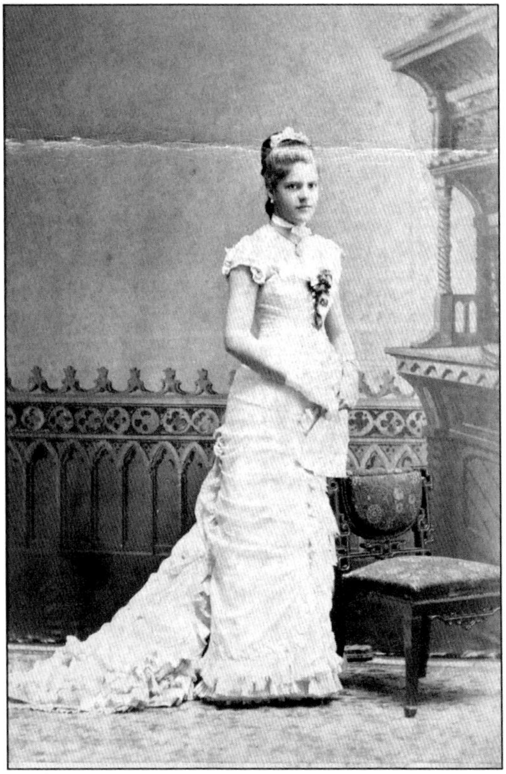

ELLA BATAVIA SMITH, C. 1889. In 1889, Ella Batavia Smith married golf course designer and realtor Devereaux Emmet in an enormous society wedding at her father's apartment on Fifth Avenue in New York City. She wore a spectacular white satin and point lace gown trimmed with pearls. There were 500 guests at the reception, which a newspaper account described as "festive" and "stunning." The Emmets eventually lived in the Stanford White–renovated farmhouse known as Sherrewogue in Head of the Harbor.

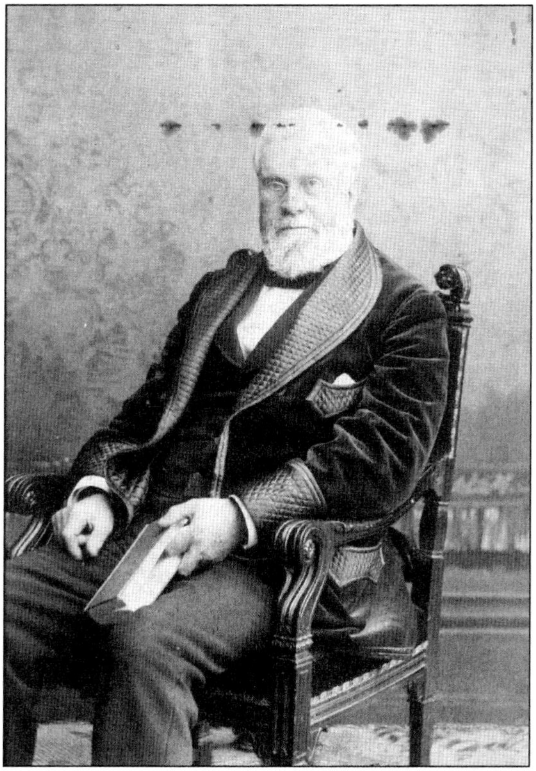

Judge John Lawrence Smith, c. 1880. John Lawrence Smith (1816–1889) was a respected jurist, bibliophile, and authority in local history. His *History of Smithtown* (1882) remains a significant work for local researchers to this day. He later became a county assemblyman, a district attorney, and a state supreme court justice. Many of his important papers and possessions, including his family homestead, are in the collection of the Smithtown Historical Society.

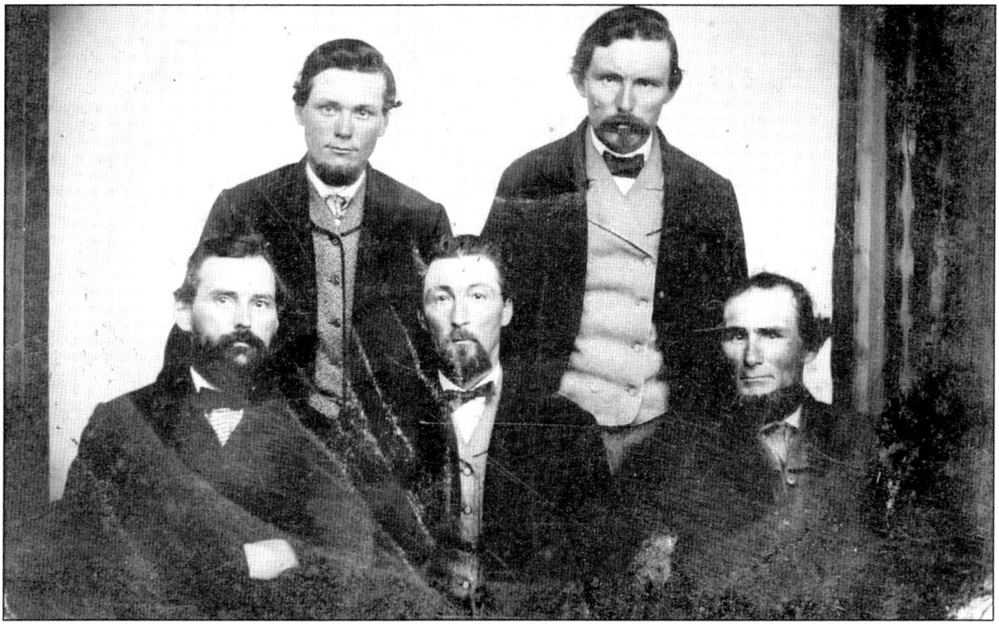

Newton Brothers, c. 1858. The Newtons were principally farmers who owned land in St. James. They eventually found other ways to profit from the growing post–Civil War tourist economy. William (standing, left) became a hunting guide and eventually the superintendent of the Wyandanch Game Club. Benjamin (center) ran a stagecoach from the St. James General Store to the Long Island Rail Road station at Brentwood.

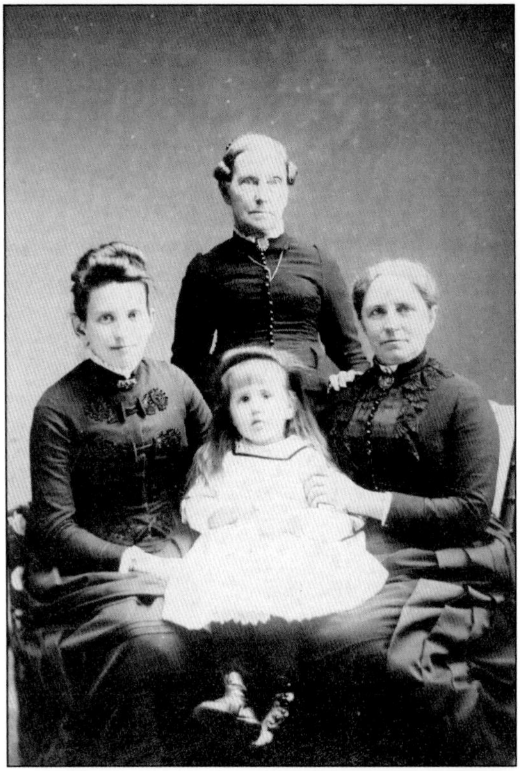

SMITHTOWN WOMEN, C. 1886. Pictured here from left to right are (first row) Julia Strong Lawrence (1859–1932), Elizabeth (Bessie) Lawrence (born in 1883), and Mariette Strong (1836–1920); (second row) Rhodetta Arthur (1817–1897). Rhodetta's husband, Franklin, was the village blacksmith and dentist. Several of Rhodetta's quilts are now in the collection of the Smithtown Historical Society.

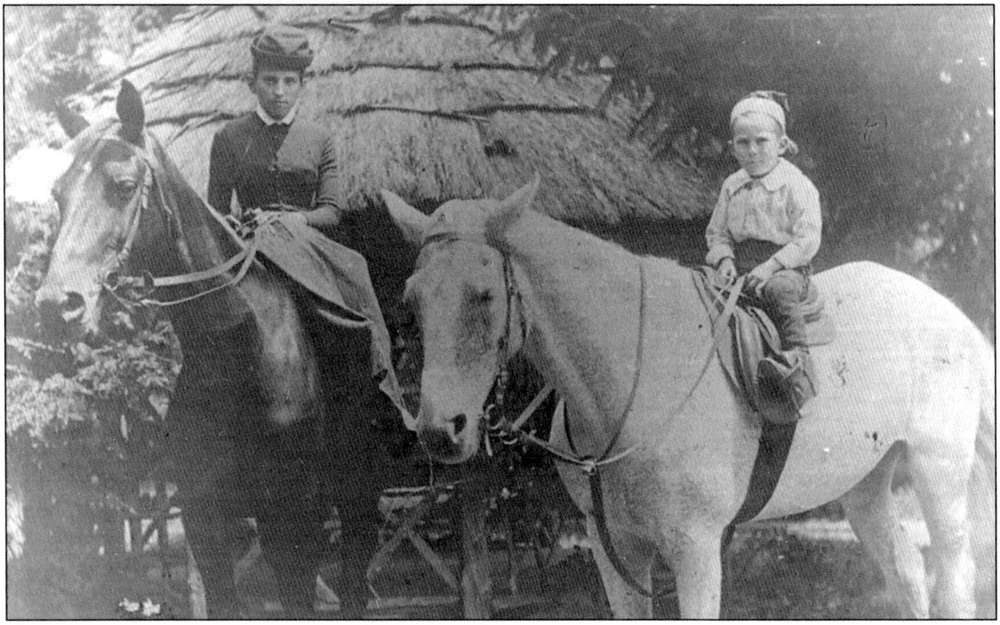

JULIA STRONG LAWRENCE AND SON, C. 1885. Julia and her son Arthur, one of her three children, sit on horseback on a lazy summer's day at Richard H. Handley's house in Hauppauge. Handley (1848–1914) was an extraordinary collector of rare books and documents of Long Island history, materials that eventually made their way into the Smithtown Library's Richard H. Handley Collection. (Smithtown Library.)

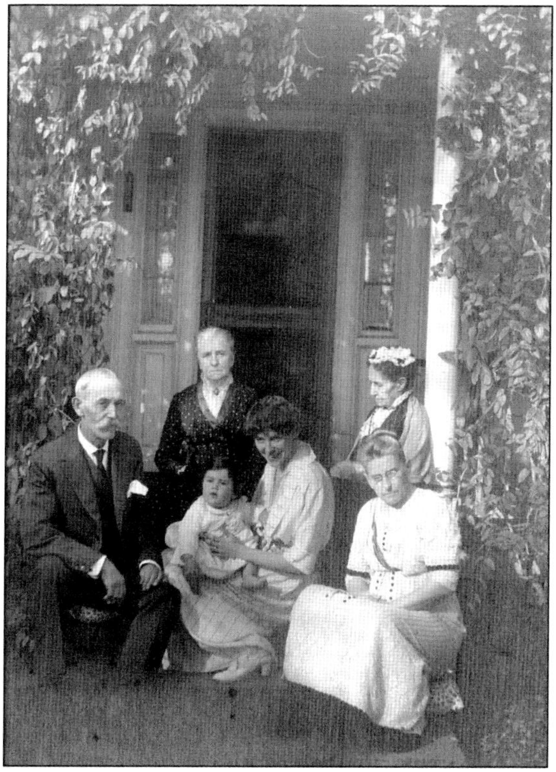

FRANKLIN O. ARTHUR HOUSE, C. 1914. The family is gathered for a portrait at the house on Middle Country Road. From left to right are Charles E. Lawrence (1852–1923), Mariette Strong, L. D. Rockwell (baby), Marcia Rockwell, Elizabeth Smith Lawrence (1832–1915), and Julia Strong Lawrence.

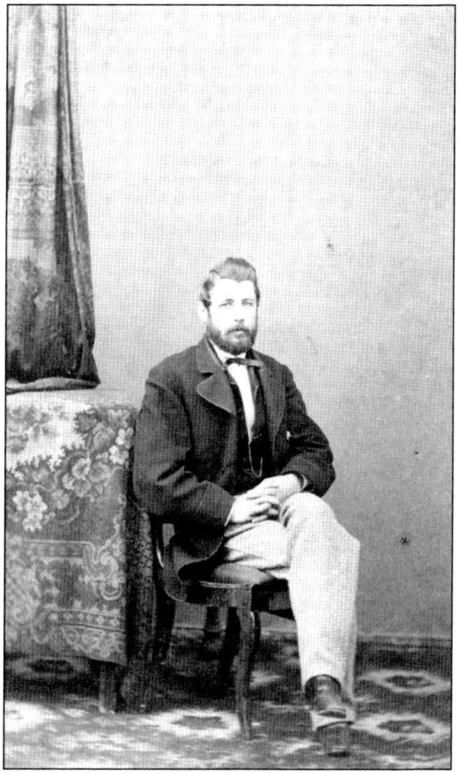

JESSE BLYDENBURGH, C. 1870. Jesse Blydenburgh (1832–1900) left Smithtown at the age of 20 in search of a life of adventure in California at the tail end of the gold rush. A letter from his aunt warned him against "foolish, and sinful pleasures, and profane unholy, language" that she feared he would fall victim to in San Francisco. Blydenburgh stayed on the straight path well enough to lead to a series of successful business ventures, ultimately trading petroleum and other products in China. He came back to Long Island later in life.

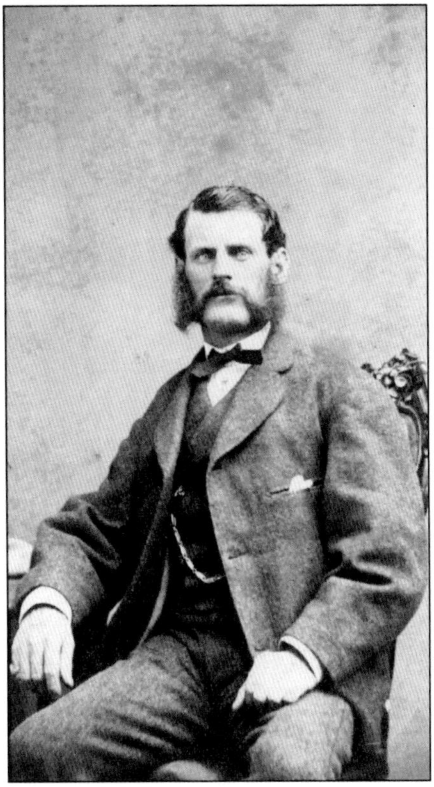

WILLIAM JUDSON BLYDENBURGH, C. 1868. Jesse Blydenburgh's younger brother William J. Blydenburgh (1833–1878) followed him west and eventually opened a trading post in Shanghai. A letter from William to Jesse in August 1868 reports, "I think I shall like Shanghai better than any place I have been yet." In another letter from Hong Kong earlier that same summer, William writes, "business is excellent" but that "nothing new or interesting has occurred except a tremendous noise made yesterday in honor of the Queen's birthday."

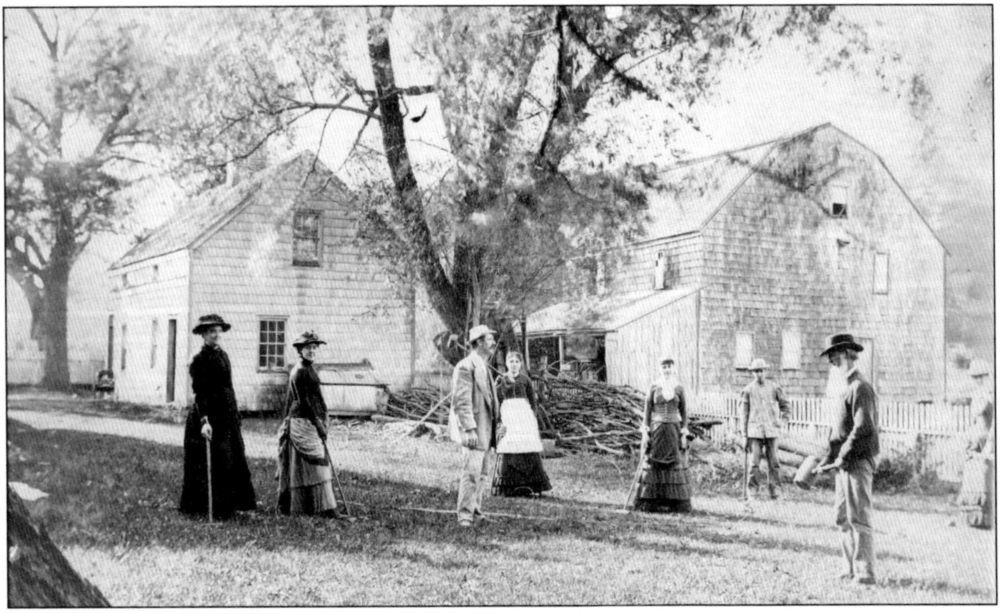

WHEELER FAMILY, C. 1880. The identities of the people in this photograph are difficult to pin down, although a descendant suggests the man standing in the middle wearing the light suit is likely Treadwell F. Wheeler, who was miller of the "old gristmill" seen at the right of the photograph. (Smithtown Library.)

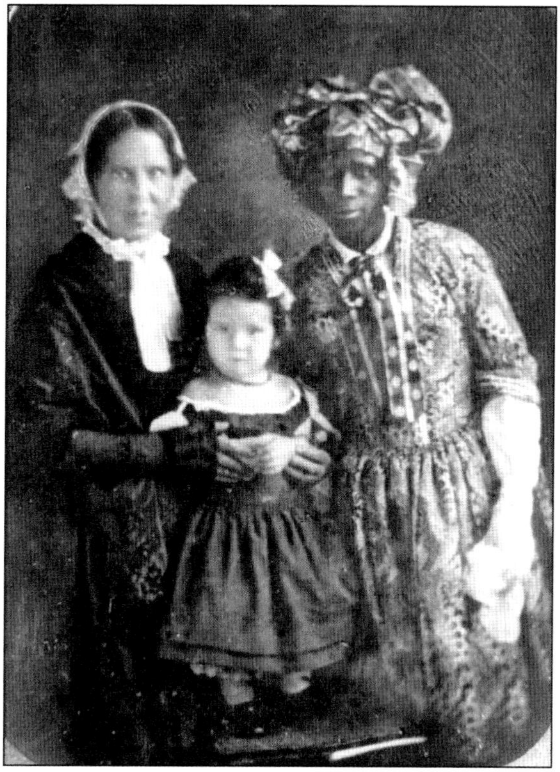

"NANNIE OLD RUTH, TOOTIE, AND I THINK MAY, APRIL 1852." The identification under this daguerreotype from Judge John Lawrence Smith's family, written by Bessie Smith White, is suspect, as Madeline May was born in 1854 (the little girl in this photograph is likely Louise Nicoll, who was born in 1849). Nonetheless, it is a fascinating picture, especially in its depiction of the African American servant who may have been one of the local descendants of slaves or a former slave herself.

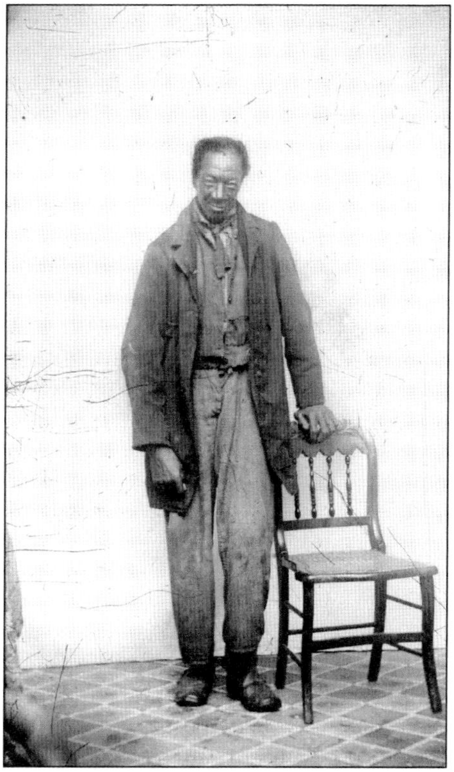

JAMES HUNTER, C. 1860. Born into bondage around 1795, James Hunter presumably lived his entire life in Smithtown. His last census listing appears in 1870, where he shows up as a "farm laborman" living with his 68-year-old wife, Sarah, and his 28-year-old son Frank. Hunter worked for several area families, including Benjamin Newton's.

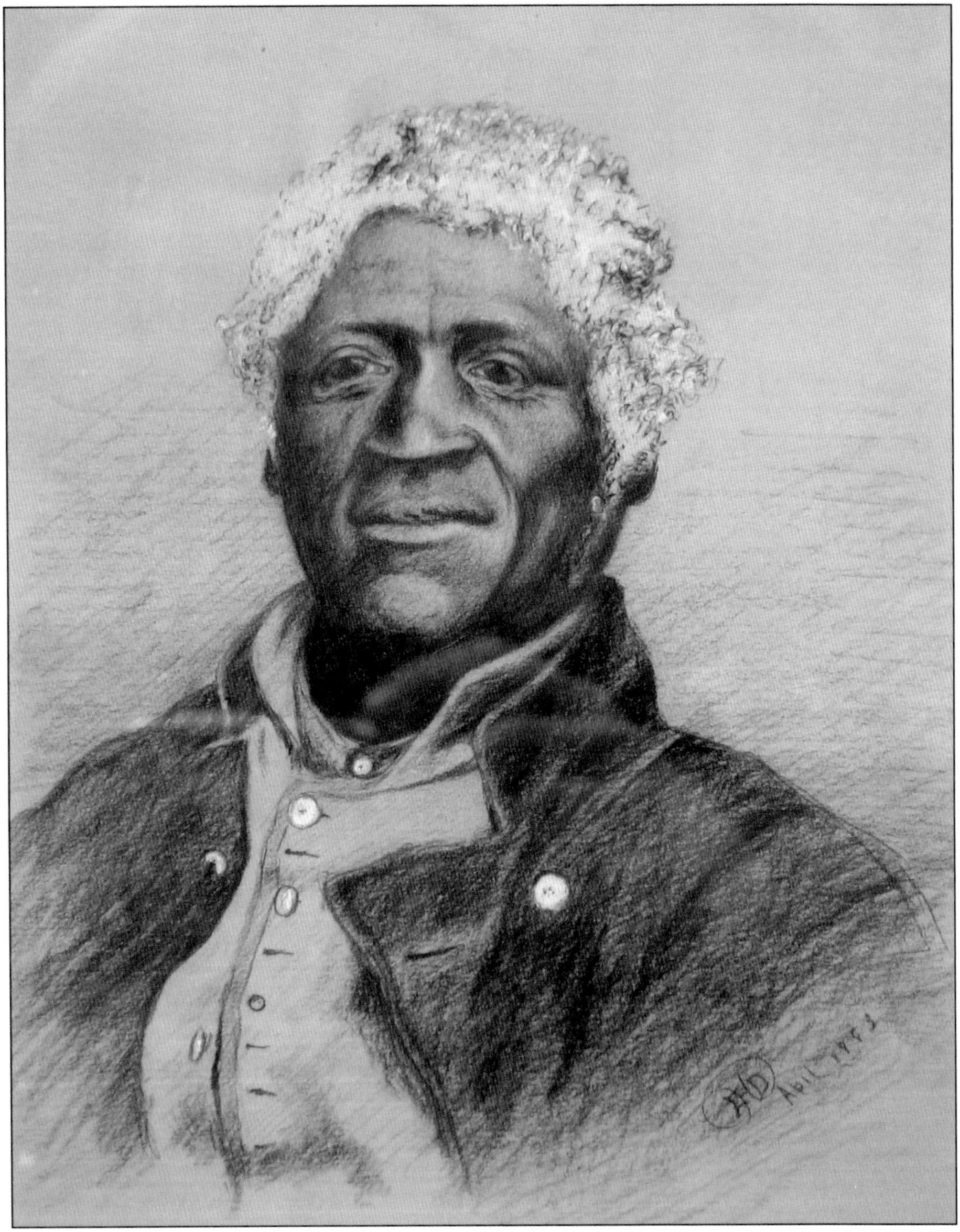

CHARLES DOBBS, C. 1882. A gift of Anna Hawkins to the Smithtown Library, this drawing was executed by Edward H. Davis of California. According to the back of the image, Charles Dobbs was "an old faithful servant" of the Hawkins family. (Smithtown Library.)

JAMES CLINCH SMITH, C. 1910. Smithtown residents were shocked when they opened their papers on April 16, 1912, to find that one of their prominent neighbors had been lost in the wreck of the *Titanic*. James Clinch Smith (1856–1912), a son of Judge John Lawrence Smith, was a debonair and well-liked member of the Fifth Avenue set. He had inherited the family homestead in Smithtown Branch and had married the talented Chicago-bred socialite Bertha Barnes.

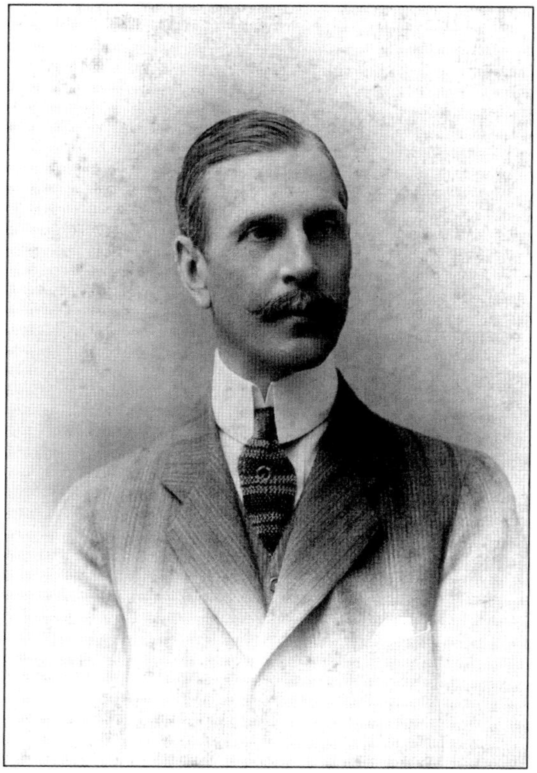

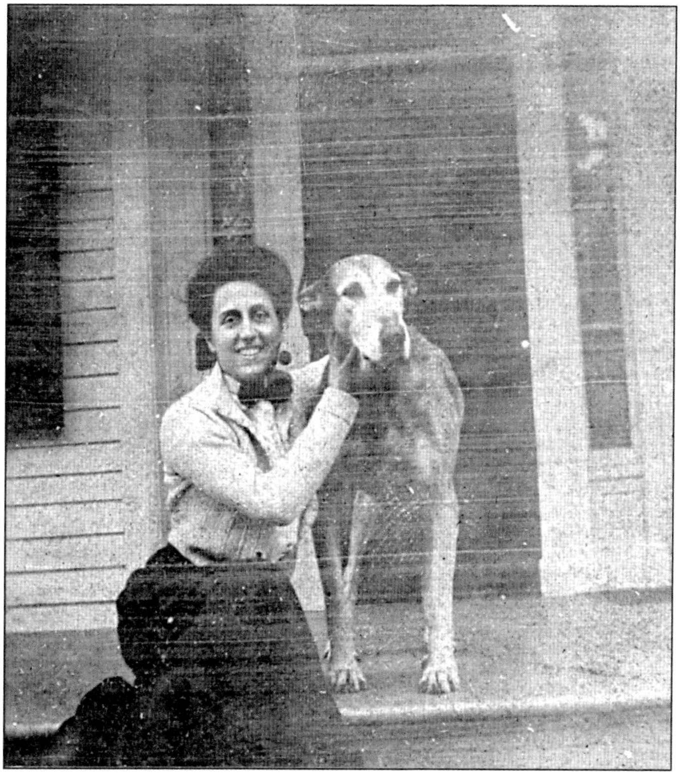

ELIZABETH LAWRENCE STETSON, C. 1906. Elizabeth (Bess) Lawrence Stetson (born in 1883) lived in the Franklin O. Arthur House for many years after marrying Paul Hamilton Stetson in 1932. She was a landscape designer and gardener and was a leading force behind the North Shore Garden Club, which began in the early 1930s. (Smithtown Library.)

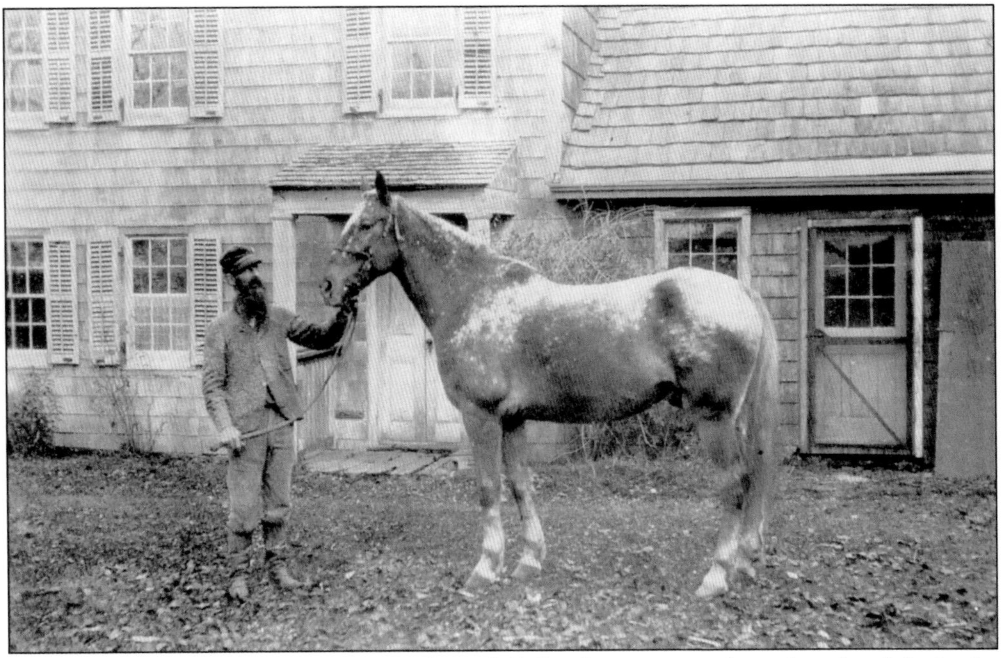

GEORGE LAFAYETTE BOOTH, C. 1890. One of 14 Smithtown men who enlisted to fight in the Civil War, George Lafayette Booth (1839–1919) was enrolled in Company H of the 127th New York State Volunteers. He saw action as a private mainly in South Carolina and was mustered out after three years of service in June 1865.

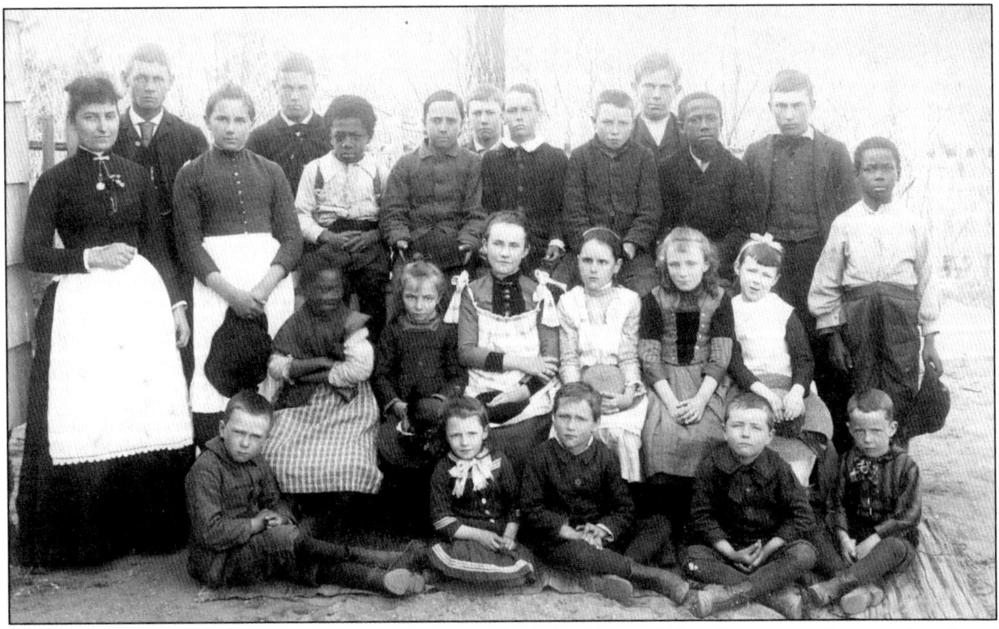

HEAD OF THE RIVER SCHOOL, C. 1888. Head of the River School was on the north side of Meadow Road in Smithtown just past the intersection of Jericho Turnpike. The building still stands today and is a private residence. Teacher Essie Brush is pictured here with her students. In the days before universal high school education, one-room schoolhouses like these were the sites of learning for young people ranging in age from 5 to 16.

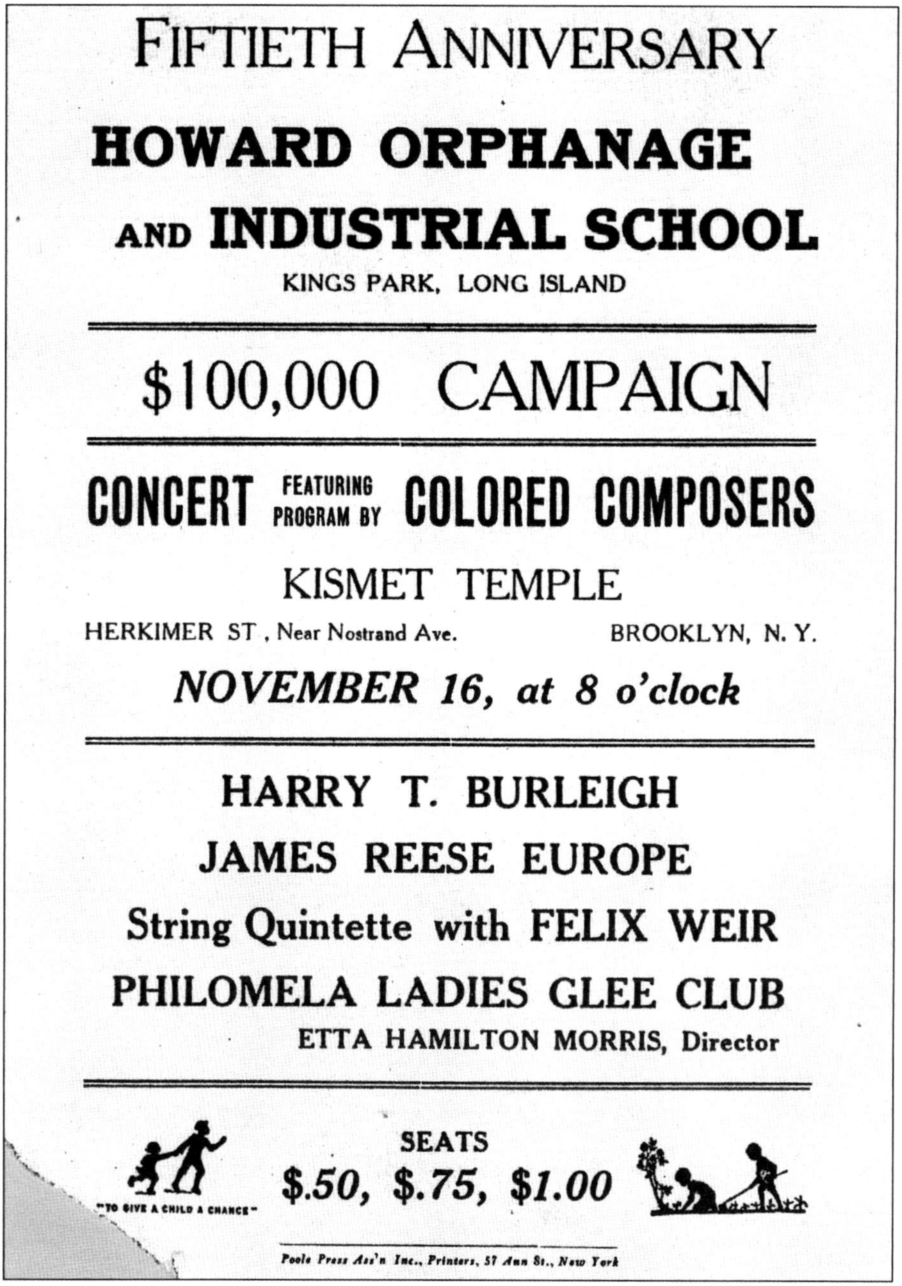

HOWARD ORPHANAGE AND INDUSTRIAL SCHOOL, C. 1917. Founded in 1866, the Howard Orphanage and Industrial School, originally known as the Howard Colored Orphan Asylum, moved to St. James in 1906. After a fire destroyed the St. James location in 1910, the organization moved to Indian Head Road in Kings Park. The institution offered a Booker T. Washington–style uplift education, focusing on agriculture and training in the trades. The orphanage struggled to stay afloat due to financial difficulties. In the winter of 1918, the bottom fell out when the school did not receive a shipment of coal to heat its buildings. When the hot water radiators failed, several children suffered from frostbite and had to have their feet amputated. Scandalized and severely in debt, the school was closed, and its equipment was auctioned off in March 1918.

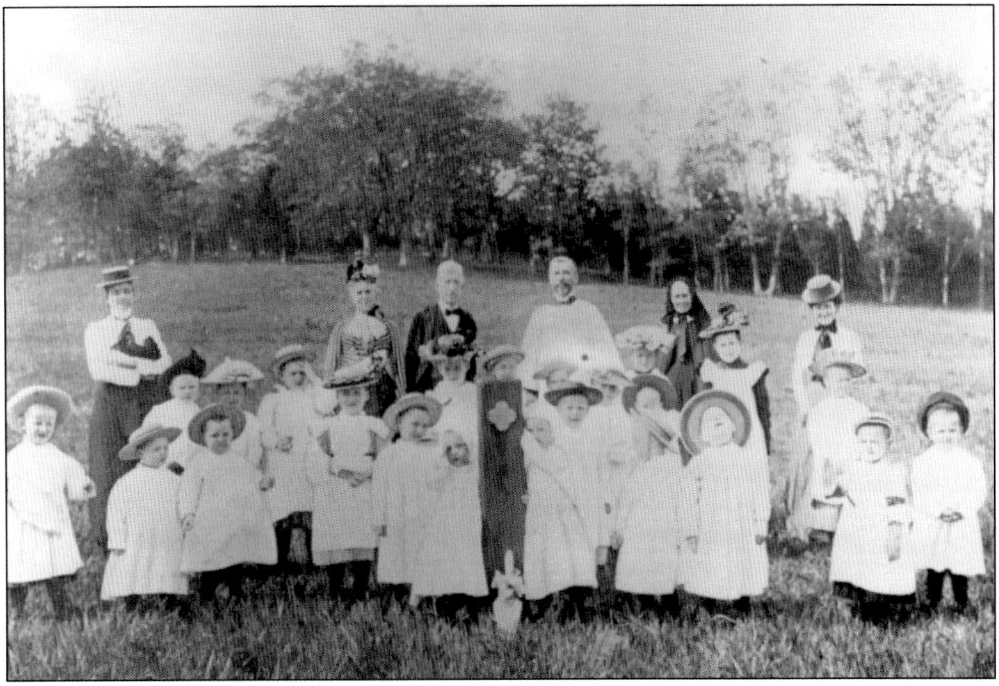

NEW BABIES SHELTER AND LAWRENCE HOUSE. The Society of St. Johnland had numerous care facilities for children that operated throughout its existence, right through the early 1950s. In these charming publicity photographs, children are gathered in white cotton summer clothes to emphasize the purified setting. The Babies Shelter in the Lawrence House, which is being inaugurated in the photograph from about 1900, above, and seen in the photograph from about 1915, below, burned to the ground in 1934. All the children and staff were safely evacuated, but the building and its equipment were completely lost. (Below, Smithtown Library.)

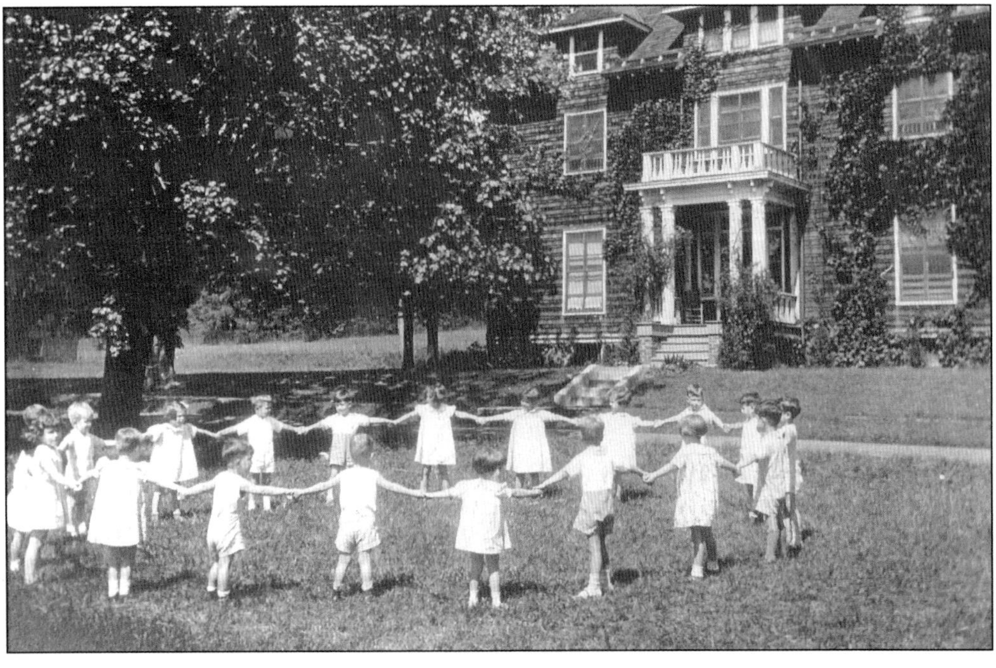

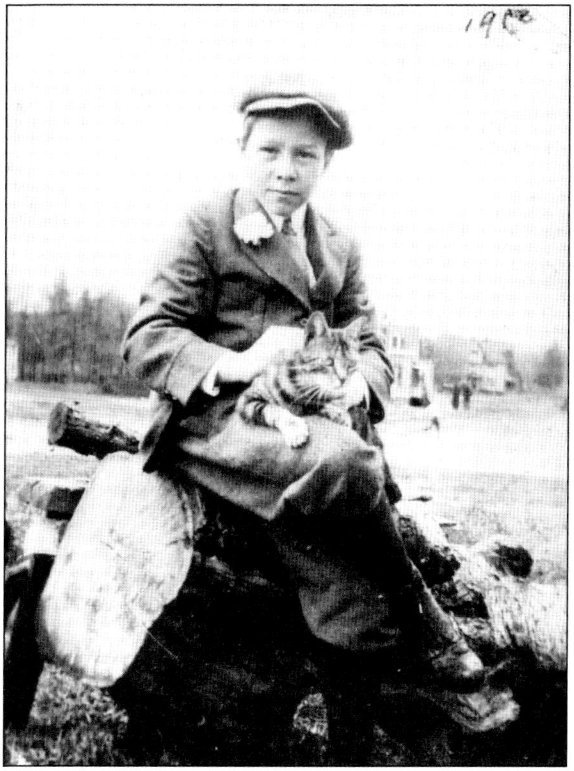

HOBART H. SMITH AND CAT, C. 1912. Hobart H. Smith (1905–1995) lived at the St. Johnland complex from 1910 through 1917. In the distant background of the photograph are the Chisholm House and Sunbeam Cottage, two facilities for children at St. Johnland.

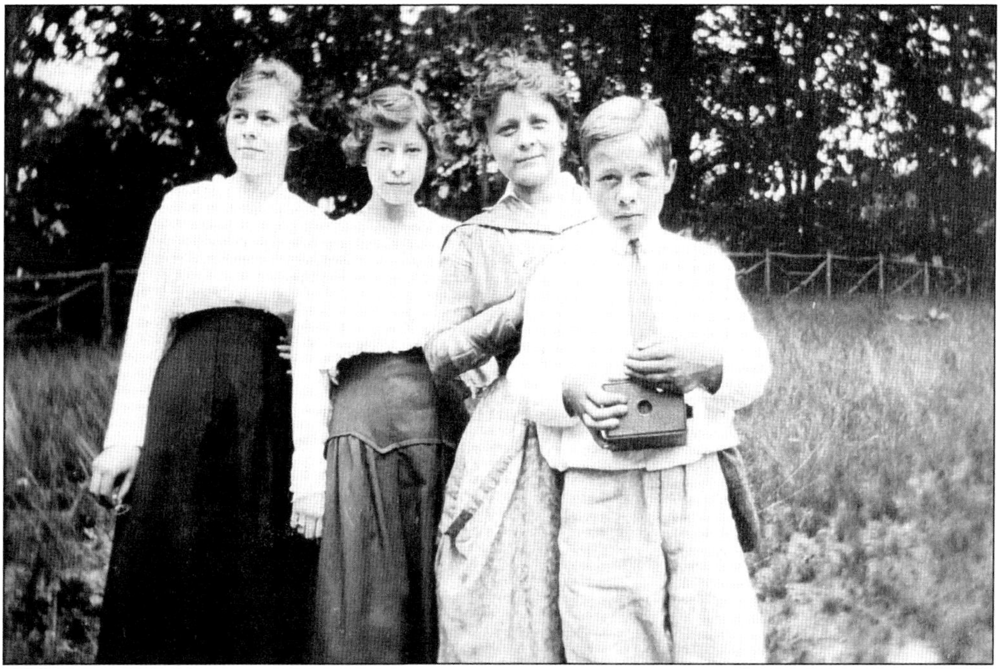

ST. JOHNLAND, C. 1916. Gathered here for a family photograph, from left to right, are Bertha Smith (1901–1936); Harriet Smith (1898–1990); mother Bertha T. Smith (1875–1968); and Hobart H. Smith.

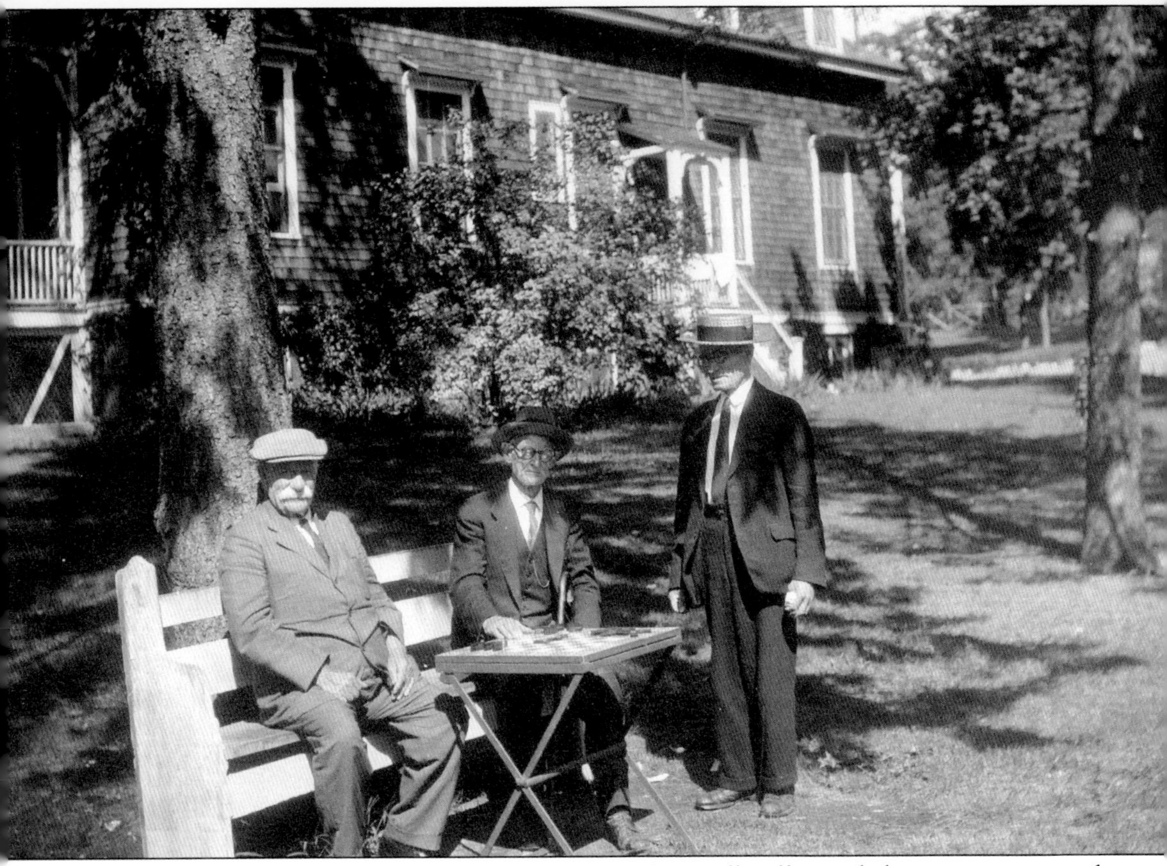

RETIREMENT HOME AT ST. JOHNLAND, C. 1920. Originally offering shelter, instruction, and assistance to underprivileged children, the Society of St. Johnland eventually opened separate retirement homes for men and women. The Home for Aged Men had a reading room and a smoking and amusement room with dominoes, chess, backgammon, and a billiards table. These gentlemen seem to prefer the great outdoors, taking shade under one of St. Johnland's magnificent old-growth trees.

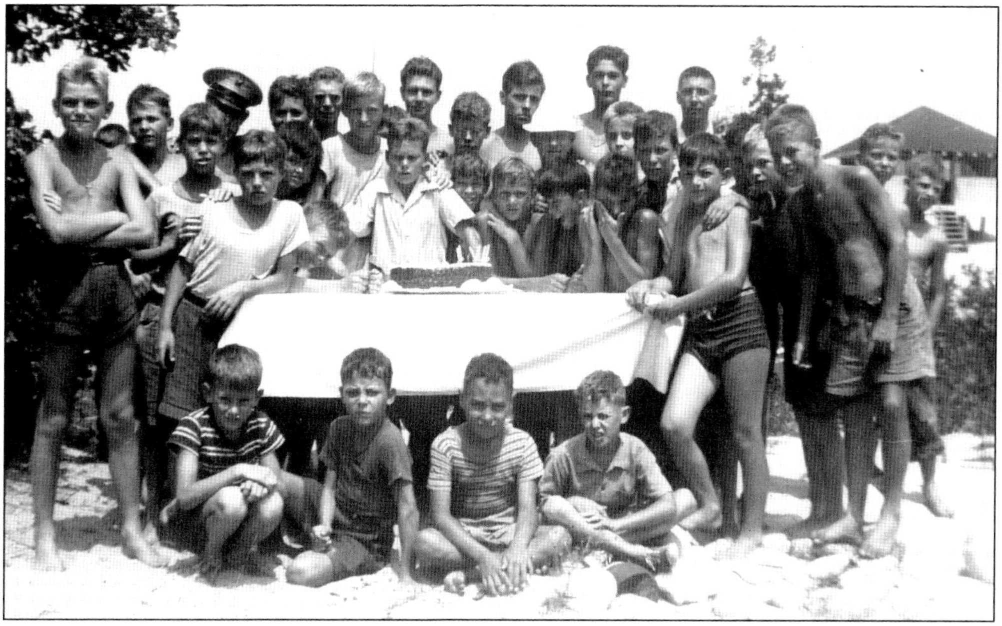

Birthday Party at St. Johnland, c. 1944. The Society of St. Johnland also had terrific outdoor recreation resources in its Kings Park spot nestled beside the Long Island Sound and the Nissequogue River. Alice Page Thompson (1868–1951), St. Johnland's superintendent from 1911 until 1946, began the society's summer camp for New York City boys and girls. Children swam daily and enjoyed rowing and putting on plays.

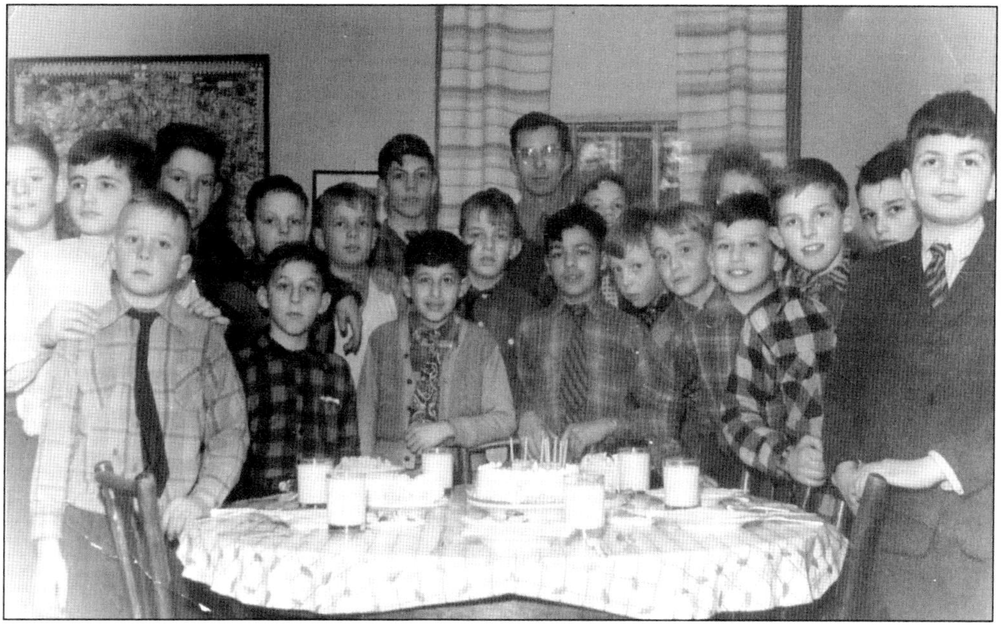

Stuart Eastland's Birthday at St. Johnland, c. 1948. Peter Beauchamp, one of the boys from Manhattan who attended the camp during its World War II years, remembered that it "was the greatest. I always looked forward to camp. We all did. I liked the scavenger hunts . . . the beach, the diving board at the creek, the row boats, digging for clams with your toes in the muck." St. Johnland discontinued its summer camp a few years after World War II.

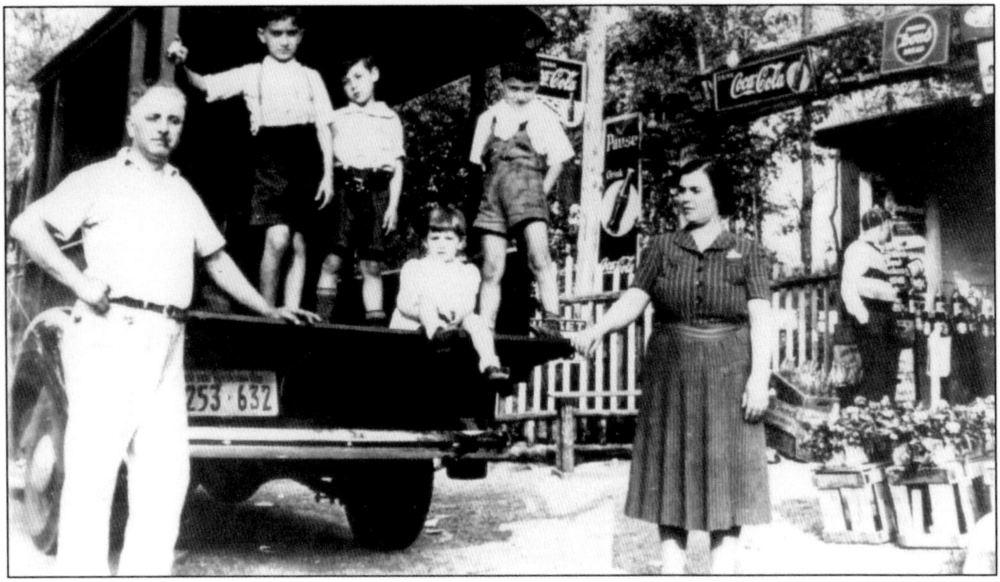

GROUP GATHERED AT SAN REMO, C. 1925. San Remo is a small but beautiful tidal community nestled along the Nissequogue River. Its original settlers were Italian immigrants who answered the advertisements running in their native-language Brooklyn newspaper *Il Corrierre*. The newspaper's publisher bought 194 acres of land in 1922 and subdivided it into 20-by-100-foot lots, selling them to residents for about $300 apiece.

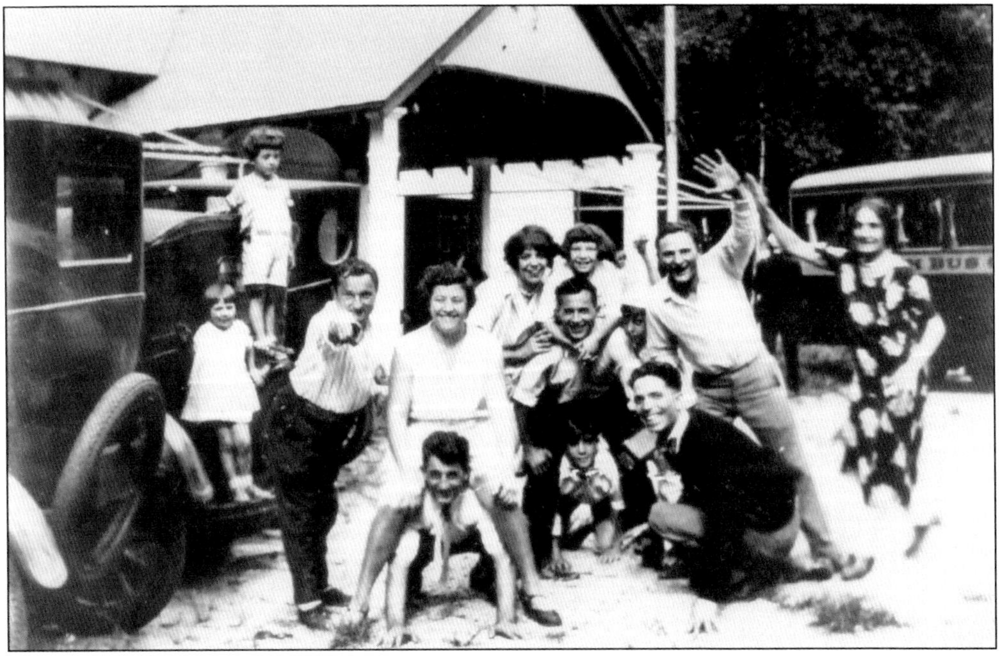

SAN REMO, C. 1925. San Remo's conditions were primitive in its early years but enjoyable nonetheless. Early residents built shacks out of crate wood and tar paper. Some eschewed the house in favor of pitching a tent on the beach. During the Great Depression, many residents lost their property due to nonpayment of taxes, but Italian families soon revived the community into the beautiful, successful enclave that exists to this day.

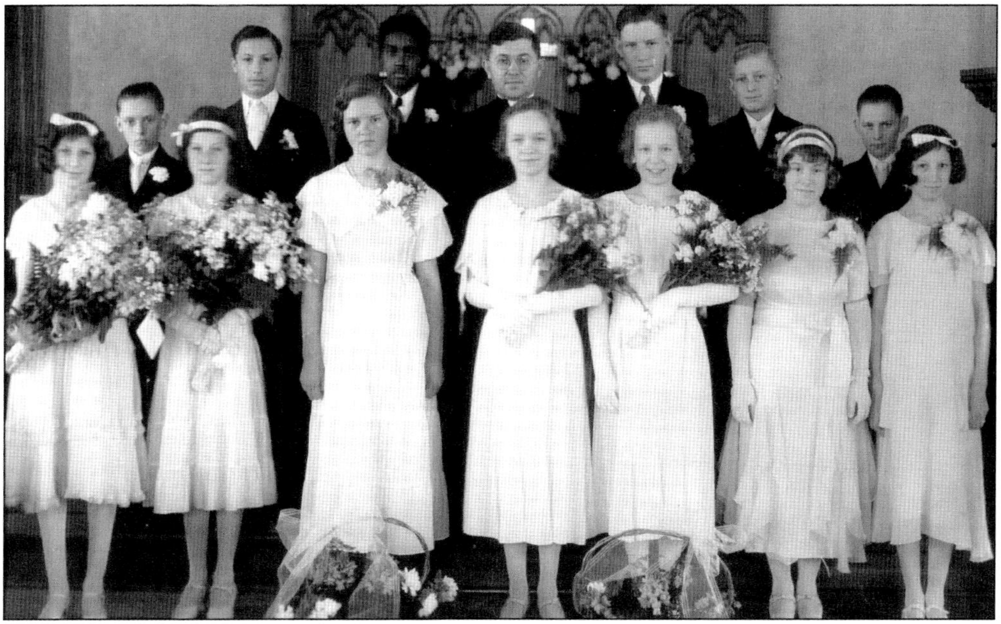

ST. JAMES LUTHERAN CHURCH, C. 1932. The St. James Lutheran Church organized itself in 1923 after the mission board of the Atlantic District of the Lutheran Church-Missouri Synod canvassed the St. James area. With surnames of its congregants like Knudsen, Gunderson, and Nooey, the church appealed, in part, to the growing numbers of Scandinavian residents in the village.

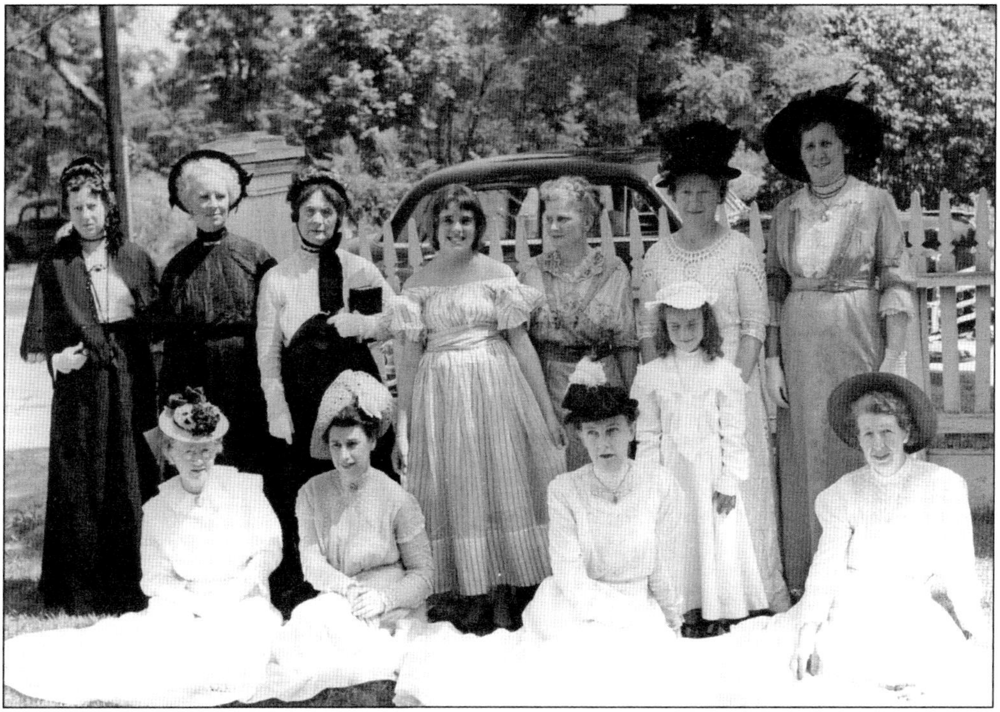

SMITHTOWN PRESBYTERIAN CHURCH, C. 1957. Members of the Smithtown Presbyterian Church, gathered and dressed in 19th-century clothing, stand on the church's front lawn.

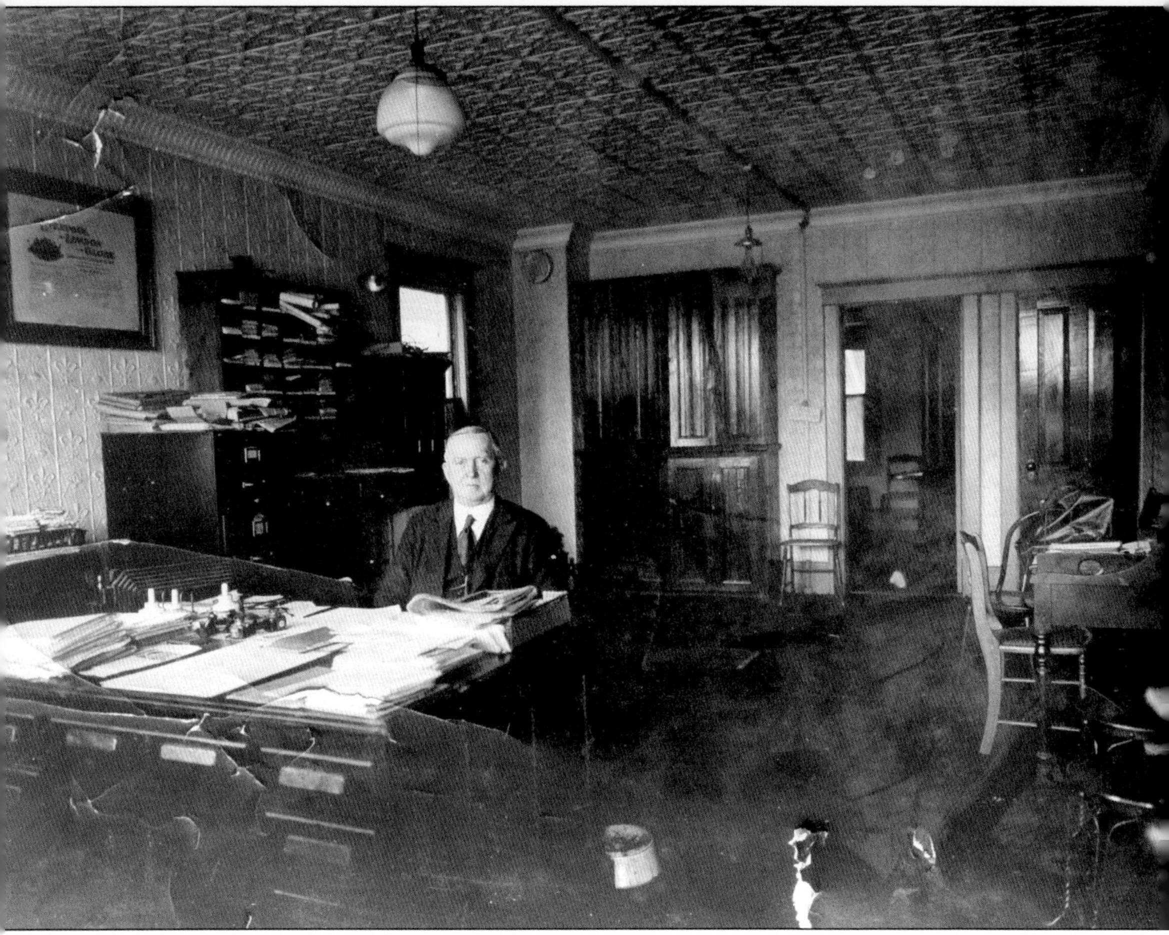

JUDGE JOHN F. KELLY, C. 1934. The Kings Park justice of the peace, elected on the Republican ticket for many years, Judge John F. Kelly was one of the first residents of Kings Park to purchase a home on Church Street just south of the Catholic church. Seen here, Kelly's office, located on the south side of Main Street, was where he ran an insurance and real estate business. He also held court here and was reputedly as intimidating a public official as this photograph would seem to suggest.

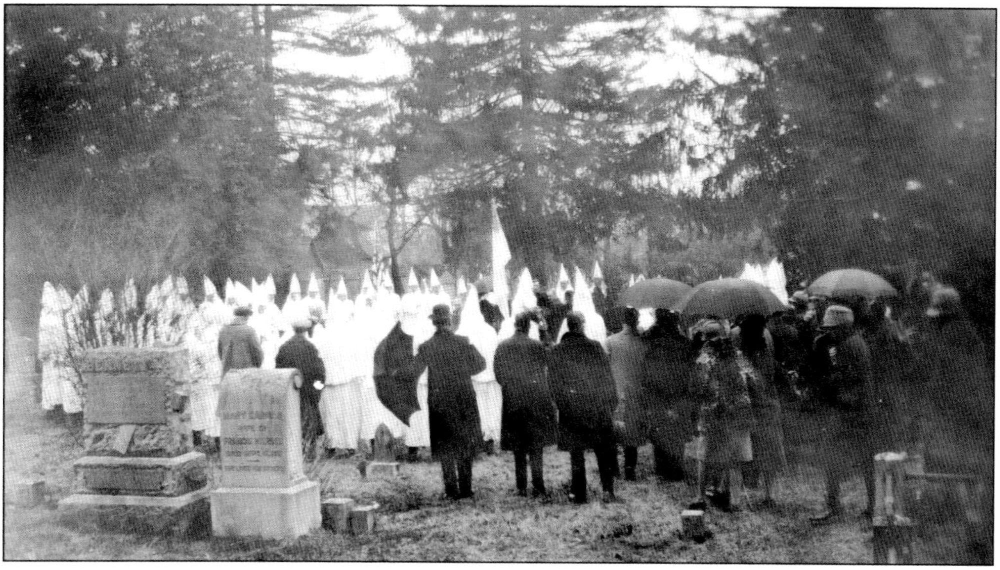

FUNERAL OF CHARLES E. SMITH, C. 1927. Across Long Island, the Ku Klux Klan's primary attention was directed more toward Catholic and Jewish immigrants than the smaller numbers of African American residents. In Smithtown, crosses were burned on the front yards of local immigrant families and in the vicinity of the St. James Catholic Church. In 1923, Lawrence Deutzman denounced the Klan in newspaper editorials and at a town hall meeting. A cross was later burned in a vacant lot across the street from his home on Edgewood Avenue. This Ku Klux Klan funeral was held at the Episcopal church in St. James.

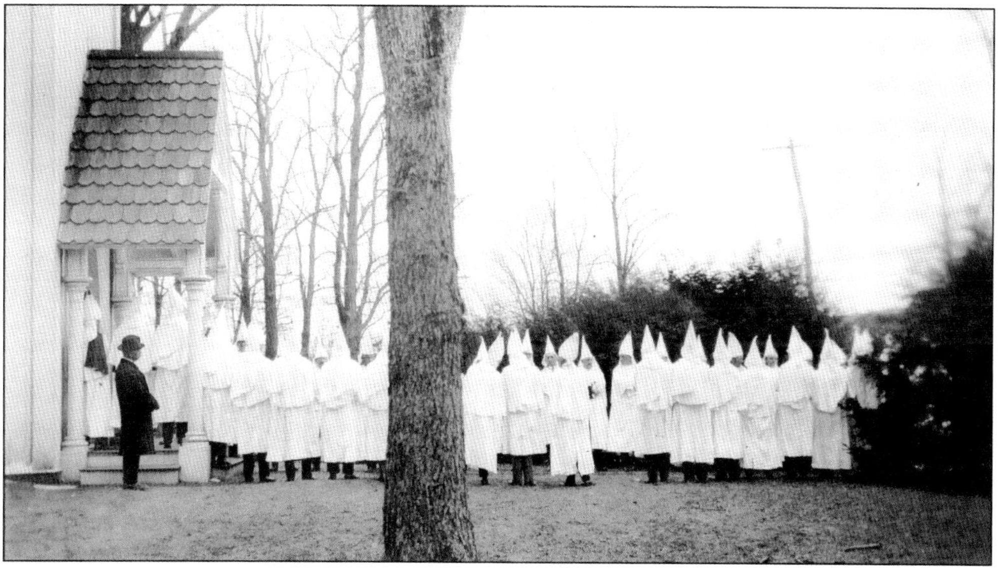

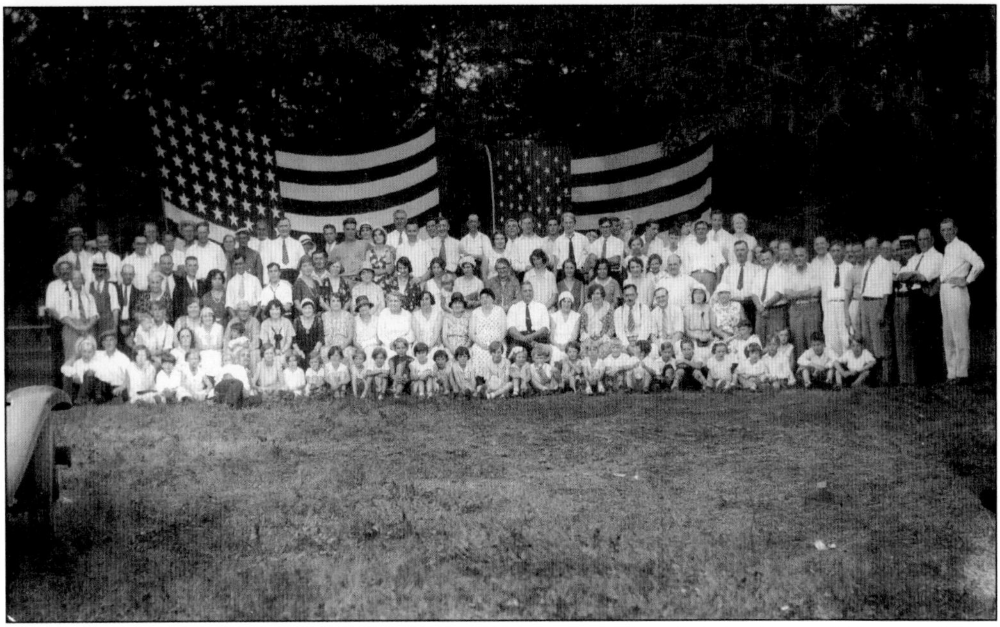

Sons of Norway, c. 1930. In June 1924, 28 Norwegians founded the Sons of Norway, Loyal Lodge 252 in St. James. This fraternal organization originally gathered in Mechanics Hall on Lake Avenue and conducted its early meetings exclusively in Norwegian. During the 1930s, the group constructed its Norway Hall headquarters in St. James on the corner of Seventh Street and Fifth Avenue.

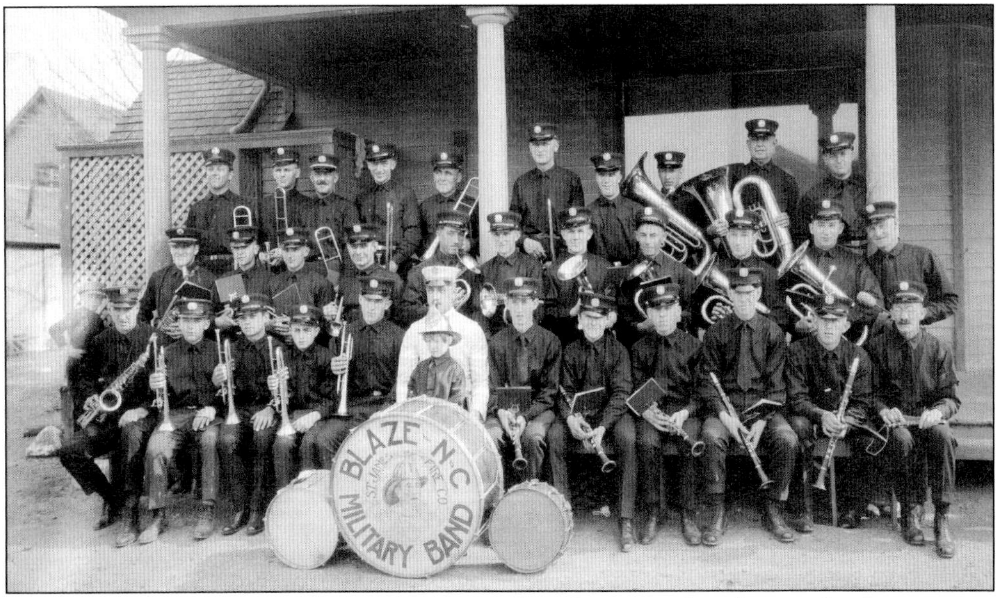

St. James Fire Department, c. 1925. As is often the way with volunteer fire departments, the St. James Fire Department was organized in 1922 after a serious fire that destroyed a local home and grocery store located where the King Kullen grocery store is now situated. The early department's bugle corps was an active part of the fund-raising effort to get new equipment, performing for money at local events and the annual village carnival. As seen here, however, camaraderie was as much a motivation for the bugle corps as money.

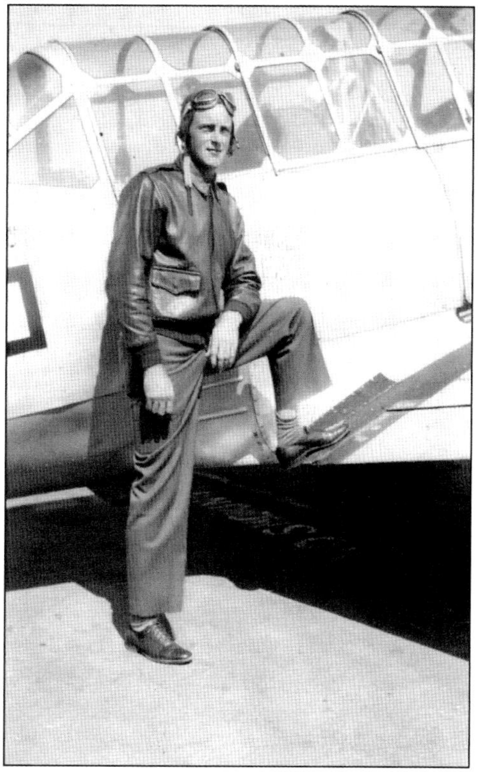

Richard L. L'Hommedieu, c. 1944. The L'Hommedieu name has been in Smithtown since the 1690s, and Richard L'Hommedieu (1920–1990) lived in the area for nearly his entire life, except for the portion that he served in the Army Air Corps during World War II. After the war, L'Hommedieu became a lieutenant in the Smithtown Fire Department while employed full time for the Hazeltine Electronics Corporation in Greenlawn as a template maker, working on the Apollo project among others.

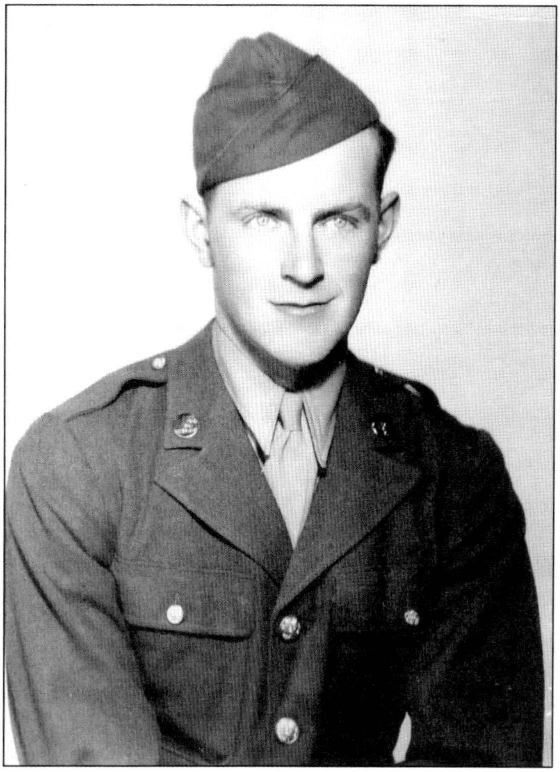

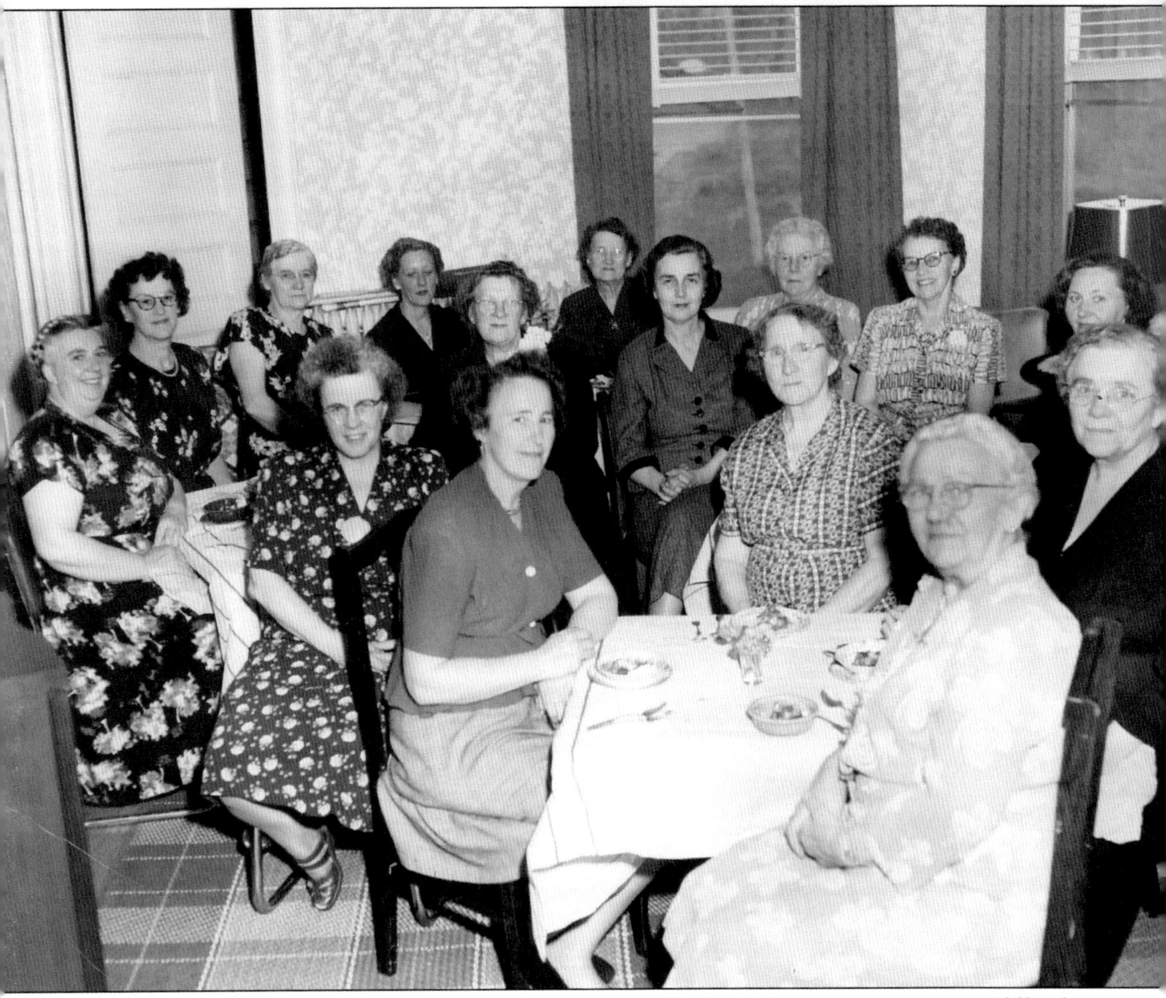

SAVE THE CHILDREN FEDERATION MEETING, C. 1942. Volunteerism among middle-class women during the 1920s, 1930s, and 1940s paved the road to the formation of many local charitable institutions and societies, including the Smithtown Historical Society. The woman sitting fourth from right in the back of this photograph (dark dress with black buttons and collar, no glasses) is Virginia Malone (1898–1978), the owner and publisher of the *Smithtown News* and town historian for 12 years.

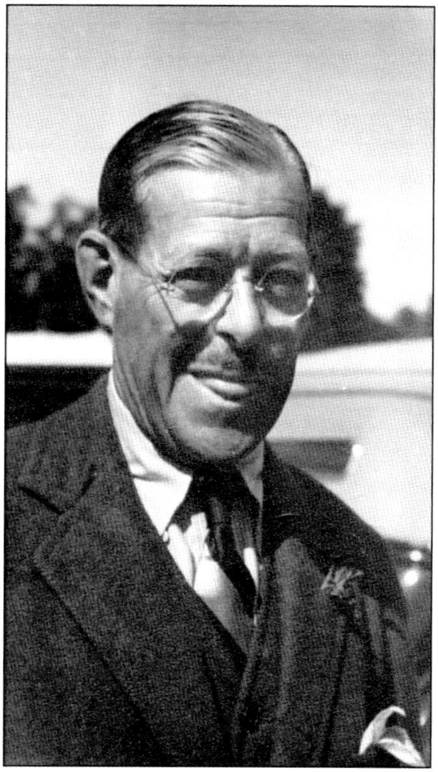

VAIL BLYDENBURGH, C. 1940. One of the founding forces of Smithtown's preservation movement, Vail Blydenburgh (1874–1943) was a successful businessman in the fur and textile trade. As the Colonial outfit attests, Blydenburgh was passionate about local and family history. He was a leader in the creation of the Smithtown Village Green shortly before his death. His house and property, the 53-acre Sweetbriar Farm along the Nissequogue River, eventually became the Sweetbriar Nature Preserve.

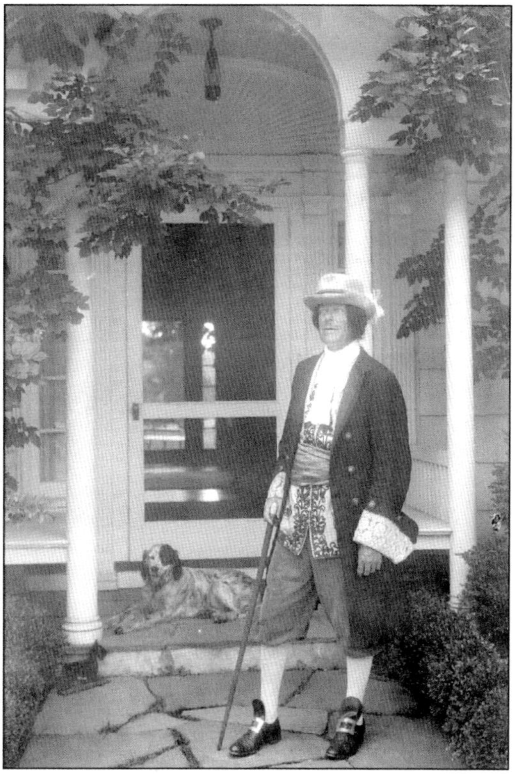

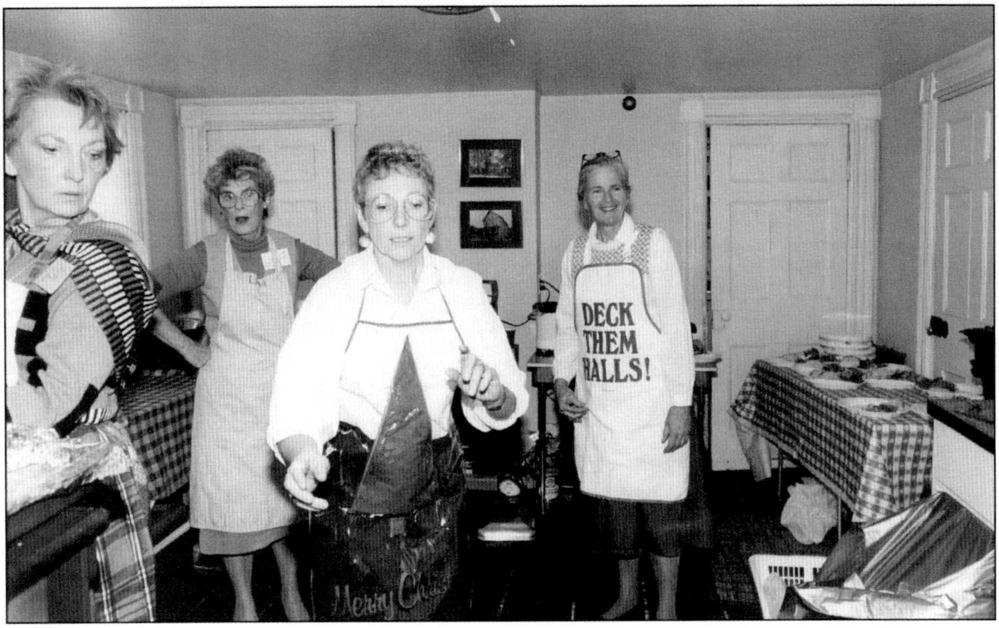

SMITHTOWN HISTORICAL SOCIETY VOLUNTEERS, C. 1988. Originally a schoolteacher, Louise Hall (far right) served as volunteer, bookkeeper, and finally director of the Smithtown Historical Society, a position she held for over 20 years. Under Hall's leadership, the society made significant steps toward its emergence as a professional organization. Since her retirement in 1999, Hall has remained extremely active as a volunteer.

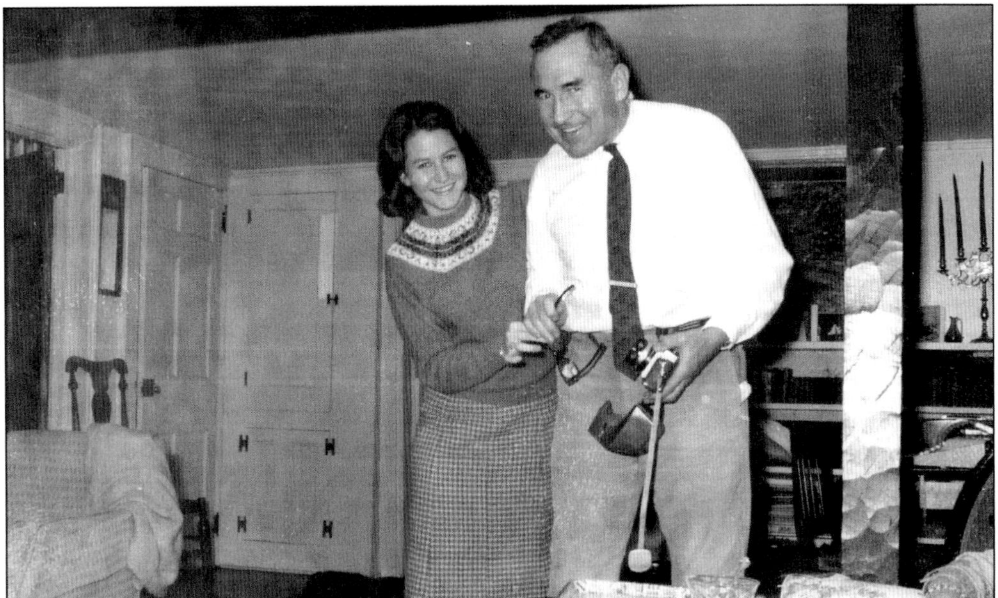

JOAN ROCKWELL AND FATHER, C. 1965. Charles Embree Rockwell (1916–2001) harbored a lifelong dedication to the care of local history. After serving as a United Airlines pilot from 1941 until 1976, Rockwell retired to become a gentleman farmer and focus on his life's work of preserving several family houses and the family farm, which he described as "more or less a memorial to the old families."

Three

Getting There

Prior to the 1870s, Smithtown was very much a bucolic outpost connected to the urbanity of New York City solely by dusty roadways and the rolling waters of the Long Island Sound and Nissequogue River. This all began to change in 1872 when the Long Island Rail Road arrived in Smithtown. Faced with reduced travel time and stress, travelers from New York City were free to consider previously inaccessible areas like Smithtown, St. James, and Kings Park as plausible destinations for a day trip. The arrival of more people in town helped spur economic and business development around and within Smithtown. While initially travelers made the trek east to take advantage of the abundant fresh air and fertile hunting grounds and fishing streams, gradually some realized the residential potential of the country setting and decided to settle in the area.

Within 30 years of the Long Island Rail Road's arrival in Smithtown, automobiles began appearing on the dirt roads of the town. Despite the initial fierce resistance to the new horseless carriage, by the 1920s, the automobile was well on its way to replacing the horse and buggy as the primary mode of transportation. Town officials were compelled to focus on paving and improving Smithtown's vast network of roads to better serve automobile traffic. By the 1930s, all the ingredients were in place for Smithtown to realize a boom in both population and land development. Before long, the rustic charm of 19th-century Smithtown gradually gave way to the suburban present.

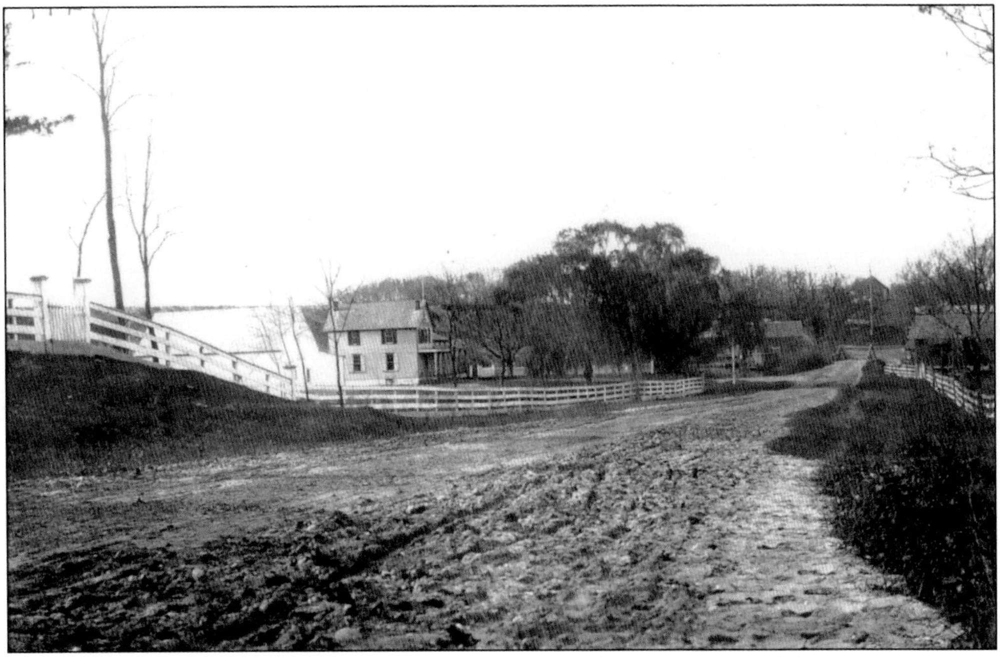

Jericho Turnpike, c. 1878. Looking west to where the statue of the bull now stands, this sweeping pastoral vista makes a stark contrast to the congestion and commercial signage that characterizes the area today. The Smithtown section of the turnpike, as with most other roads in town, remained unpaved until the 1920s.

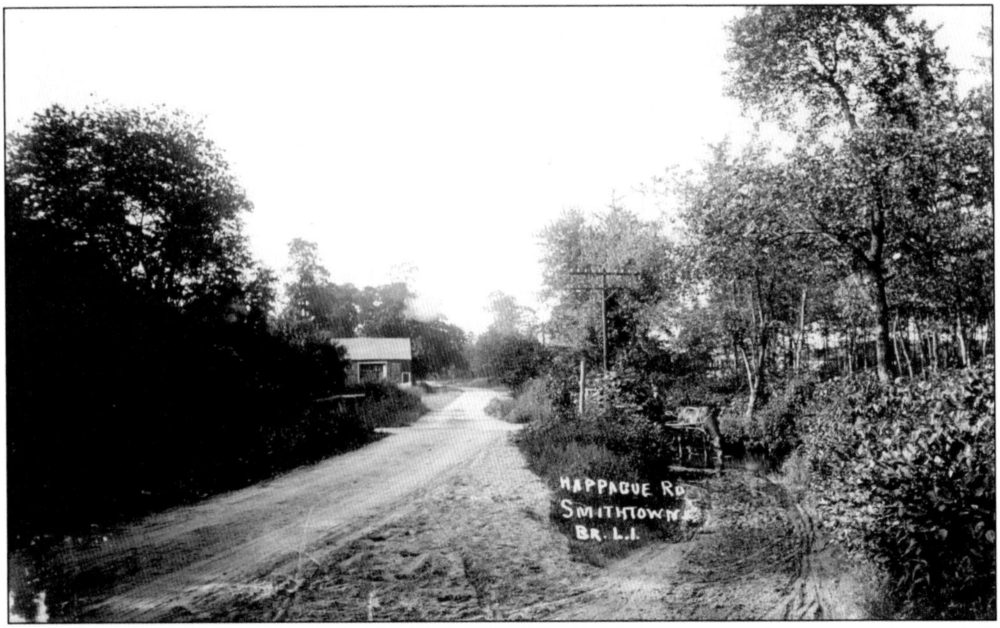

Old Hauppauge Road, c. 1910. Hauppauge Road, now more commonly known as New York Route 111, was an important roadway that provided travelers an easy route from Smithtown to Hauppauge as well as points south. It first begins to appear on local road maps as a paved road in the mid-1920s. Modern drivers may look with envy at this quiet scene of the area just south of where the Smithtown Post Office stands today.

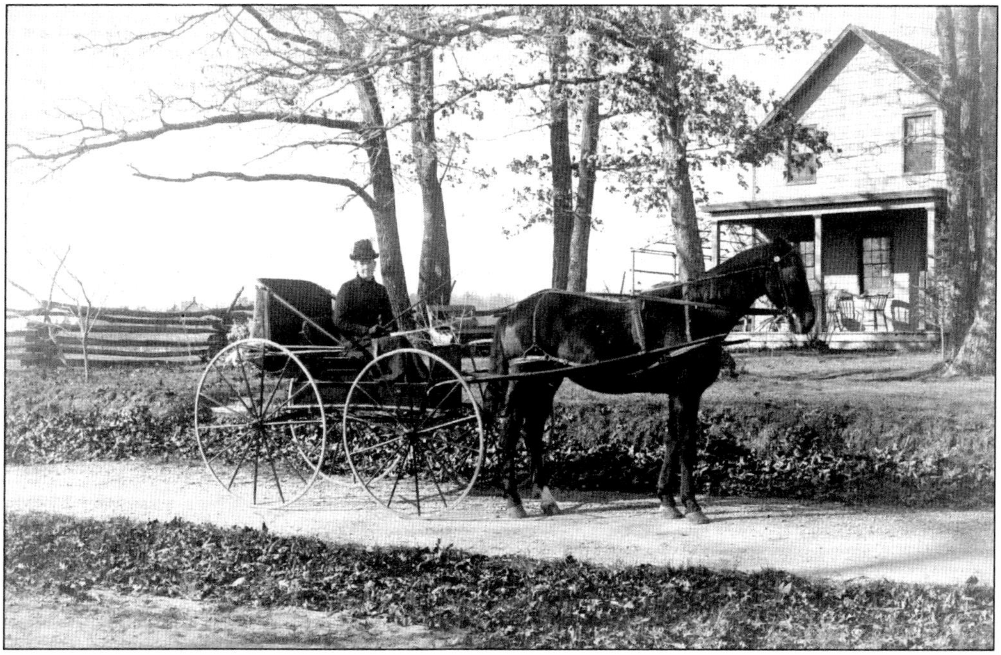

WOMAN AND HER BUGGY, C. 1890. Prior to the advent of the automobile, the most common means of vehicular transportation was the horse-drawn buggy. The unidentified woman here is stopped outside what was known as the Call House located near the current intersection of Bank and Main Streets in Smithtown's central business district.

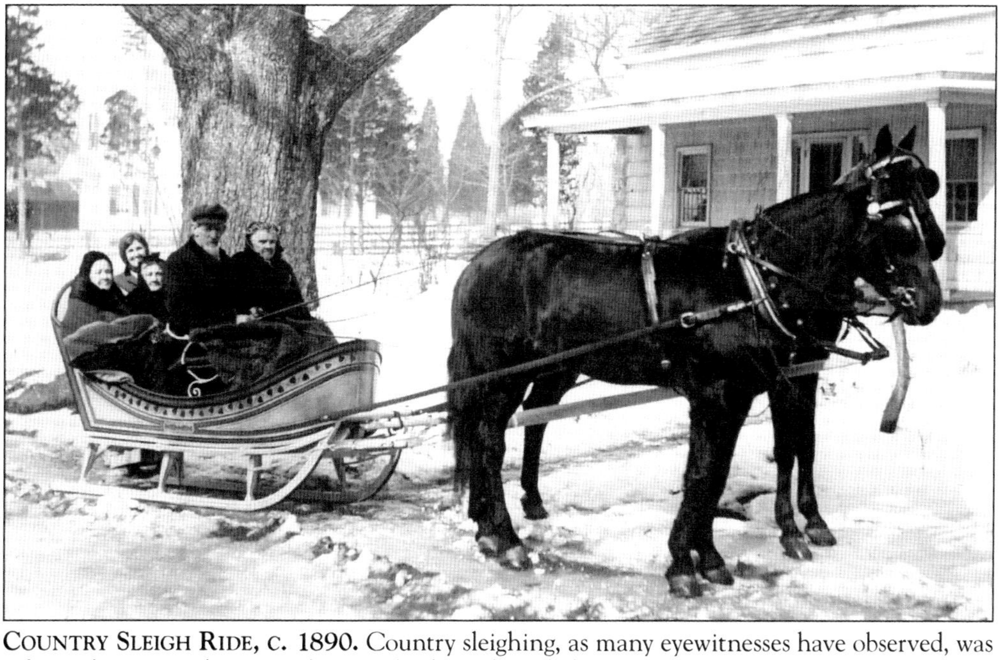

COUNTRY SLEIGH RIDE, C. 1890. Country sleighing, as many eyewitnesses have observed, was a favored pastime along Smithtown's back roads and channels. Alma Blydenburgh's 1833 diary entry for January 17 notes, "Mr. Floyd been to the river and took Em and myself for a sleigh ride. Good sleighing!" The sleigh seen here is now in the collection of the Long Island Museum in Stony Brook. (Smithtown Library.)

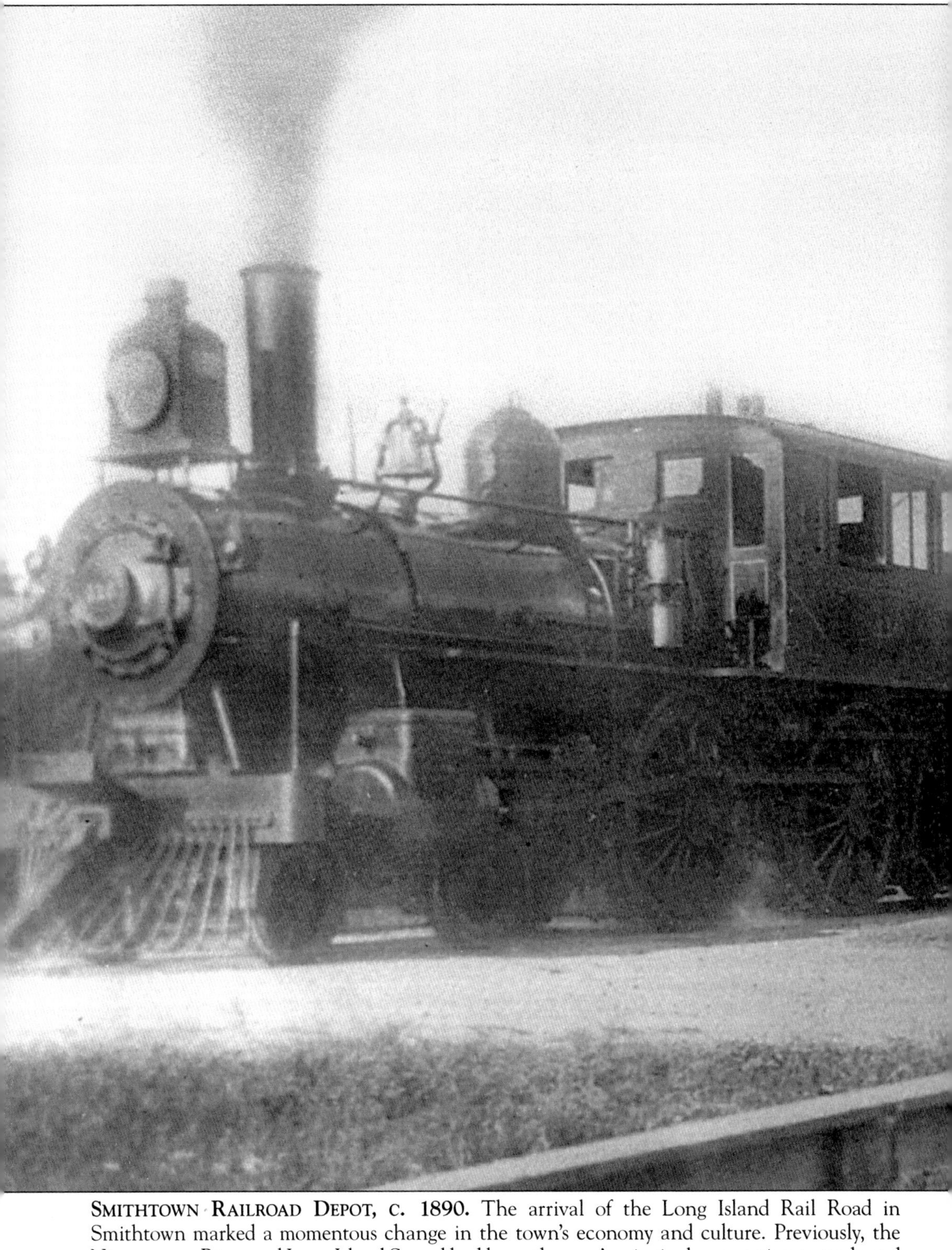

SMITHTOWN RAILROAD DEPOT, C. 1890. The arrival of the Long Island Rail Road in Smithtown marked a momentous change in the town's economy and culture. Previously, the Nissequogue River and Long Island Sound had been the area's principal connection to trade and

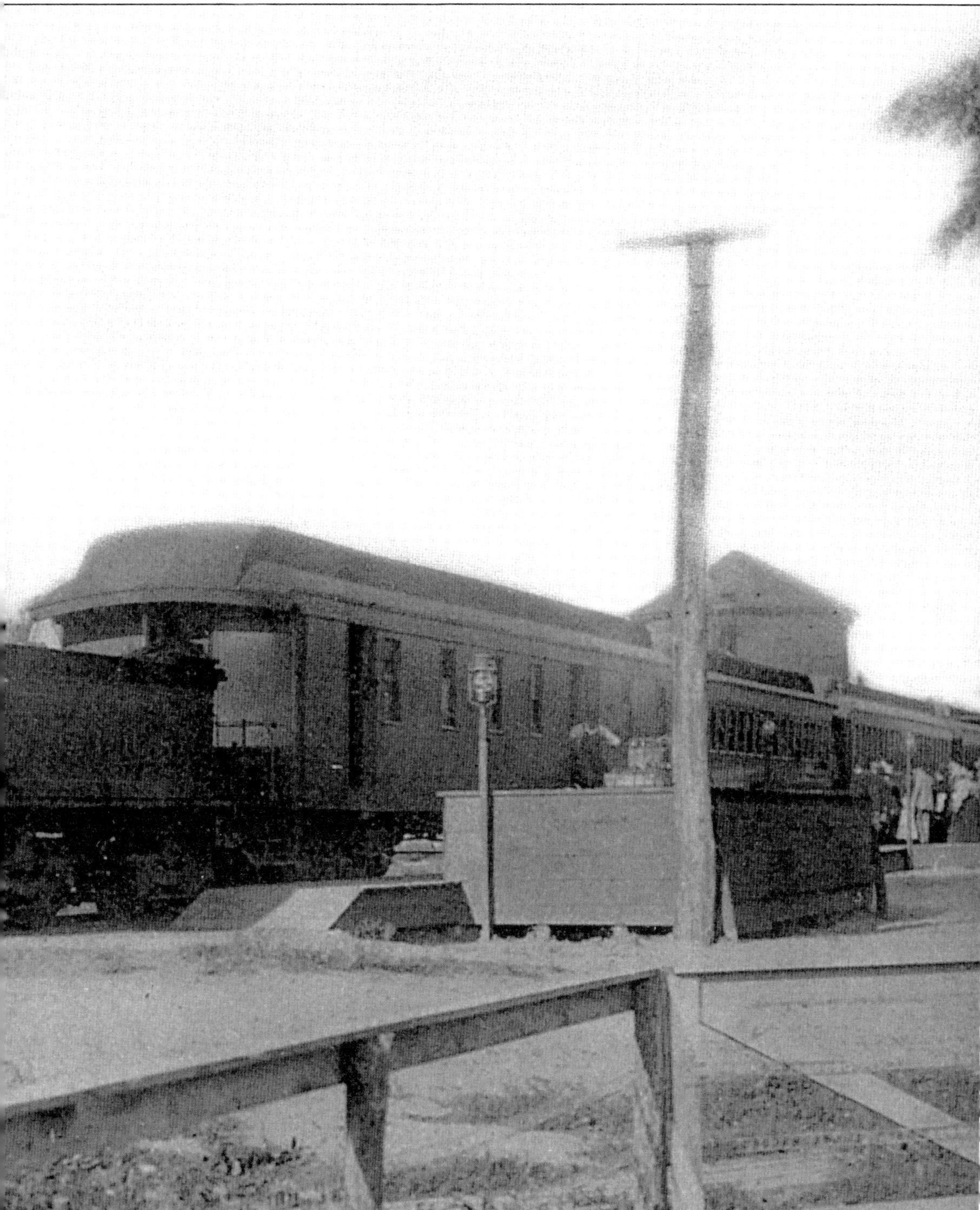

travel routes. After 1872, local farmers could load wagons full of produce onto flatbed railroad cars headed for New York City. In turn, city residents discovered Smithtown as a summer tourist spot. (Earl Scott.)

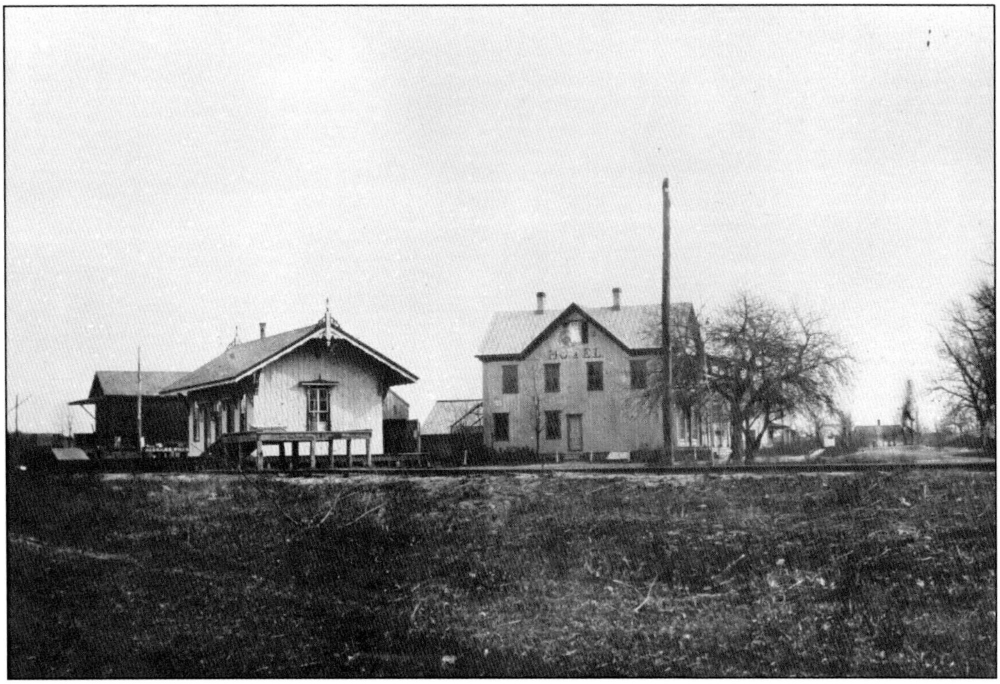

SMITHTOWN'S RAILROAD STATION, C. 1878. Trainor's Hotel, seen here at right, was located next to the Smithtown railroad depot. For many years, it provided weary travelers with convenient accommodations until it burned to the ground on December 5, 1909. It was never rebuilt.

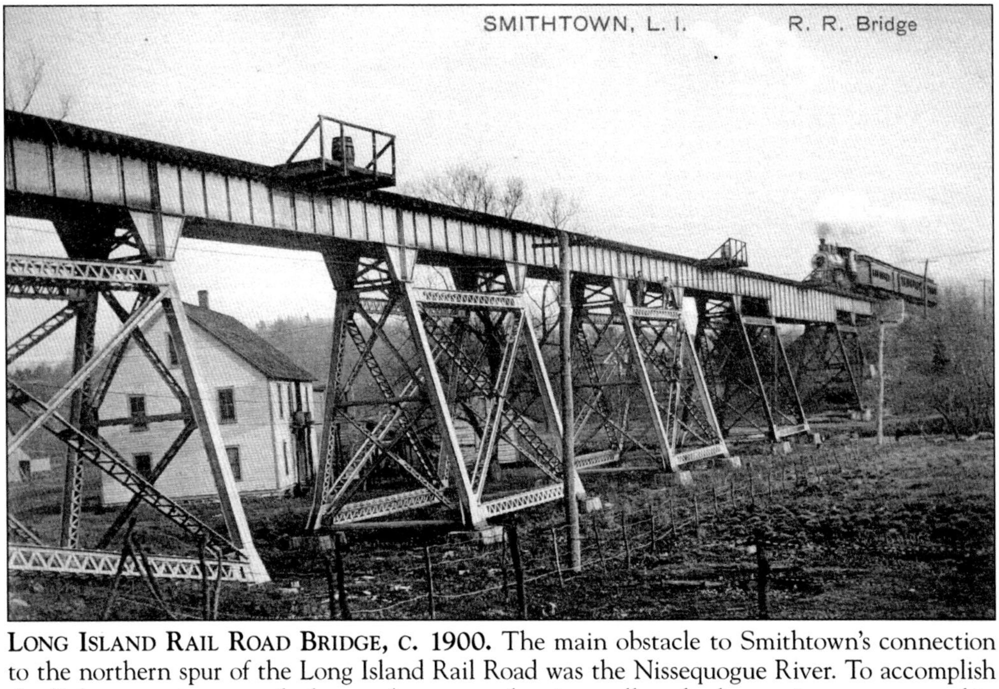

LONG ISLAND RAIL ROAD BRIDGE, C. 1900. The main obstacle to Smithtown's connection to the northern spur of the Long Island Rail Road was the Nissequogue River. To accomplish the linkage, engineers crafted a trestle to span the river valley, the largest iron structure of its kind on Long Island. The monumental structure stood over 50 feet high and spanned a distance of 490 feet.

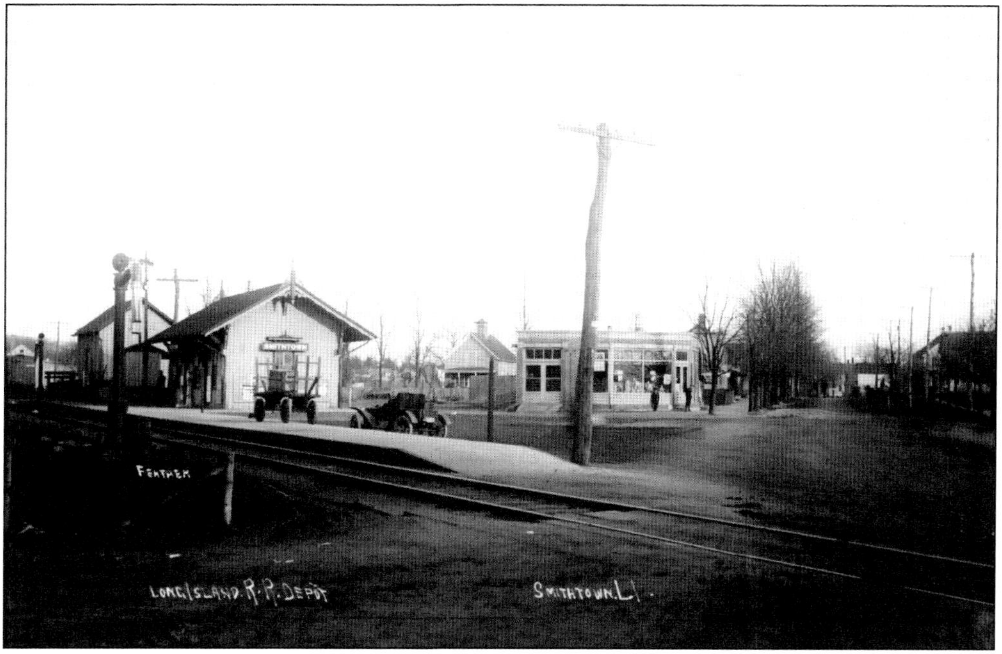

RAILROAD STATION AND MAIN STREET, C. 1910. The Smithtown railroad depot is seen here sitting to the left of the railroad crossing at Main Street. In 1937, an underpass was constructed to eliminate the intersection and reduce the potential danger it caused to motorists and pedestrians.

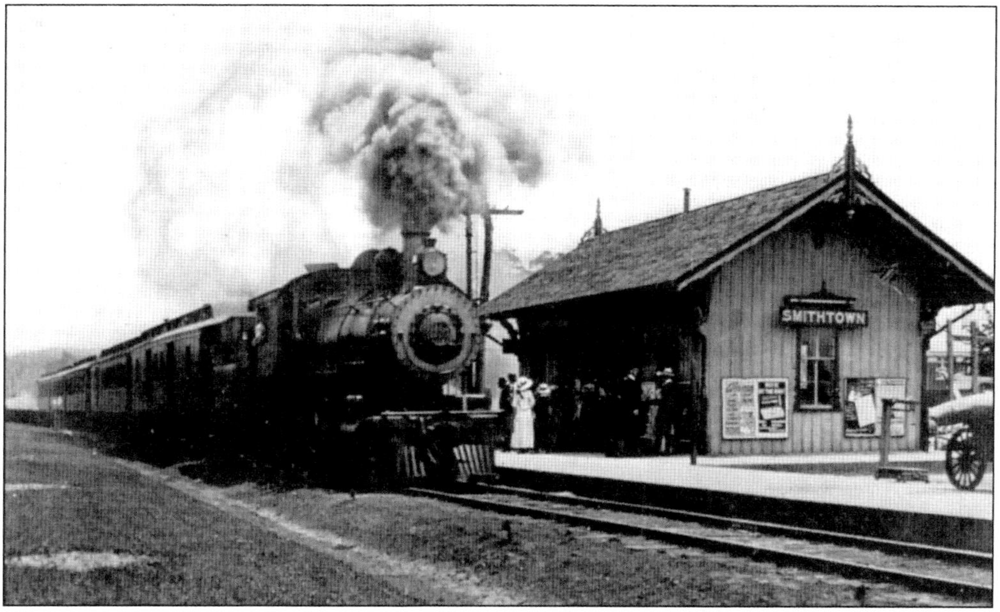

TRAIN IN SMITHTOWN STATION, C. 1910. Smoke dramatically billows from the train as it pulls into the Smithtown station to accept its waiting passengers. The original ornately detailed Victorian-era station house seen here no longer functions as a train station. It was replaced by a more modern structure in the 1920s. The first station was sold, relocated to Lawrence Avenue in Smithtown, and converted to a private residence.

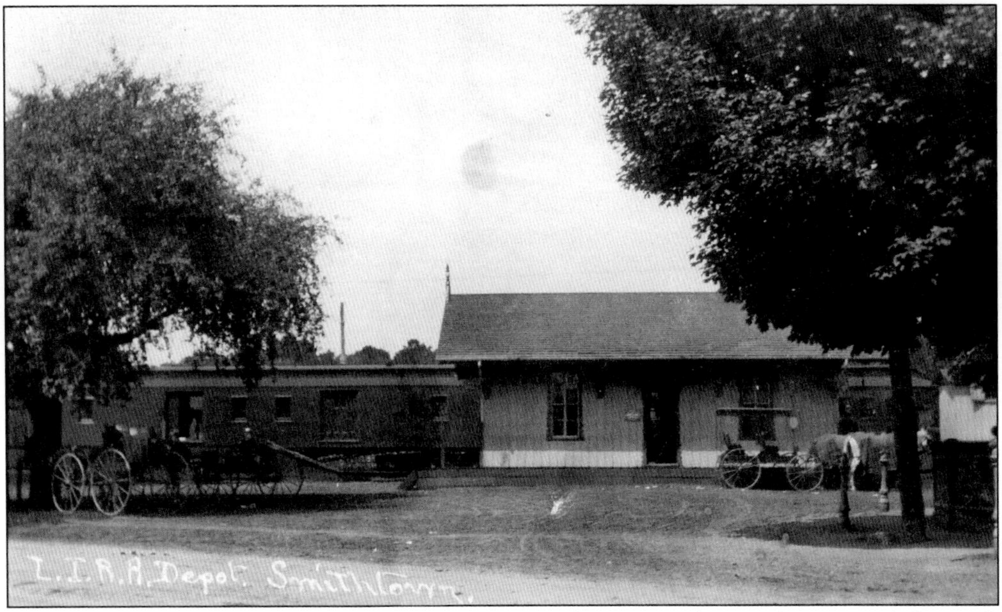

SMITHTOWN RAILROAD STATION, C. 1904. Horse-drawn omnibuses, the taxis of the 19th century, await the arrival of the train and its passengers into the Smithtown station. While automobiles were present in Smithtown by this time, they had not replaced the horse-drawn apparatus as the primary means of conveyance.

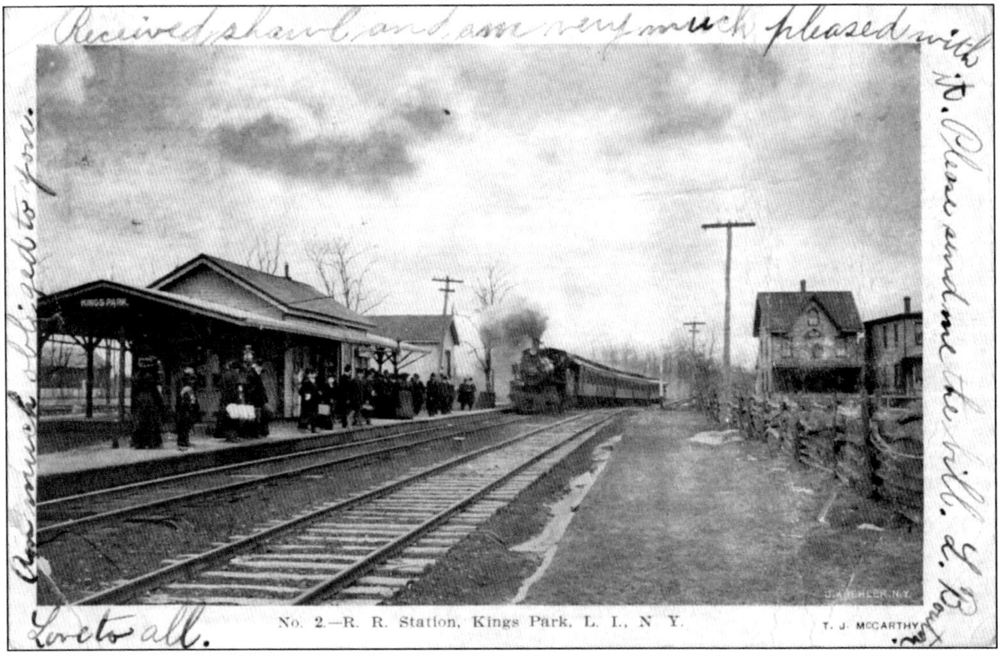

KINGS PARK RAILROAD STATION, C. 1900. Initially christened St. Johnland after Dr. William Augustus Muhlenberg's Society of St. Johnland, the central business district of what is now Kings Park first began to develop around the new railroad station in the 1870s. In 1891, the railroad station and burgeoning community were renamed Kings Park in connection with the recently founded Kings County Farm and Asylum.

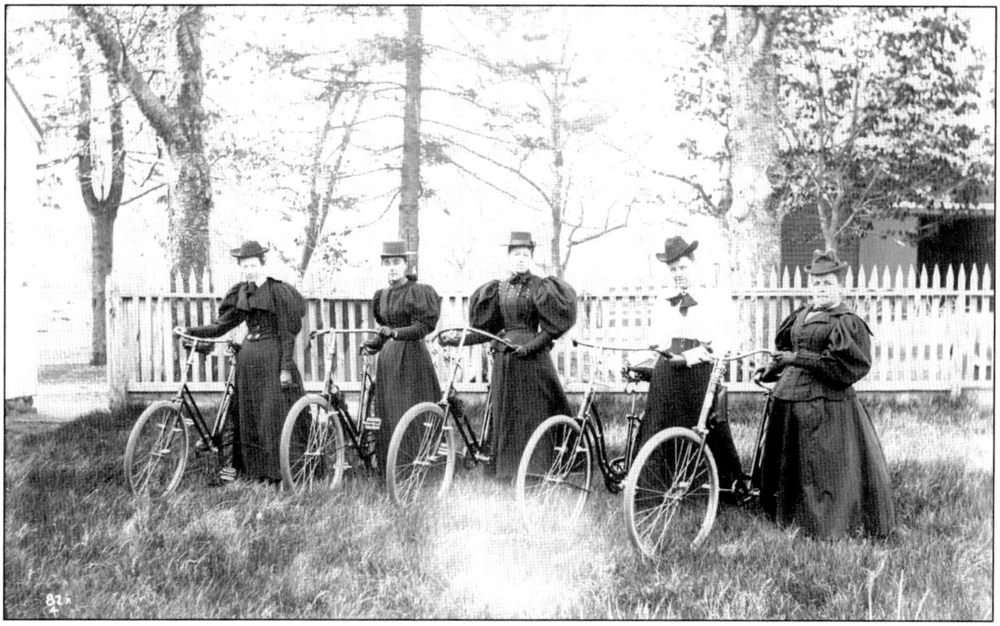

LADIES AND THEIR BICYCLES, C. 1895. Bicycles first became a popular fad in the Smithtown area in the 1890s. Within 20 years, however, the trend had become a nuisance in the eyes of town officials. In 1911, Smithtown's town board issued a motion banning bicyclists from riding on town sidewalks. Any rider caught violating the order could be levied a fine in amounts up to $5. (Smithtown Library.)

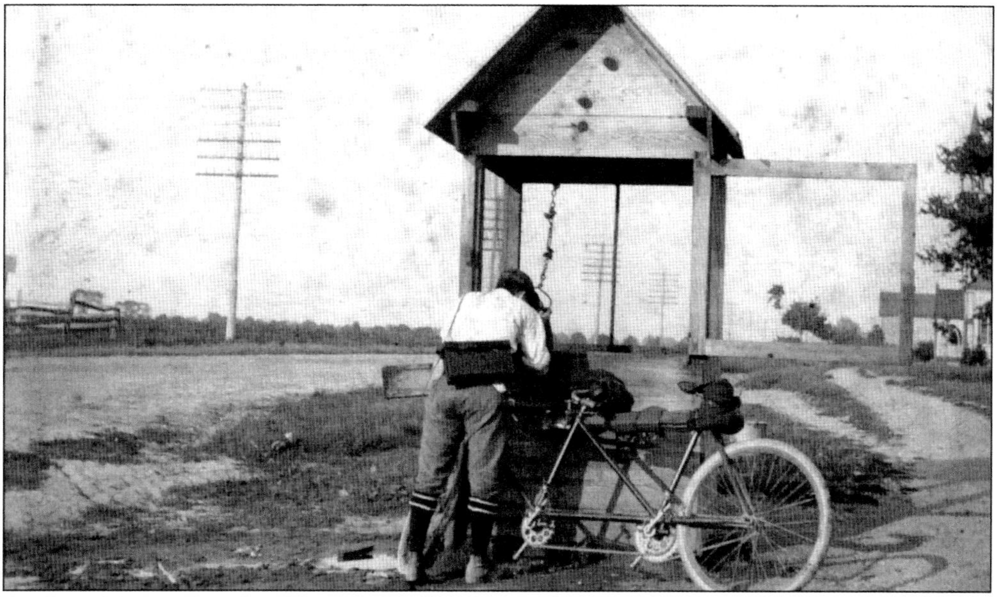

JERICHO TURNPIKE, C. 1900. By the late 1890s, bicyclists were urging both the Town of Smithtown and Suffolk County to follow local millionaire Richard H. Handley's example and construct dedicated bicycle paths to allow riders greater safety and comfort as they wound through town. Handley, an early bicycle enthusiast, had personally funded the construction of a bike path from his estate in Hauppauge out to Smithtown. Eventually Suffolk County constructed such a path along Jericho Turnpike.

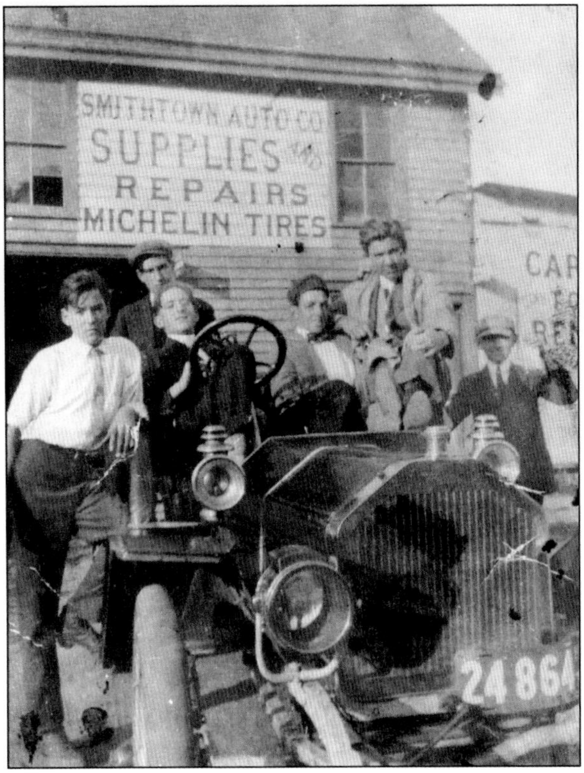

SMITHTOWN AUTOMOBILE COMPANY, C. 1915. The first automobile to appear in Smithtown was a 1901 Locomobile Steamer owned by a Dr. George T. Fanning of Smithtown Branch. Within the year, Coe D. Smith and Richard H. Handley had followed Fanning's lead, and Smithtown's automotive era was officially underway. Less than 20 years later, these young men proudly pose with the 1910 Buick they had toiled to fix up.

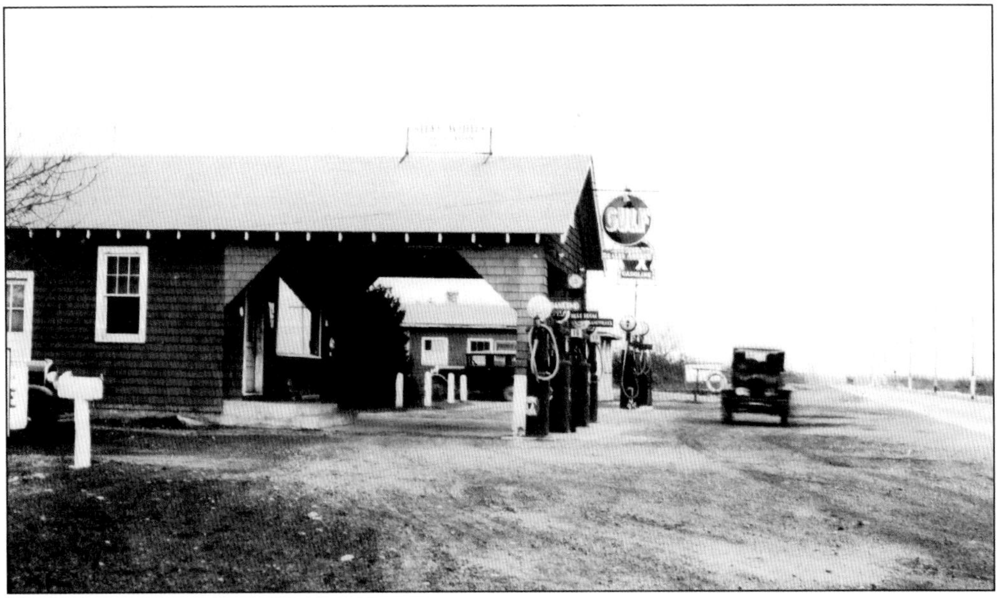

WHITE'S GAS STATION, C. 1932. The town's first filling stations arrived shortly after automobiles. Local resident Frank Brush describes Smithtown's first gas station: "The Standard Oil Co. installed a 275 gal. tank and hand pump at Huntting's general store [in 1904]. By turning a handle you would pump up one gallon then reverse it and run it down for another gallon." Steve White's gas station, seen here, employed similar pumps.

VANDERBILT MOTOR PARKWAY, C. 1906. One of the most important leaders of the early automobile era was Arthur Raynor Pardington (at right), an engineer who lived in Smithtown. Pardington designed the world's first limited access roadway, the Vanderbilt Motor Speedway (below), for his friend and business partner William Kissam Vanderbilt. The highway stretched nearly 60 miles from Ronkonkoma through Smithtown all the way to the Queens border and was the first road constructed with the use of reinforced concrete. Pardington also went on to finish the first transcontinental highway in the country, the Lincoln Highway (Route 30, officially dedicated in 1913). He died in 1915.

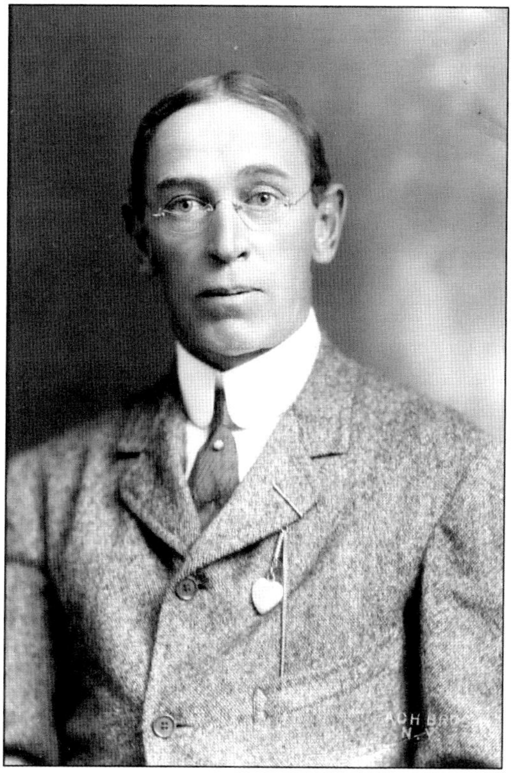

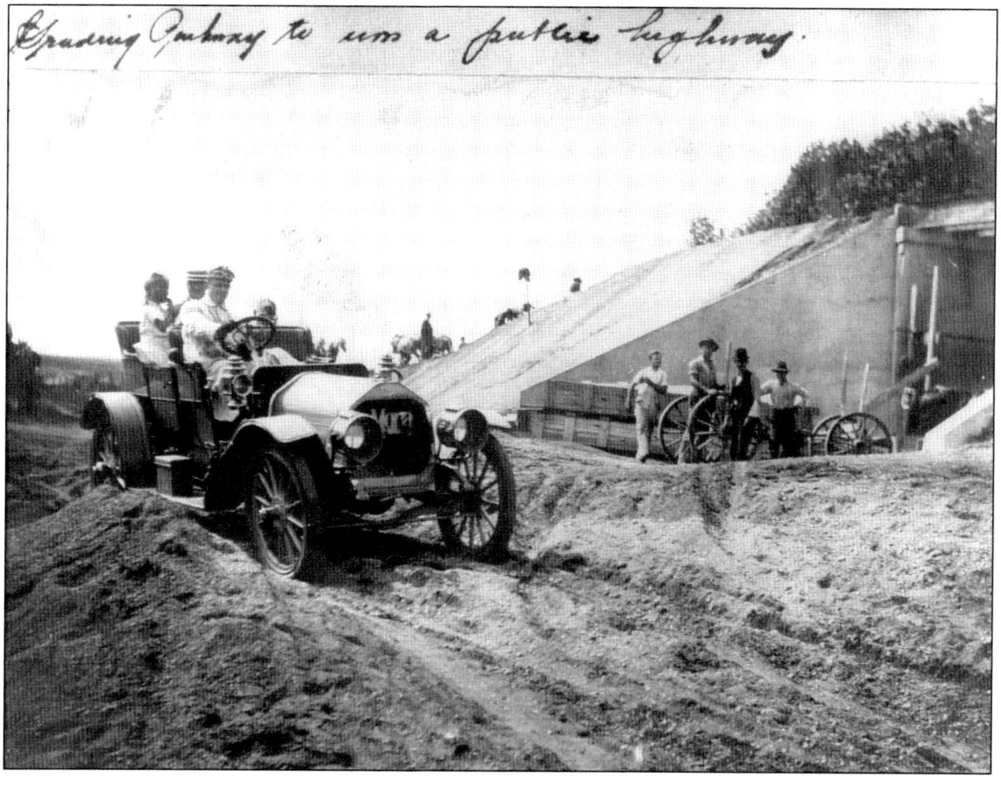

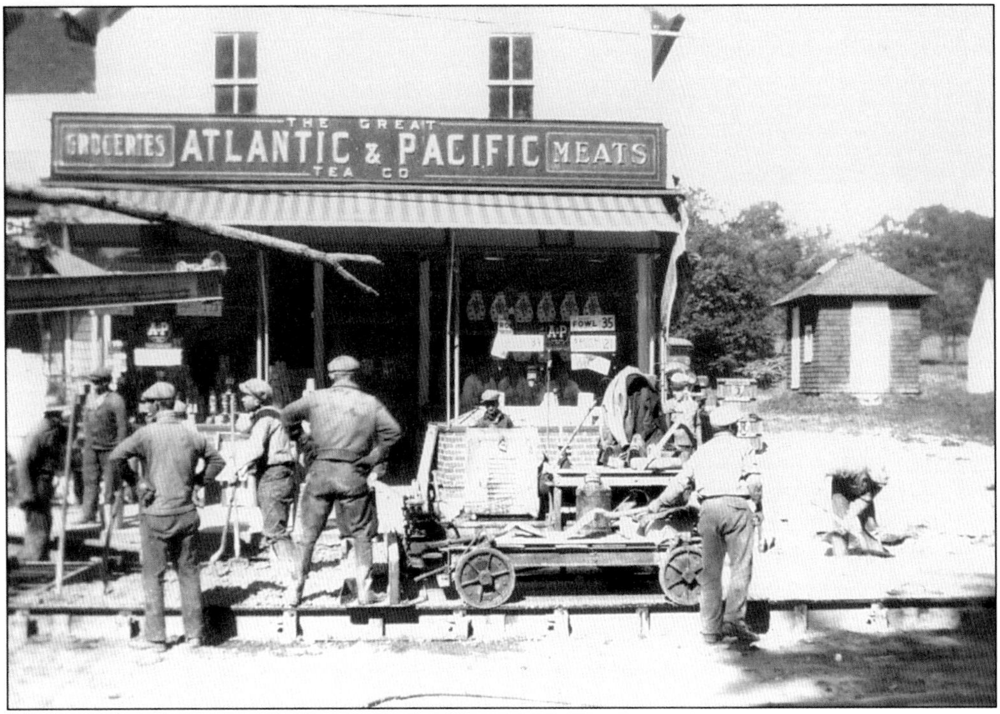

Smithtown Highway Department, c. 1927. As the automobile rapidly gained acceptance in Smithtown, it became clear that the town's network of roads was becoming outdated. By the 1920s, the Smithtown Highway Department had begun to acquire machinery to help keep up with the demand of creating and improving roadways suitable for car use. By the end of the decade, the highway department had successfully paved many of Smithtown's main roads. Above, the crew paves Main Street in front of the A&P. Below, highway superintendent Frank Valentine (standing in front of the tractor) and crew work to create an automobile-friendly road. (Above, Lee Corbani.)

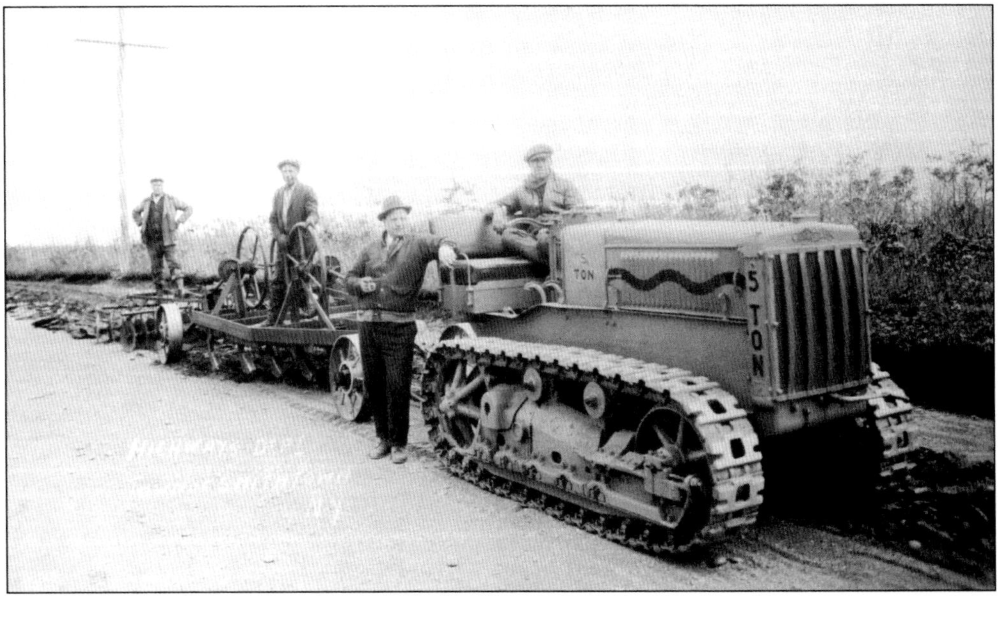

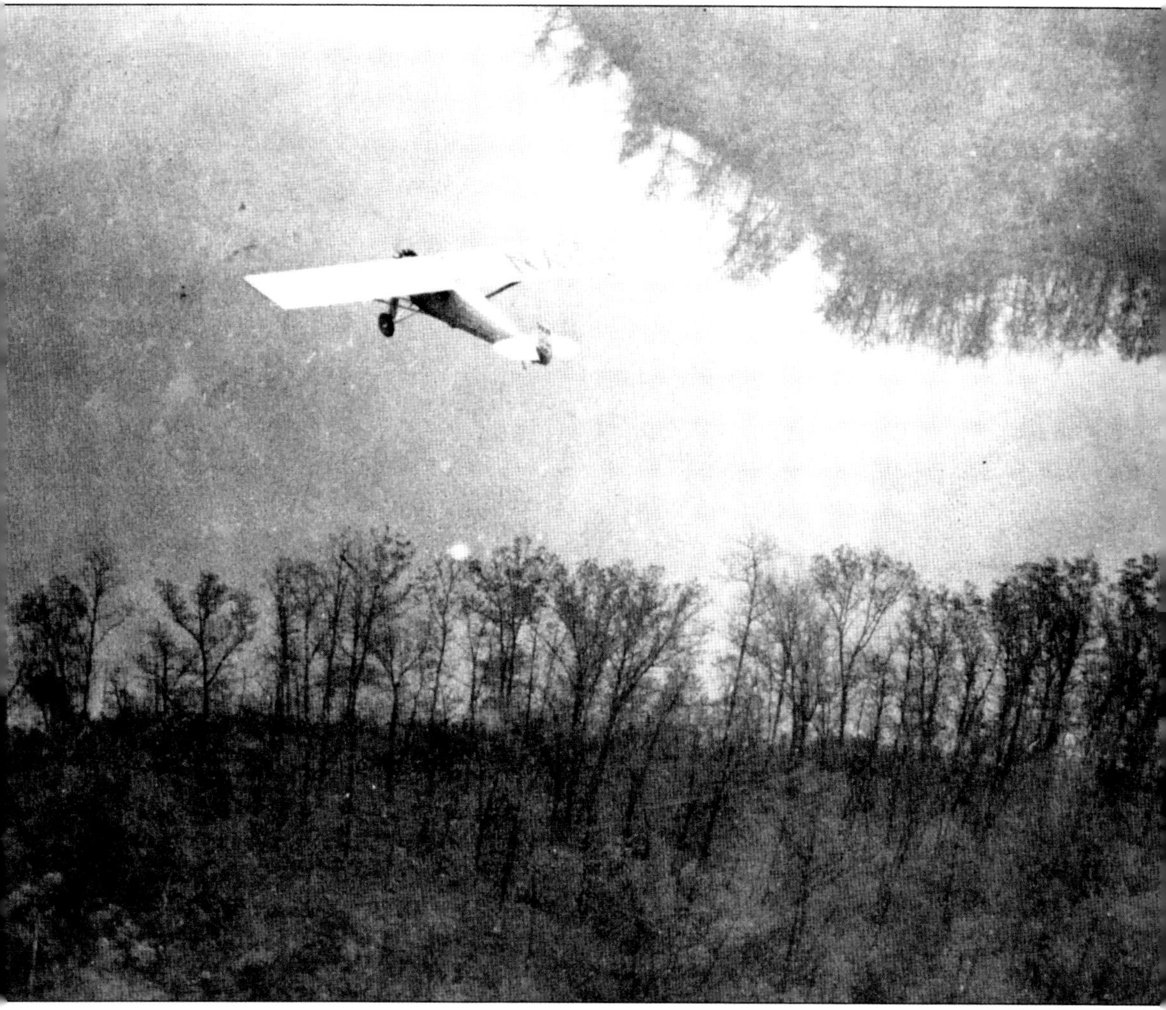

CHARLES LINDBERGH, 1927. This iconic photograph, the only known picture of Lindbergh after his departure on his first solo transatlantic flight, was taken on May 20, 1927, over New Mill Pond in Hauppauge. After lifting off from Garden City, New York's Roosevelt Field, "Lucky Lindy" flew over Smithtown on his way to making history. As Lindbergh made his way over the Rockwell Farm, located at 245 Middle Country Road, a young Charles Embree Rockwell caught a glimpse of the famed aviator. Perhaps it was this moment that later inspired Rockwell to become a commercial pilot for United Airlines. (Library of Congress.)

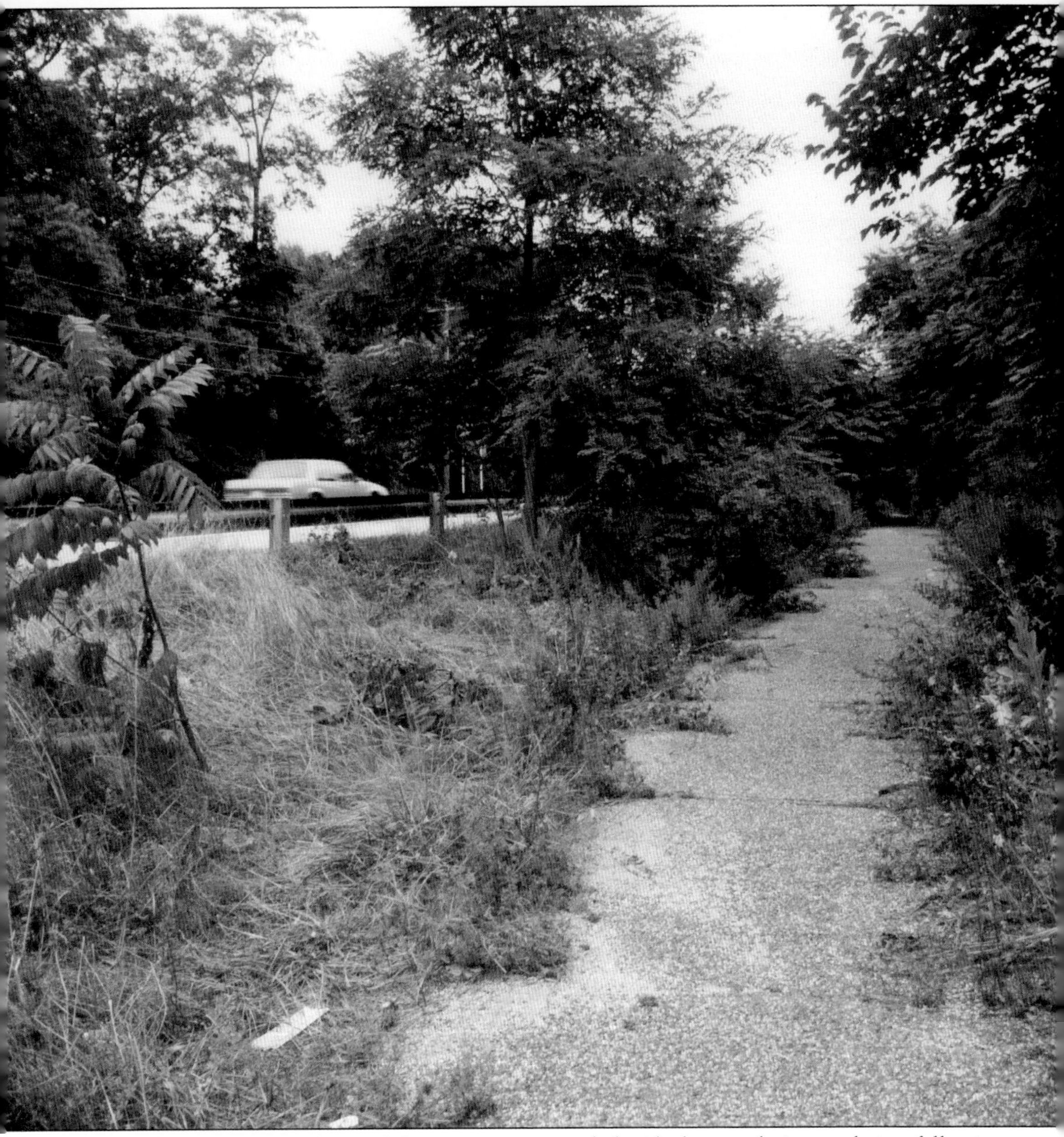

ROUTE 111, C. 1999. Automobile innovations coupled with the population explosion following World War II rendered some town roads inadequate for mid-20th-century Smithtown. As automobiles were able to move faster, roads such as Route 111 (Hauppauge Road), replete with curves and limited sight lines, became hazardous for motorists. In 1962, New York State designed a plan to remedy some of the dangers. The initiative called for the reconfiguring and straightening of Route 111 such that its new terminus would be at the intersection of Routes 25 and 25A. While there were other aspects of the plan that the town's citizens defeated (a proposed widening of Route 25), the Route 111 project was completed by 1966. Here the new and old Routes 111 sit next to each other on a stretch of the roadway south of the Branch Shopping Center.

Four

MADE IN SMITHTOWN

John Lawrence Smith described the town's agriculture as "one of the richest and most prosperous" on all of Long Island in 1882. However, he was less confident about its industry and trade, which he deemed to be "behind the age." Transportation improvements over the next several decades released Smithtown from its relative isolation and led to the growth of business districts in each of its villages by the 1920s. Hotels and tourist-oriented businesses gradually gave way to retail-oriented operations. Automobile and truck transportation on Jericho Turnpike and the Long Island Expressway by the early 1960s led to even more large-scale economic growth. Between 1956 and 1963, five shopping centers were constructed in the township. By the time the tercentenary was celebrated in 1965, Smithtown had several active chambers of commerce and a host of new car dealerships, banks, and building suppliers.

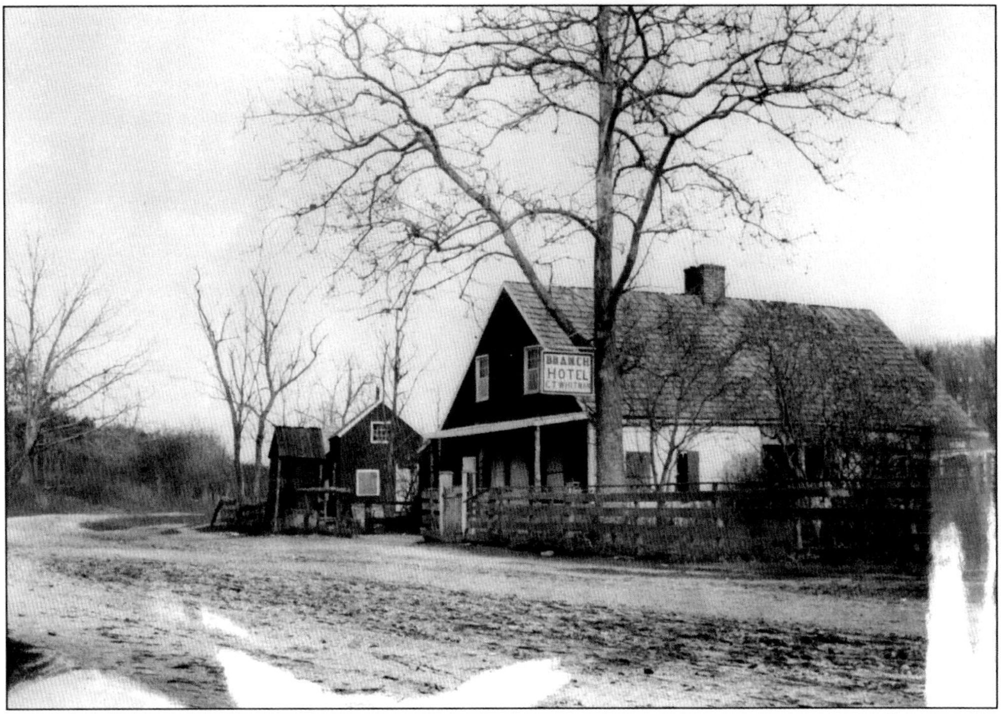

SMITHTOWN BRANCH HOTEL, C. 1878. The Smithtown Branch Hotel was located a quarter mile east of the Smithtown Presbyterian Church on the east side of North Country Road.

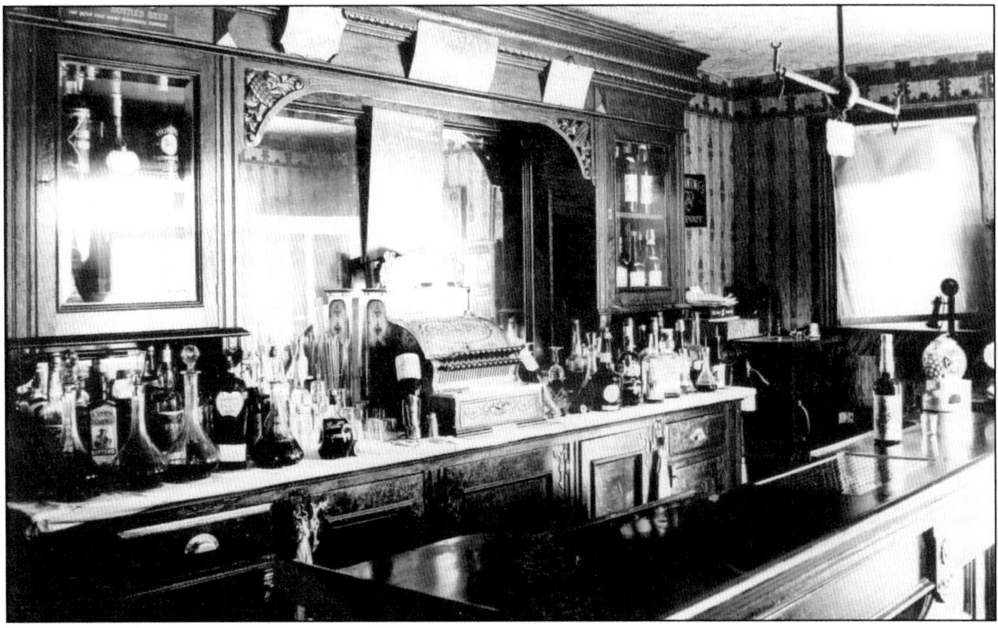

GUS KOHR'S BAR, C. 1915. Along with a beautiful wraparound veranda outside the hotel, this fully stocked bar was certainly an enticement for patrons seeking lodging during the early 1900s. Gus Kohr's North Shore Hotel was located near the present-day entrance of Sunken Meadow State Park. The structure was later cut in half, with one side remaining on the original site and the other being relocated east of Kohr Road.

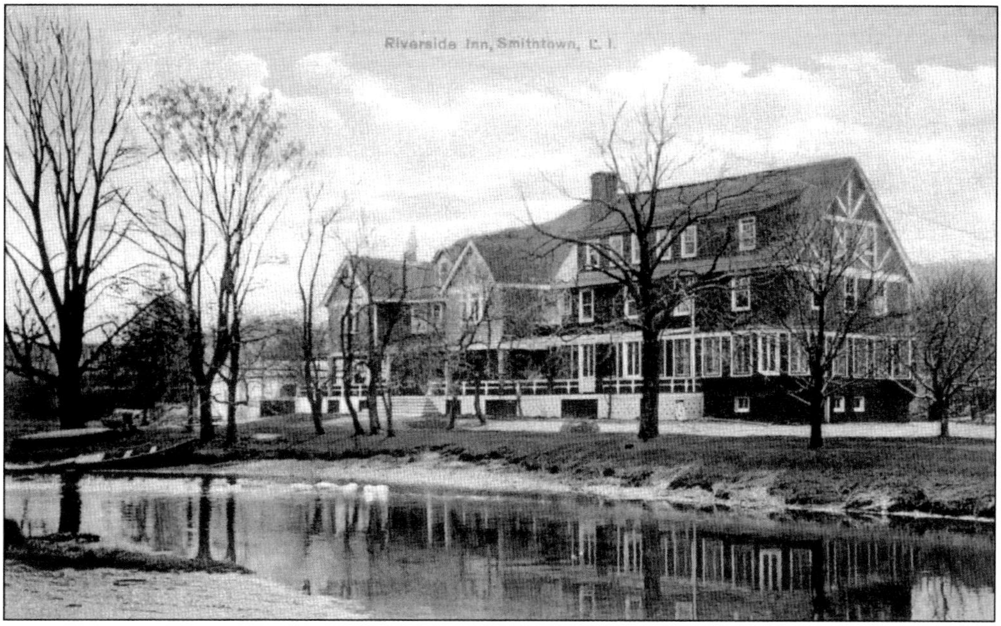

RIVERSIDE INN, C. 1905. Located at Head of the River, the Riverside Inn was owned and operated by William N. Spurge, whose father had been a hotel proprietor in New Rochelle. After the original 1875 inn burned down in 1900, Spurge reopened a much more spacious hotel in March 1901. The improved Riverside Inn featured hot and cold running water, steam heat, and acetylene gas.

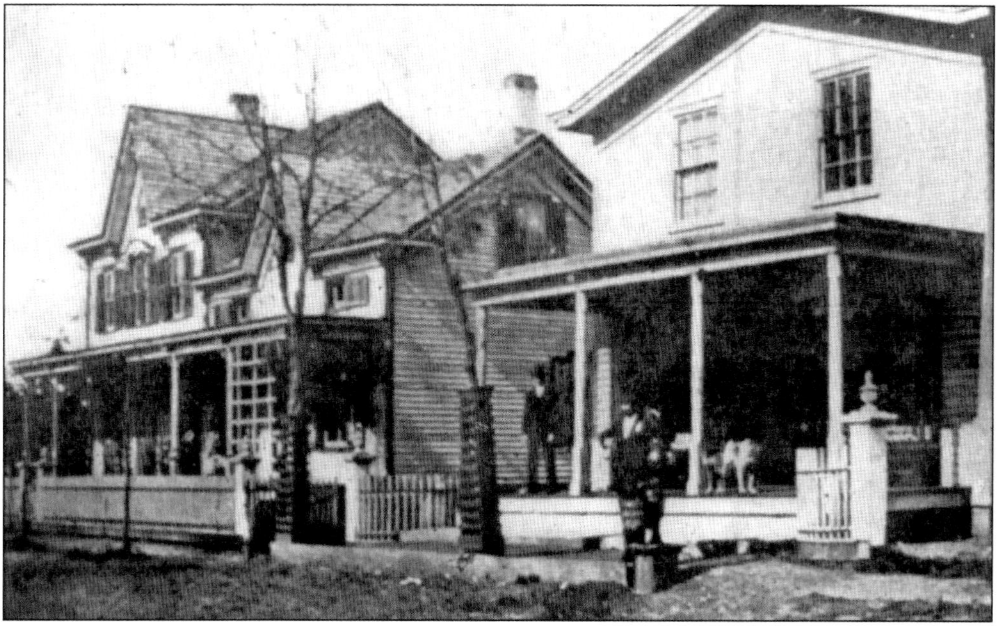

DONALDSON GENERAL STORE. The first Donaldson General Store, at right in the photograph, operated for 34 years until it was struck by lightning and burned down on August 10, 1904. A second store was constructed on the same site and operated until it too was struck by lightning and burned down. The third store built on the site eventually became Temple Beth Chai before being demolished in 1980.

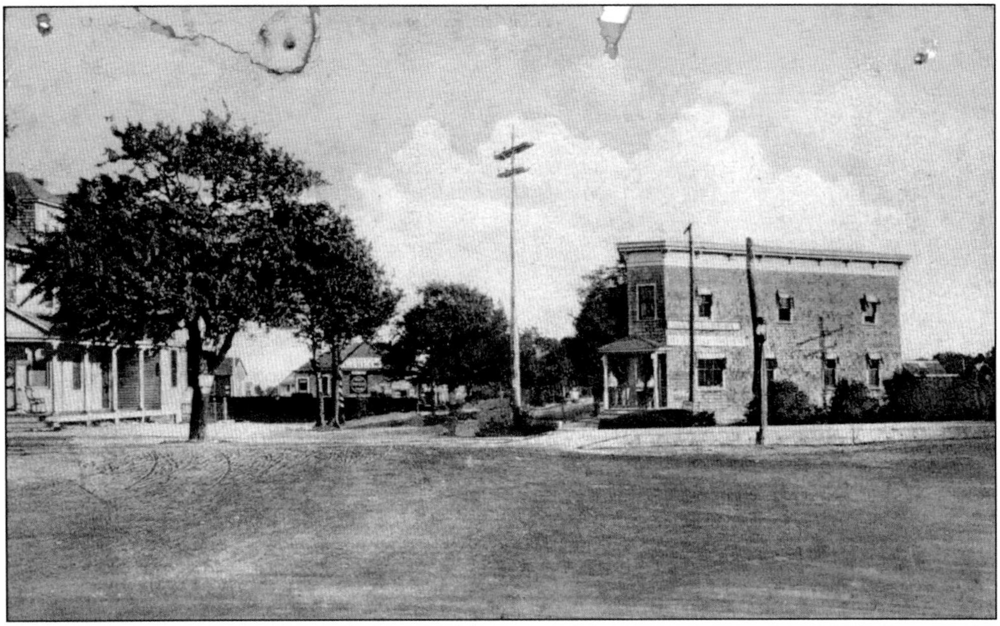

LAKE AVENUE. Joseph Amey's flatiron building at right was constructed in 1908. During the Depression, this structure housed Larry Smith's Stationery and Ice Cream Store. The Riis building at center was constructed sometime after 1917 and housed Phil's Market. The building at left is the Nissequogue Hotel, erected on the corner of Lake and Railroad Avenues in 1905. It survived until a Christmas fire in 1952.

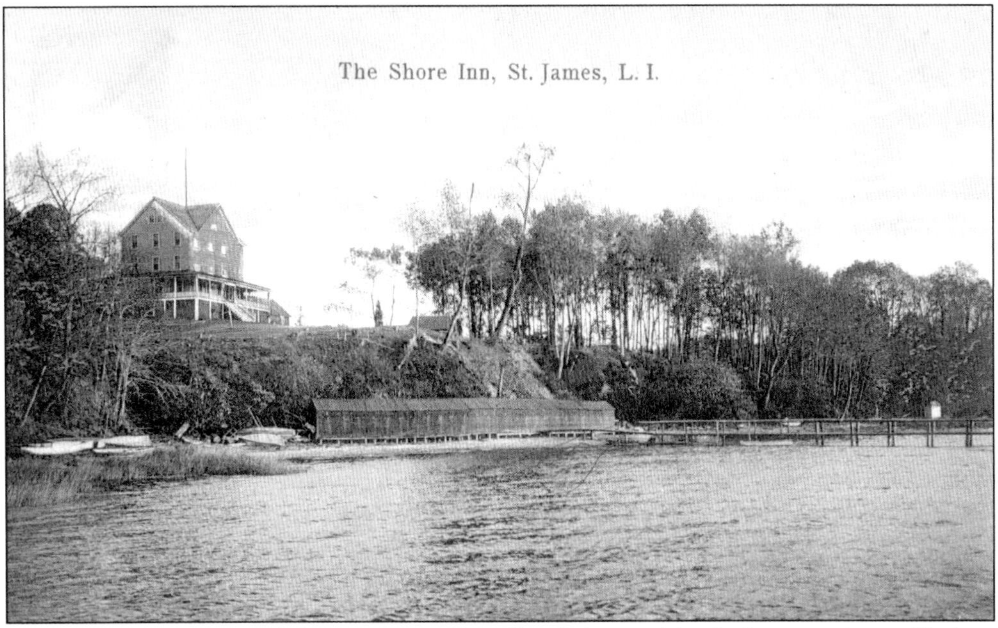

SHORE INN, C. 1910. Built by actor Tony Farrell and designed by St. James architect Herbert Smith, the Shore Inn boasted 82 rooms, each with breathtaking views of Stony Brook Harbor. According to a newspaper account, the inn's 1902 opening was accompanied by "song and dance, with ball games and clam steams, with pipe and timbrel, sea bathing and boat races, recitals by eminent comediennes and gymkhana races." (Diane Michels Henze.)

EVERETT SMITH GENERAL STORE. One of the more popular local landmarks to this day, the St. James General Store (as it is known today) was originally owned by Everett Smith, who built it in 1857. The store also became a social center of sorts and, for a short time, the local post office. In 1990, it was purchased and preserved by Suffolk County and the Friends for Long Island's Heritage.

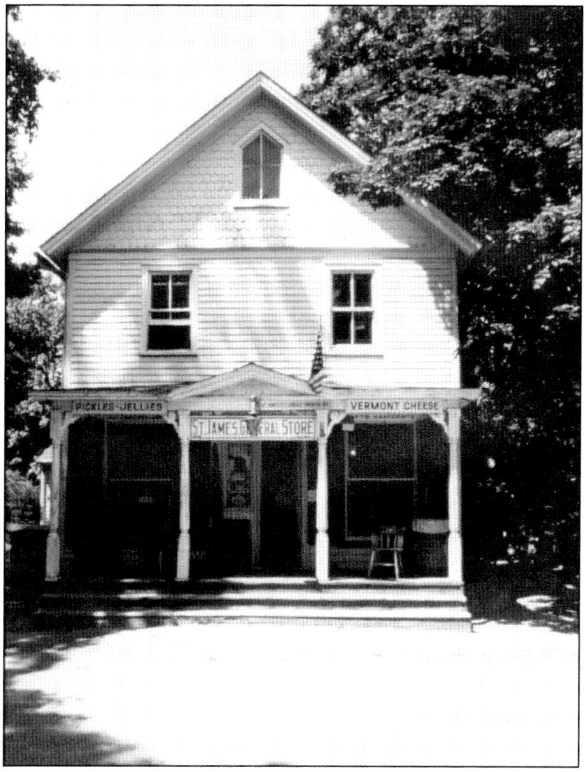

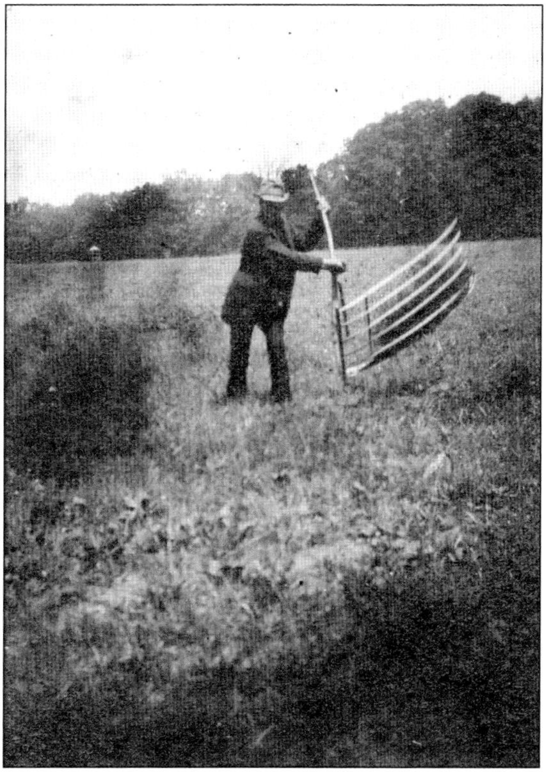

CHARLES E. LAWRENCE, C. 1903. Charles E. Lawrence (1852–1923) was labeled an "old horseman" in his obituary for his skillful training of horses as well as his breeding and raising of champion race thoroughbreds such as Baronward. Simultaneously, Lawrence ran a prosperous farm in Hauppauge. He raised oats, cabbage, potatoes, and corn and is seen here cutting and dropping hay into piles.

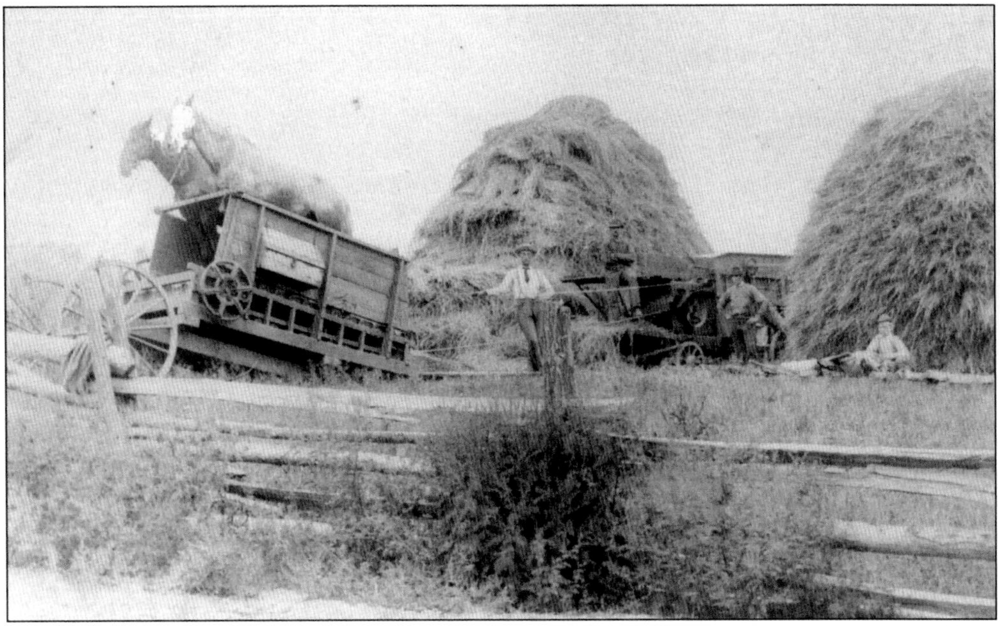

O'Berry's Farm, c. 1895 Farmers use a horse treadmill in the gathering and baling of hay. According to John Lawrence Smith, the hay was "pressed into bales of about 200 pounds and shipped to the city, by sloop or rail, and always returns the farmers remunerating prices . . . This is one of the richest and most prosperous [farming] towns in the county or on the island in comparison to the number of its inhabitants."

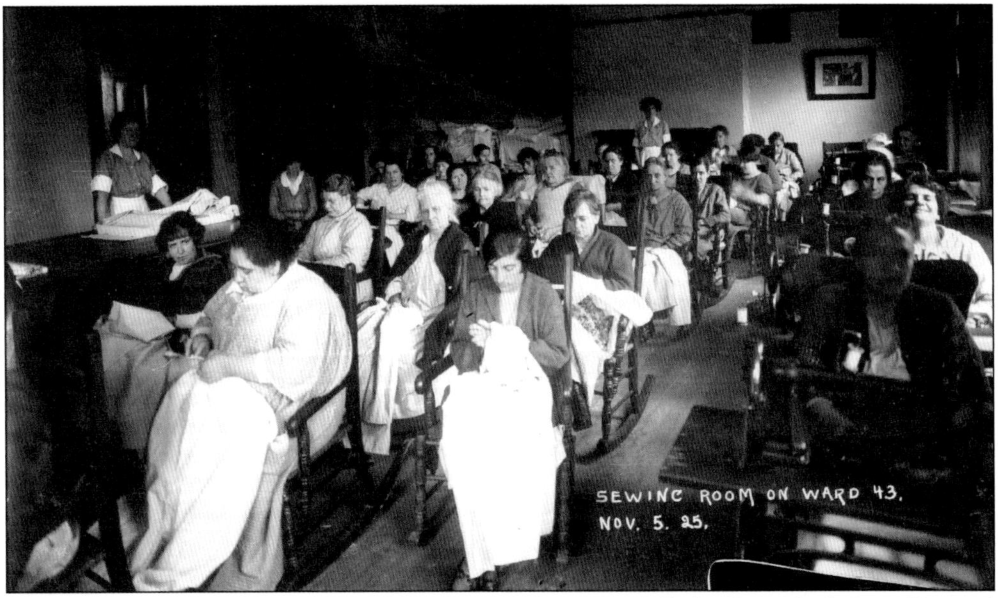

Kings Park State Hospital, c. 1917 From its origins in 1885, the Kings Park State Hospital for mental patients grew to an operation of enormous capacity. As seen here, the hospital's early-20th-century treatments emphasized vocational and other activity-based forms of therapy. Indeed, more than 70 percent of the hospital's patients were employed on the hospital grounds. Women engaged in these sewing activities were seen as benefiting from their work as well as providing economically efficient supplies for the hospital.

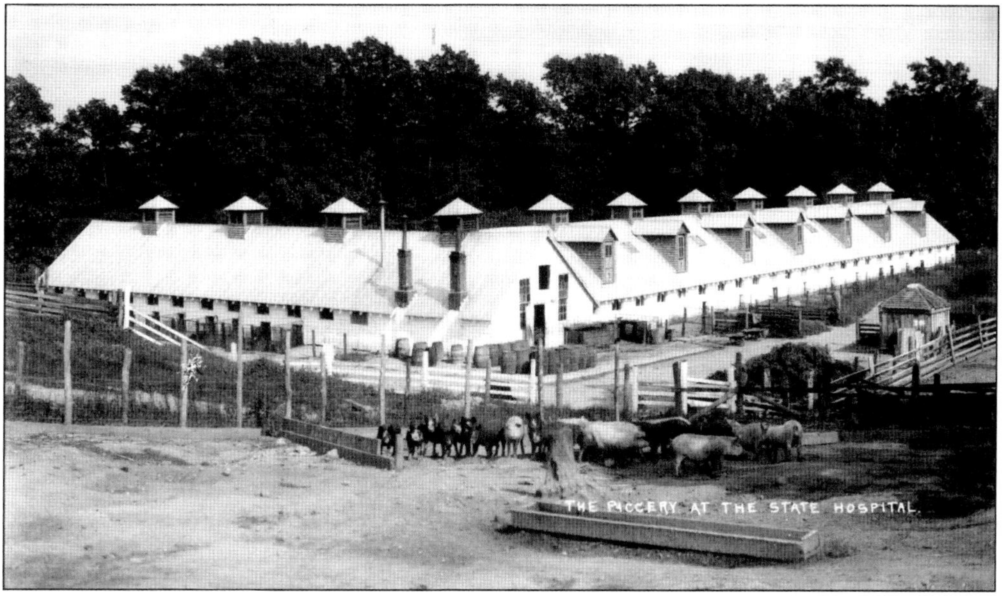

PIGS AT KINGS PARK STATE HOSPITAL, C. 1917. The hospital's farm program was extremely far-flung and included large numbers of livestock and 169 cultivatable acres by 1917. The hospital's farm also became inextricably tied to the Long Island Food Reserve Battalion during World War I, providing over $40,000 worth of food products annually to the war effort by 1918. In addition to well-regarded vegetable produce, the farm harvested substantial amounts of fresh pork, beef, and dairy products.

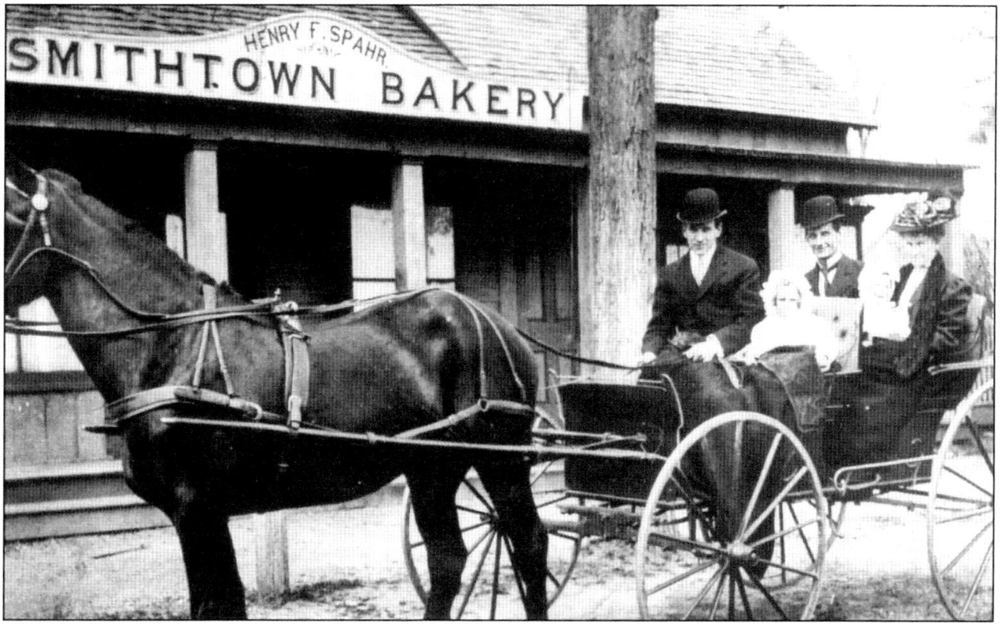

HENRY F. SPAHR AND FAMILY, C. 1910. German immigrant Henry F. Spahr originally learned to bake as a soldier in Cuba during the Spanish-American War. Spahr acquired this building—previously owned by baker Augustus Silliman—in the early 1900s. He is pictured here at the reins of his wagon along with, from left to right, little Ruth, his brother William, and his wife Ada, who holds William Jr.

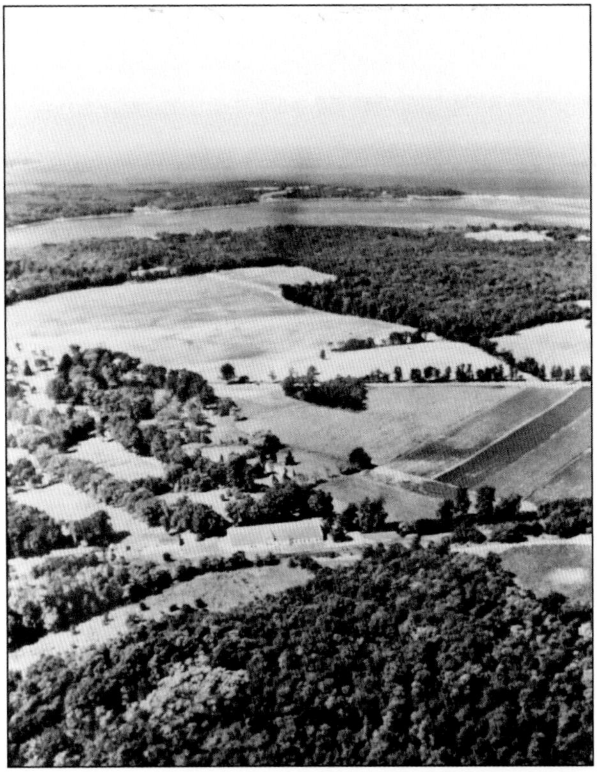

FLOWERFIELD, C. 1942. Located at the junction of Route 25A and Mills Pond Road, the 362-acre Flowerfield Bulb Farm opened in 1917 and included a five-building complex and a railroad depot for shipping. In the early 1950s, the site became related to military technology when the Gyrodyne Company of America purchased it for helicopter and other aerial manufacturing. Today much of the site has been incorporated into the campus of the State University of New York at Stony Brook, although it also now includes fairgrounds, a catering site, and a day care center.

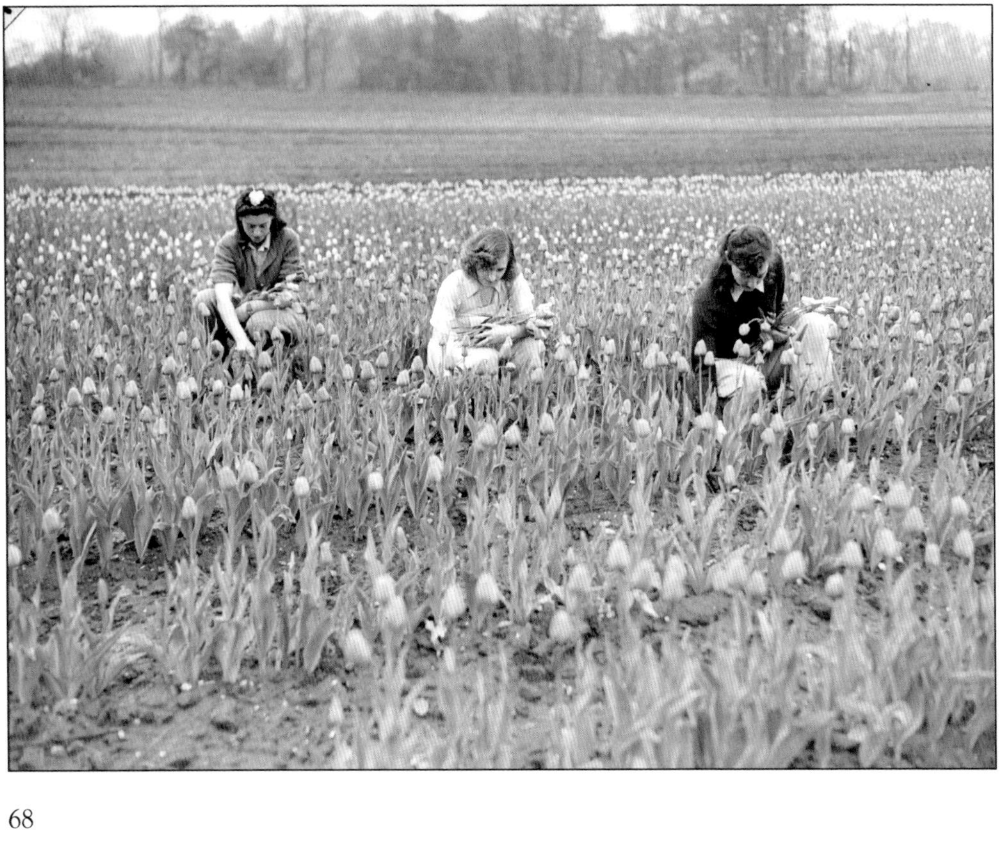

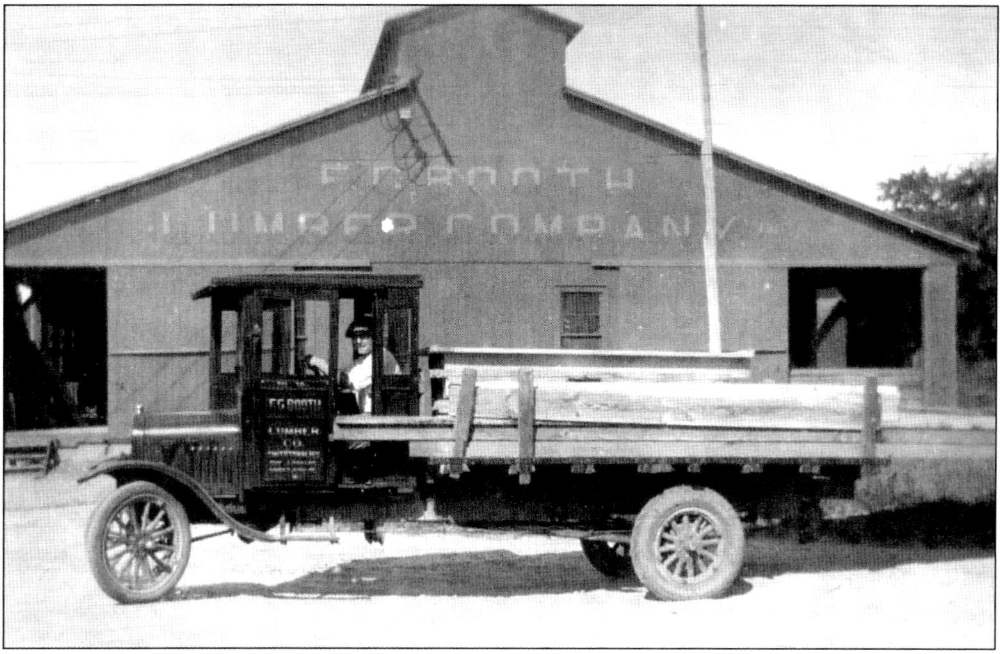

F. C. Booth Lumber Company, c. 1915. Booth Lumber had the first commercial electric installation in Smithtown in 1912. The company was located at 100 Landing Avenue and later became Nassau Suffolk Lumber Company. Today it is the site of AMF Smithtown Lanes Bowling Center.

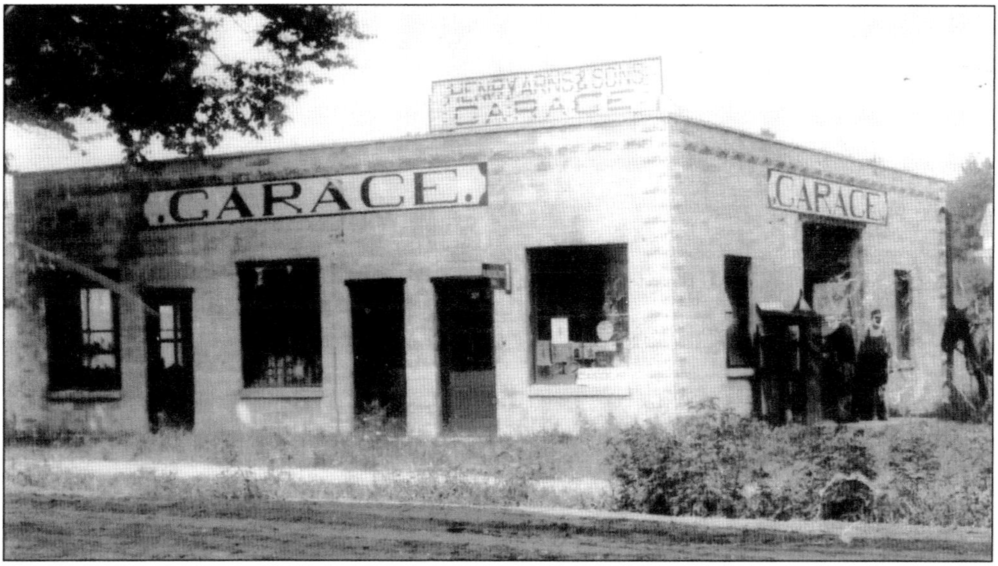

Henry Arns and Sons Garage, c. 1917. This was the first of several automobile garage shops that the Arns family owned in the 20th century. Henry Arns (1853–1929) was a German immigrant who brought his family from Brooklyn to Hauppauge in 1897. Arns was a master blacksmith who made the transition to working on automobiles by the time he opened this shop in 1913. His son William ran William Arns Garage from 1923 until the eve of World War II. The two Arnses, son and father respectively, are visible in the side doorway of this garage. (Earl Scott.)

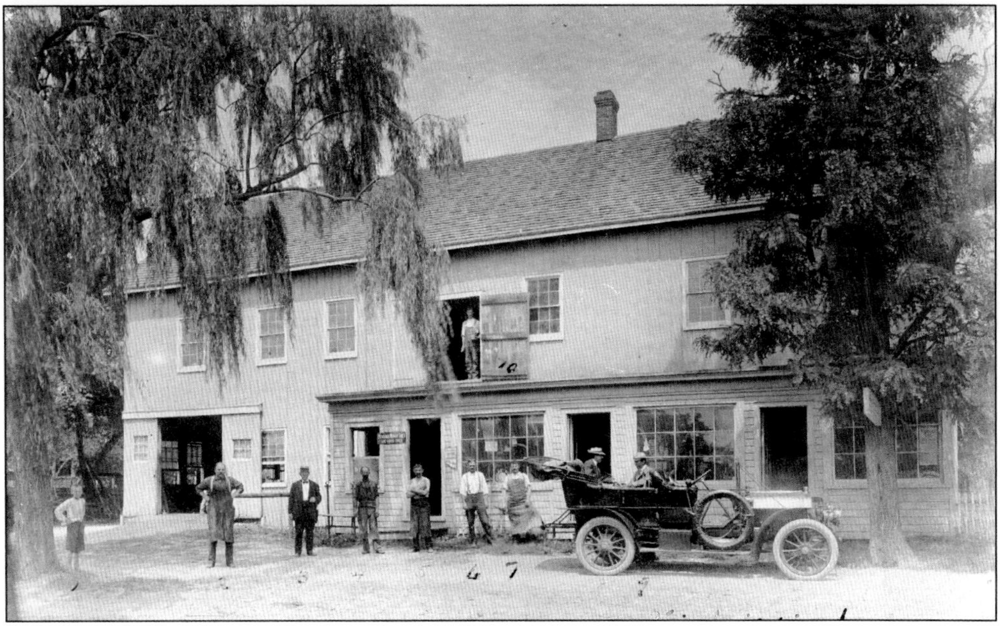

HALLOCK BLACKSMITH SHOP, C. 1908. Pictured here from left to right are Alanson Sturm, A. E. Hallock, E. Brooks Raynor, George Gentry, Luke Glavey, Luther B. Hallock, Charles Sturm, Harry Register, Ellis Newton, and John Brown (on the second floor). The enormous three-story, 75-foot-long Hallock Blacksmith Shop, located on the northeast corner of Landing Avenue and Main Street in Smithtown, was also apparently a wheelwright and carriage repair shop.

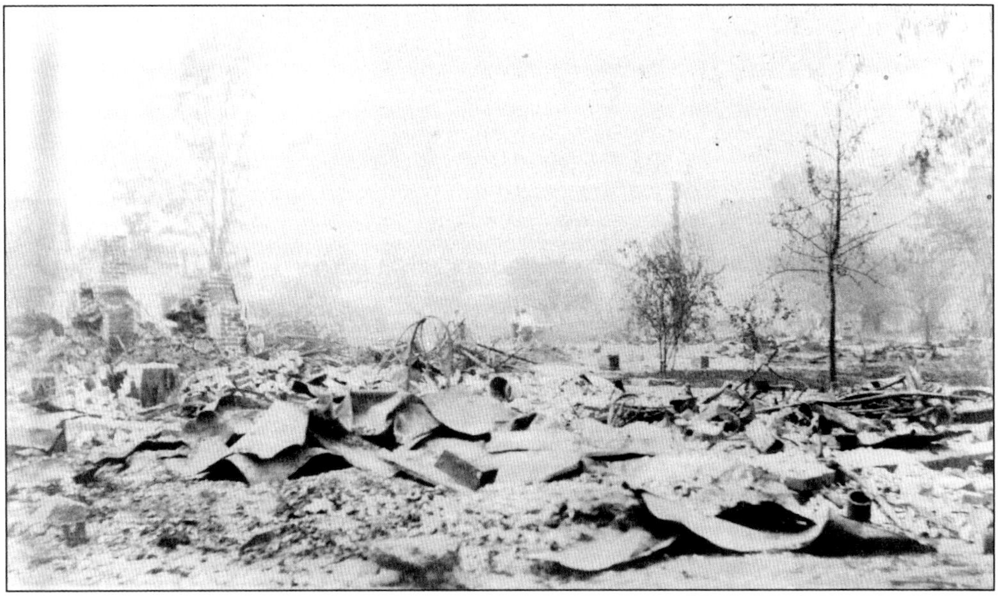

REMAINS OF THE HALLOCK BLACKSMITH SHOP, C. 1908. In one of the worst fires in Smithtown's history, a blaze began in this wooden-frame structure and consumed it in no time at all. The fire spread to other buildings but was prevented from causing further devastation by the arrival of a large chemical tank from the Kings Park State Hospital. The one positive outcome of the fire was the impetus it provided for increasing support and supplies for the newly established Smithtown Fire Department.

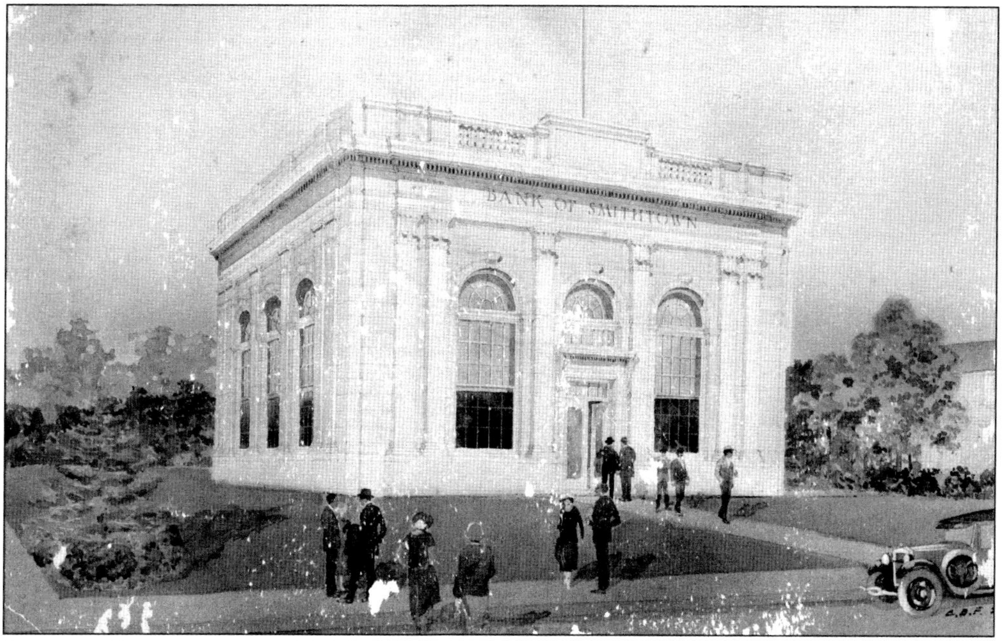

BANK OF SMITHTOWN, 1924. The bank opened its doors as the National Bank in 1910 and was originally a single 20-foot-by-30-foot room with bars on the window, a vault, and a teller's window. When it moved and reopened in the new building seen above at 1 East Main Street, it was greatly enlarged, reflecting the boom years of Smithtown in the 1920s. Notable in the bank's history was its management by Maude Huntting Bach, who succeeded her father as director in 1949 and ran the bank until 1979.

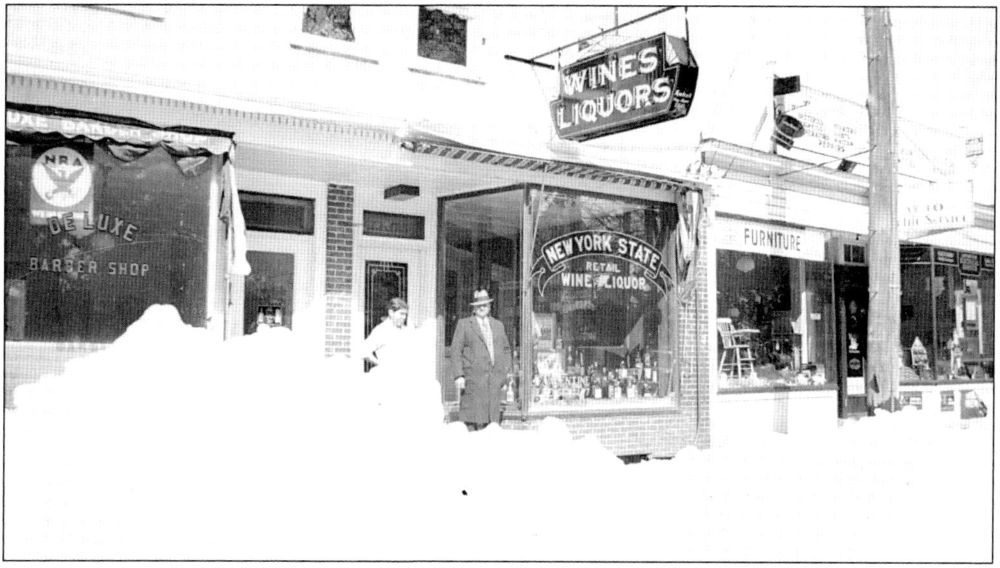

SNOW PILED ALONG MAIN STREET, C. 1934. The first liquor shop to open in Smithtown after Prohibition, Frank Valentine's Smithtown Wines and Liquors Store is seen here behind the snowdrifts, as is Joe Nicosia's barbershop. Nicosia's shop window sports a familiar NRA (National Recovery Administration) sign with the blue eagle, a mark that was considered good for business in the early New Deal years. (Lee Corbani.)

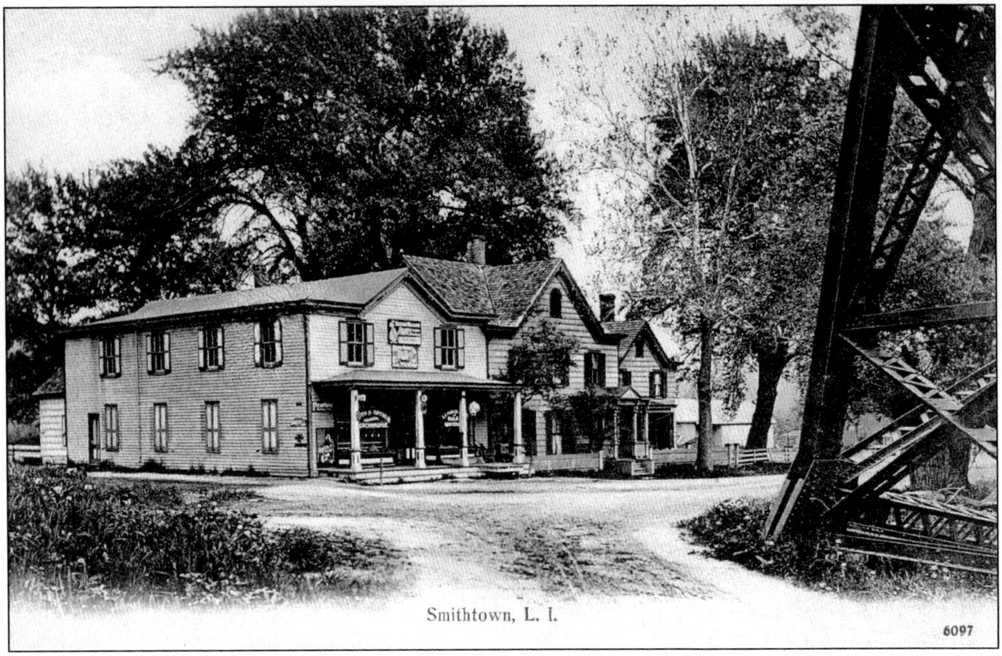

BOOTH-ARTHUR GENERAL STORE, C. 1900. According to one set of recollections, a general store existed at this site near the present-day bull statue locale since approximately 1860. Its proprietor, E. L. Arthur, sold general merchandise, lumber, and coal. The store also functioned as the Smithtown Post Office for a time. This building burned to the ground in 1912.

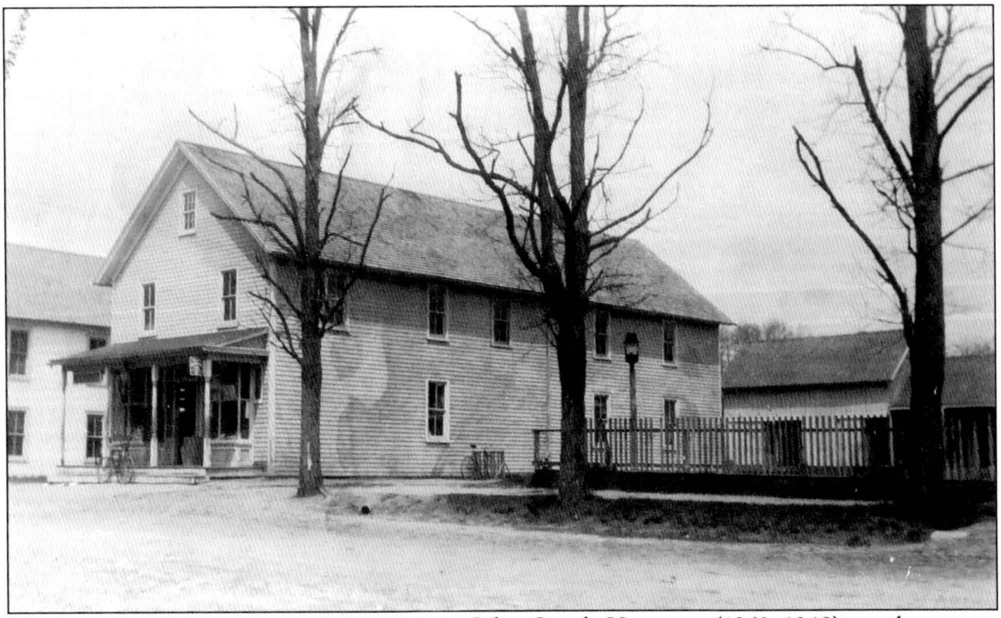

JOHN HUNTTING GENERAL STORE, 1904. John Smith Huntting (1869–1948) was born into the grocery merchant business, having a father, Joseph Reed Huntting, who earlier operated a store that sold molasses, tea, coffee, and food products. The Smithtown Historical Society owns ledgers and account books from John Smith Huntting's store in the early 1900s.

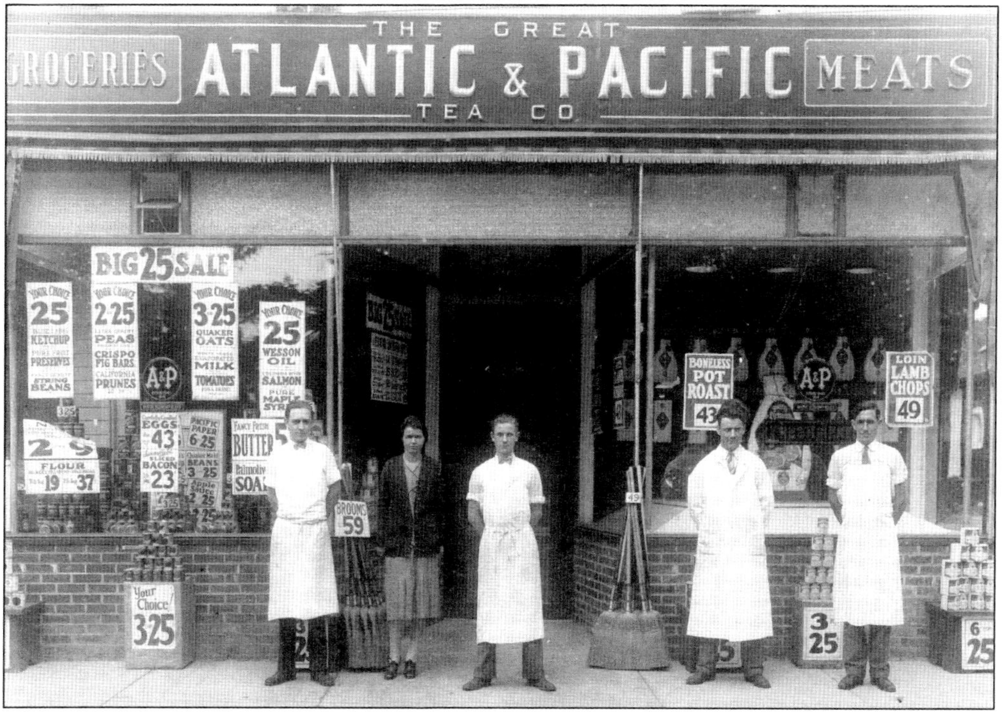

A&P Grocery Store, c. 1924. Opening in the same building that originally housed John Smith Huntting's General Store, the A&P was the first chain grocery store to open in Smithtown, (a sign of things to come). This store was one of 13,961 A&Ps nationwide by 1925, and while it thrived on mass-market cost-saving devices, there was still the air of a small-town general store. Clerks still waited on customers and brought them what they needed.

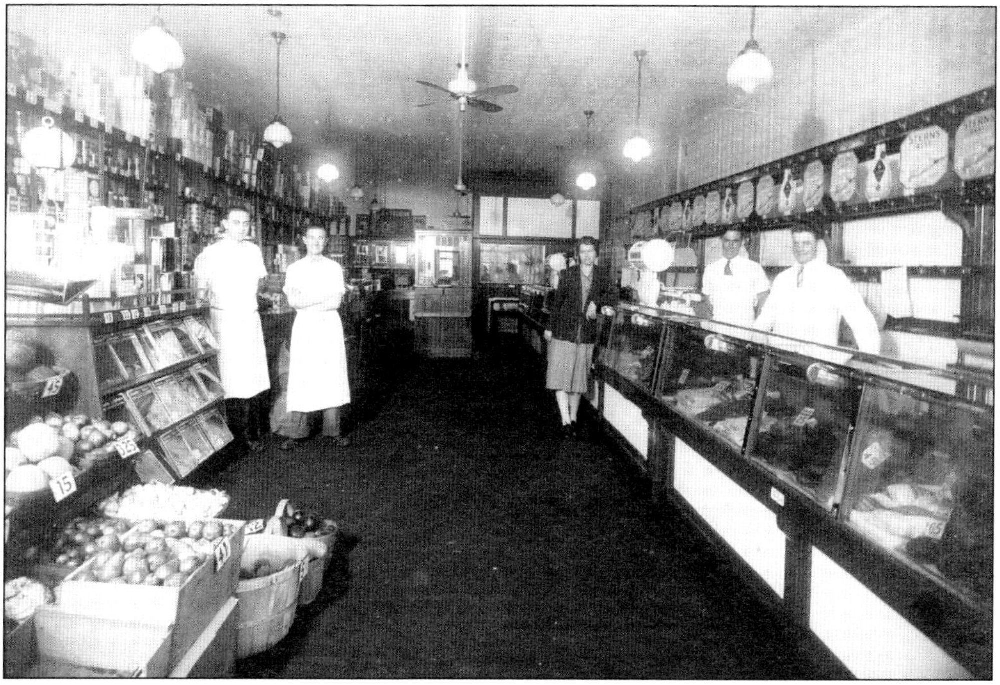

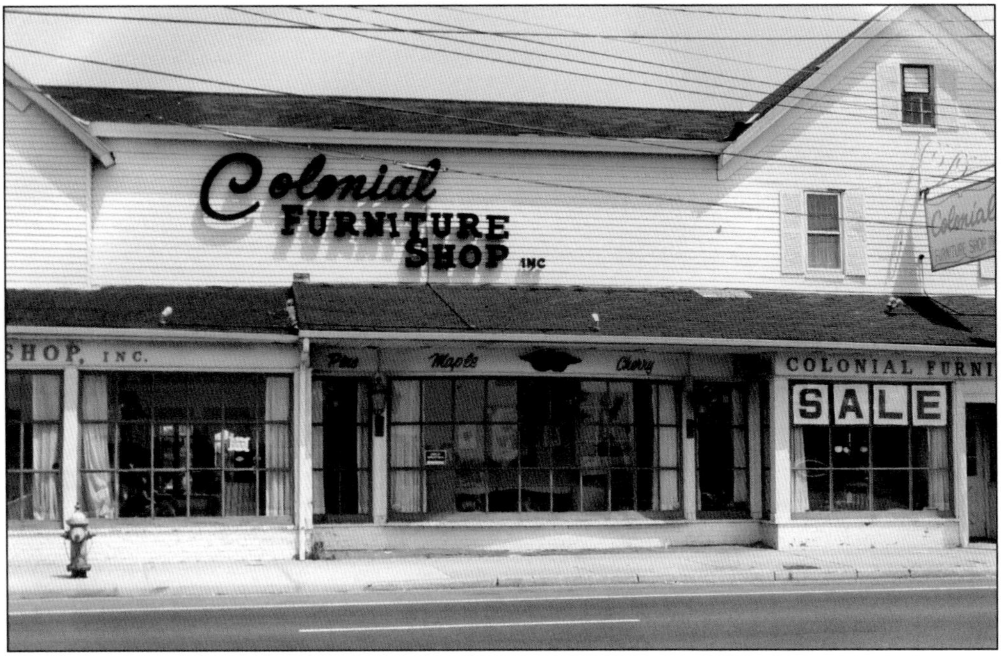

Colonial Furniture Shop, c. 1975. The Colonial Furniture Shop opened its doors in the 1950s and was the product of the convergence of both John Smith Huntting's original store and the Royal Arcanum Hall. The original rooflines of these buildings can still be seen from Main Street.

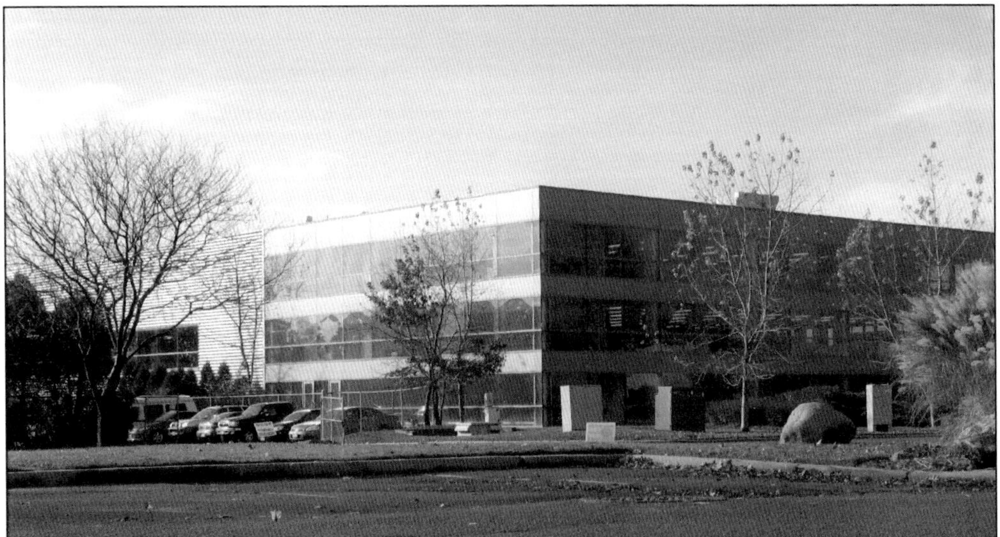

Hauppauge Industrial Park. The 1,400-acre John V. N. Klein Hauppauge Industrial Park was placed in a superb location for business, immediately off the Vanderbilt Motor Parkway and minutes away from the Long Island Expressway and Northern State Parkway. Young planner and engineer Lee Koppelman convinced both Suffolk County and Smithtown politicians that building the park was an idea with merit in 1960, when Long Island was in the midst of its suburban boom. Today the massive complex is home to more than 1,300 businesses and 55,000 employees.

Five

Prominent Landmarks and the Changing Landscape

When New York State inventoried historical sites during the bicentennial in 1976, over 650 historic structures were identified throughout Smithtown. To be included on the list, the building had to be over 50 years of age and a place where a historical person lived or a historical event occurred. Across Smithtown, in all the villages and hamlets of the town, there are many prominent landmarks. All these landmarks have a story to tell since they are a reflection of the 350 years of the community's history. The house known as Timothy House in Head of the Harbor is an example of a landmark that reflects its history. It has a small east wing with a Dutch gambrel roofline that dates back to the early 1700s, a large west wing that was added in 1800, and other wings that were added to the house in 1903. It is a house that has been lived in for many years by many generations of Smiths, and like the landscape around it, the house has seen many changes, including being moved 200 feet back from North Country Road. Each of the landmarks in this section of the book has its own story to tell and reflects the changing landscape of Smithtown's past and present.

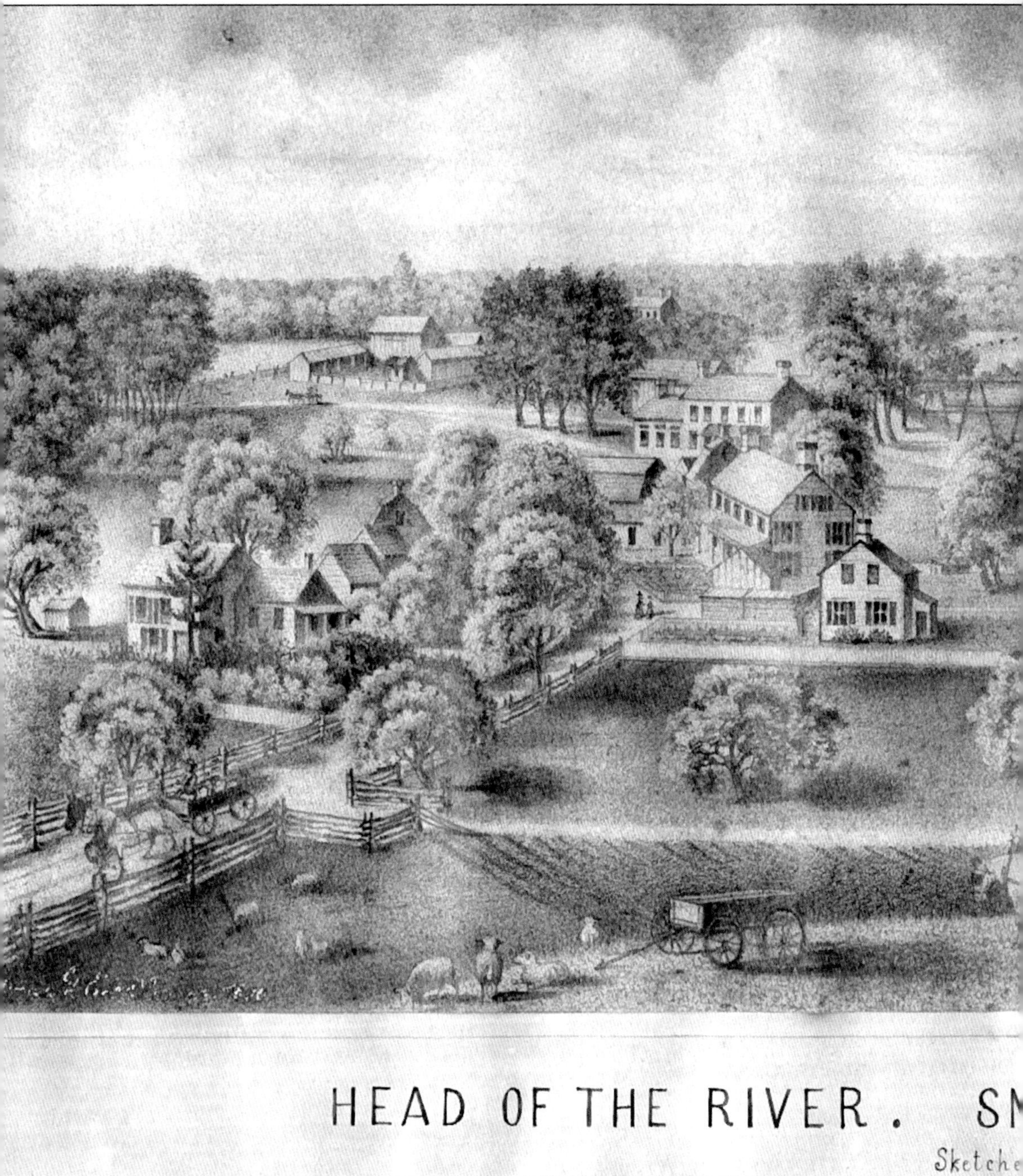

HEAD OF THE RIVER SKETCH. This aerial view looks to the north from Ebenezer Blydenburgh's farm, presently a part of the Forestwood subdivision on New Mill Road. In the left-hand corner, a horse and wagon can be seen traversing Mill Dam Road. Most of the community of Head of the River as it existed in 1874 can be seen in Edward Lange's drawing. The small house in the middle was Dr. Charles H. Havens's house (c. 1810), and north of it is the Treadwell Wheeler

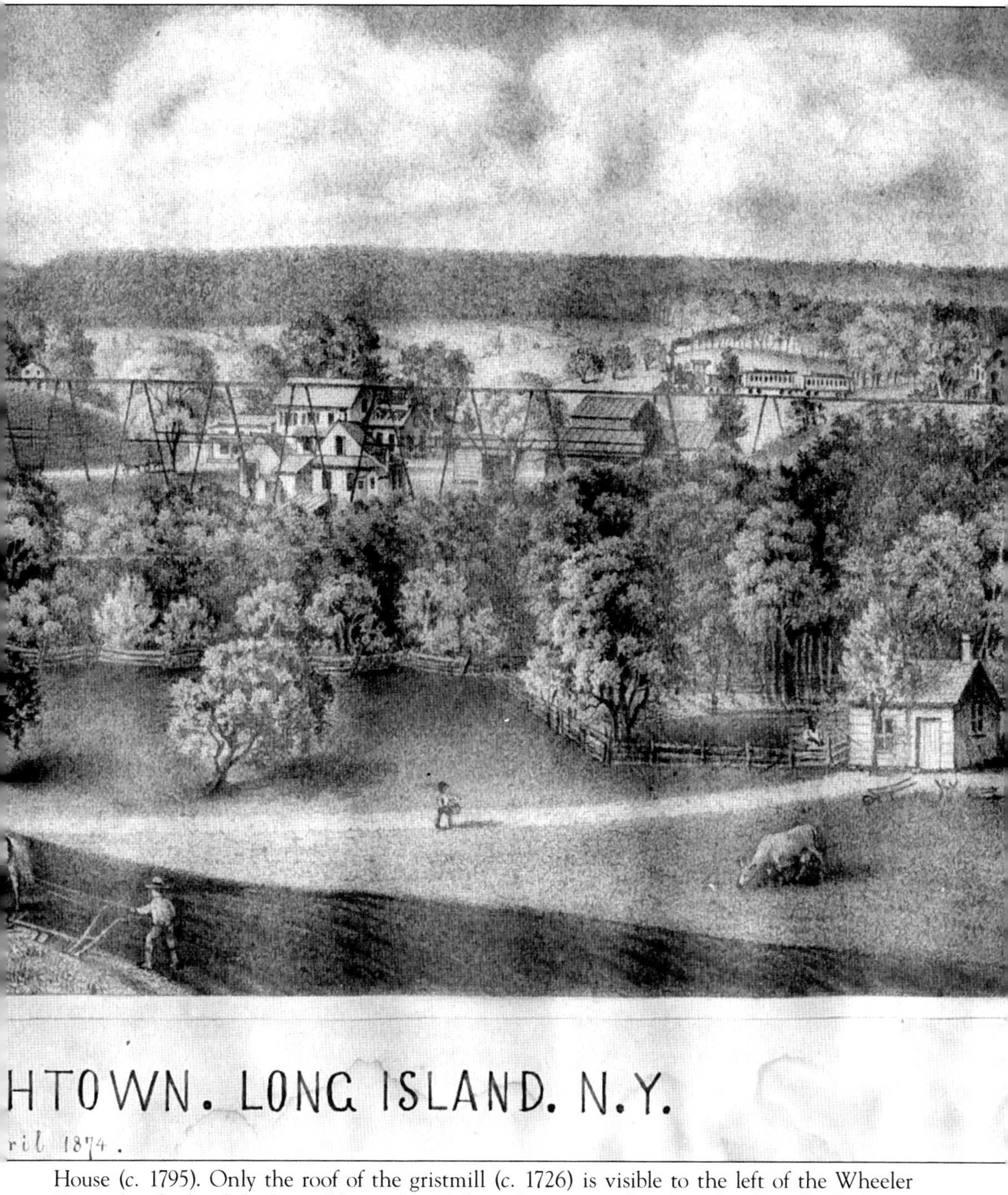

House (c. 1795). Only the roof of the gristmill (c. 1726) is visible to the left of the Wheeler House, but farther left, the mill house (c. 1726) can be seen on the edge of millpond. The house on the rise on the far side of the river is the George Phillips House (c. 1726), one of the oldest houses in Head of the River.

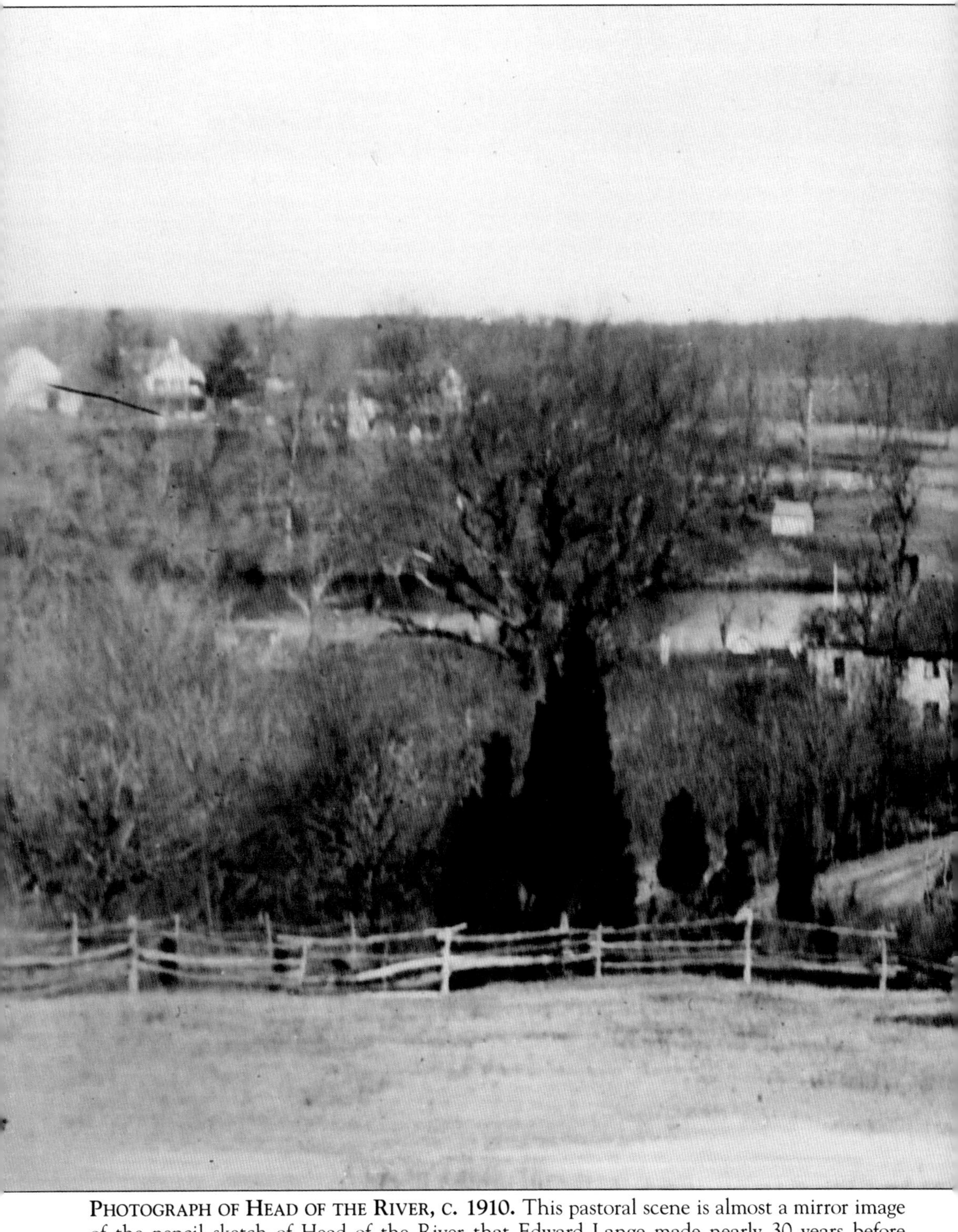

PHOTOGRAPH OF HEAD OF THE RIVER, C. 1910. This pastoral scene is almost a mirror image of the pencil sketch of Head of the River that Edward Lange made nearly 30 years before this photograph was taken. It shows that little change had come to Smithtown and that life

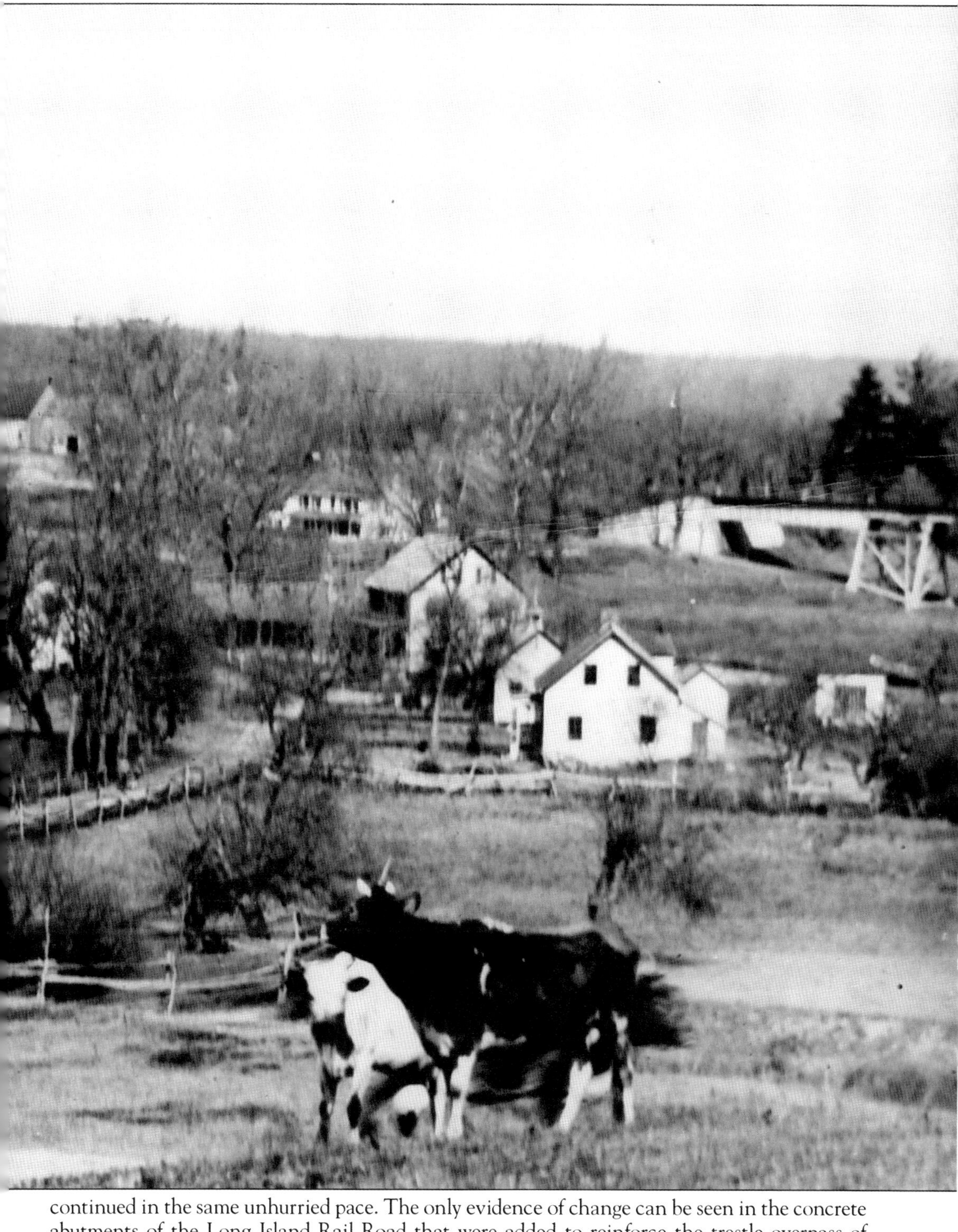

continued in the same unhurried pace. The only evidence of change can be seen in the concrete abutments of the Long Island Rail Road that were added to reinforce the trestle overpass of Jericho Turnpike.

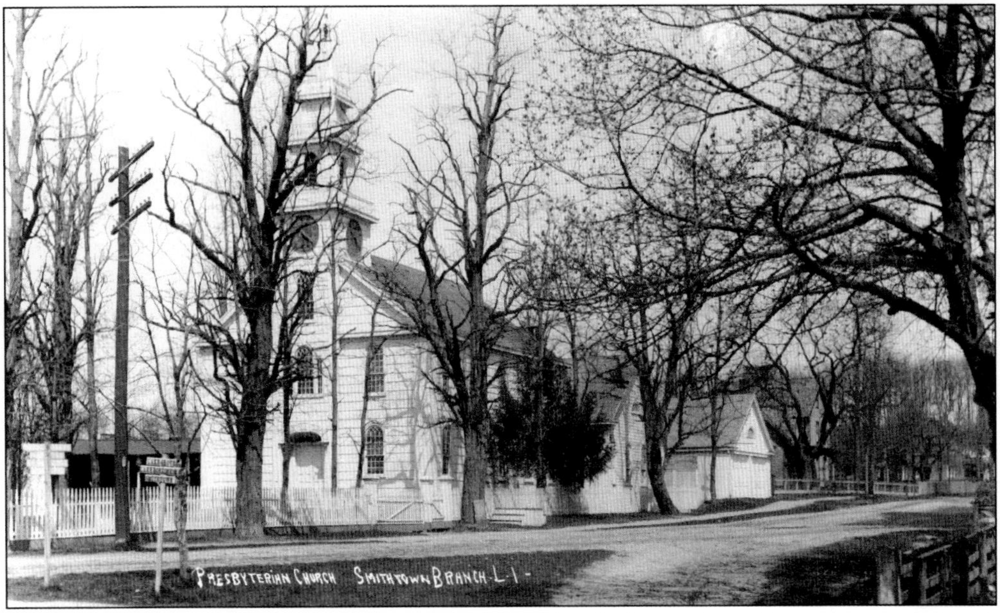

THE FIRST PRESBYTERIAN CHURCH, C. 1910. This church, founded as a Congregational church in 1675, is Smithtown's oldest. Originally established in a little meetinghouse in Nissequogue, the congregation voted to relocate in 1750 and moved into the village of Smithtown Branch. The present church, seen in this photograph, was erected and dedicated in 1827. The beautiful structure, located at the intersection of North Country Road, Middle Country Road, River Road, and Route 111, is one of Smithtown's most prominent landmarks.

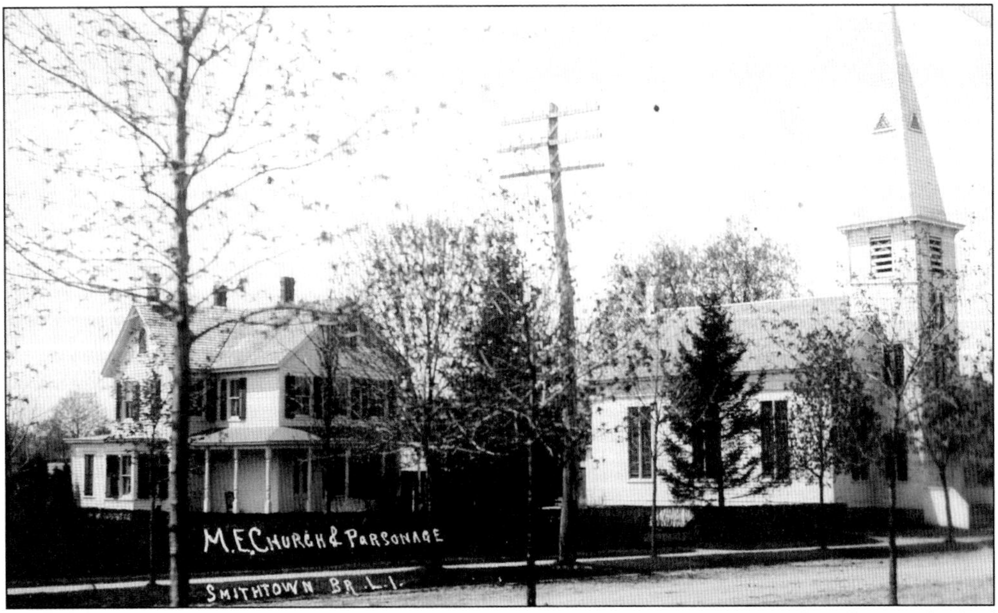

METHODIST EPISCOPAL CHURCH AND PARSONAGE, C. 1910. This is the church as it looked when it was on the south side of Main Street just east of Maple Avenue. Originally located on Judge's Lane, it was moved to Main Street in 1885. The tall steeple was added sometime between 1892 and 1894. The steeple was removed in 1935 because it was leaning precariously.

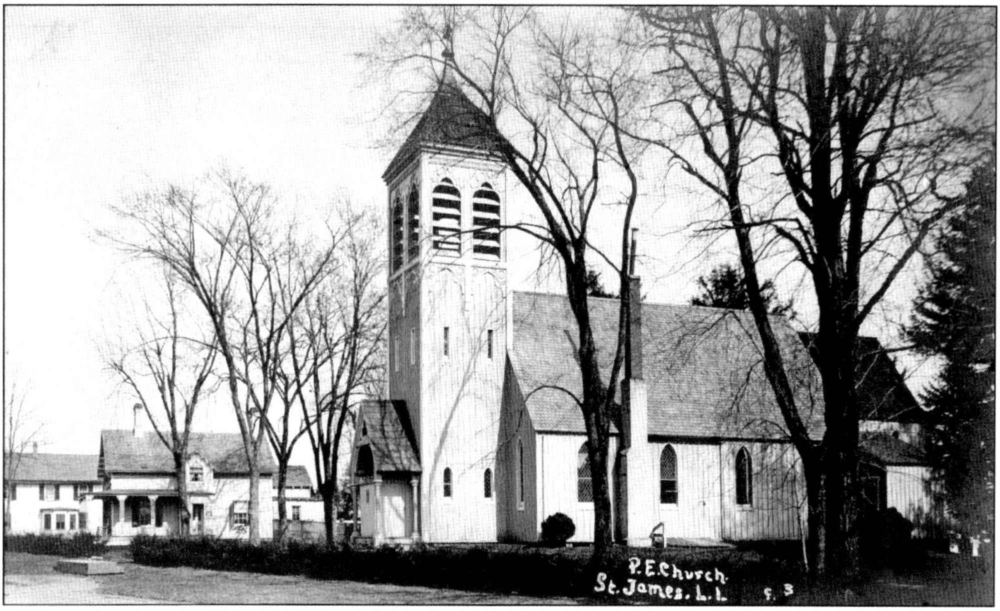

ST. JAMES PROTESTANT EPISCOPAL CHURCH. In 1853, Episcopalians living in Smithtown, Head of the Harbor, and Stony Brook came together to build a church and form a parish. Designed in Gothic Revival style by architect Richard Upjohn and constructed on two acres of land on the south side of North Country Road donated by Joel L. G. Smith, the St. James Protestant Episcopal Church was consecrated on July 3, 1854.

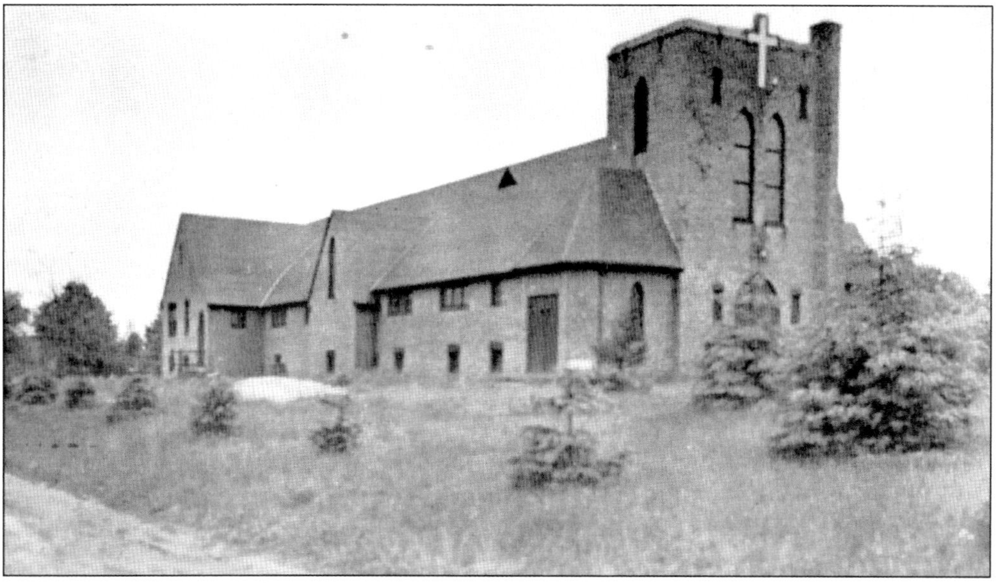

ST. PATRICK'S ROMAN CATHOLIC CHURCH, 1929. This is a view of the church as it looked shortly after construction in 1929. Built on the southwest corner of Edgewater and Mayflower Avenues, this was the third St. Patrick's Roman Catholic Church erected in Smithtown. It was constructed to replace the previous church building, which had burned down in a forest fire on June 11, 1927.

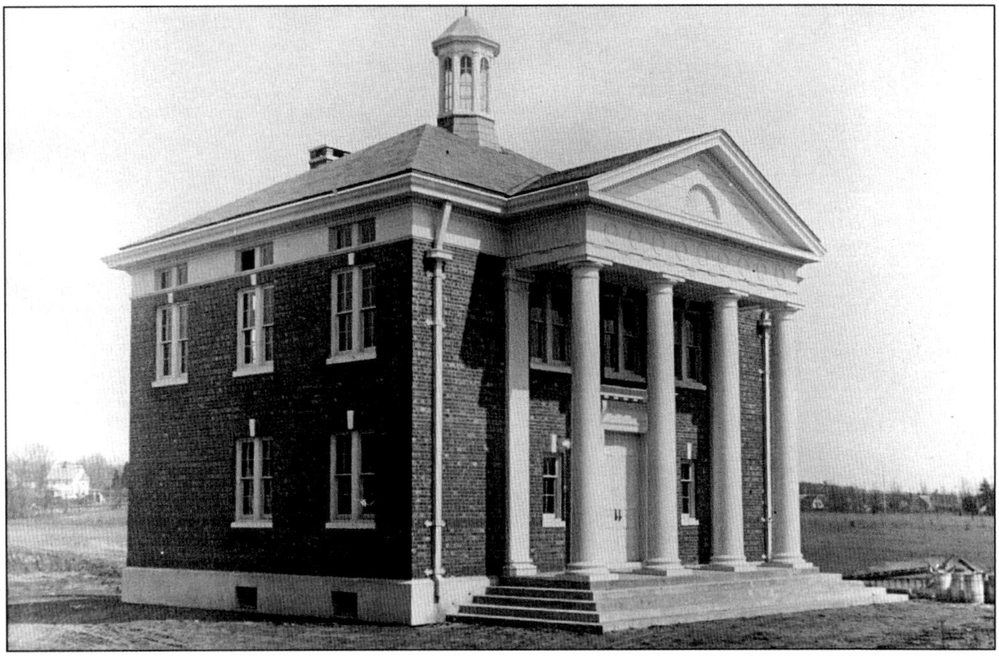

SMITHTOWN TOWN HALL, C. 1912. On August 17, 1911, the town board voted to buy a site on Main Street to construct a town hall building. Designed by Lawrence Butler and constructed by G. Everett Hand and Andrew Madison for a cost under the $9,000 budget imposed by town authorities, the completed town hall opened its doors in 1912.

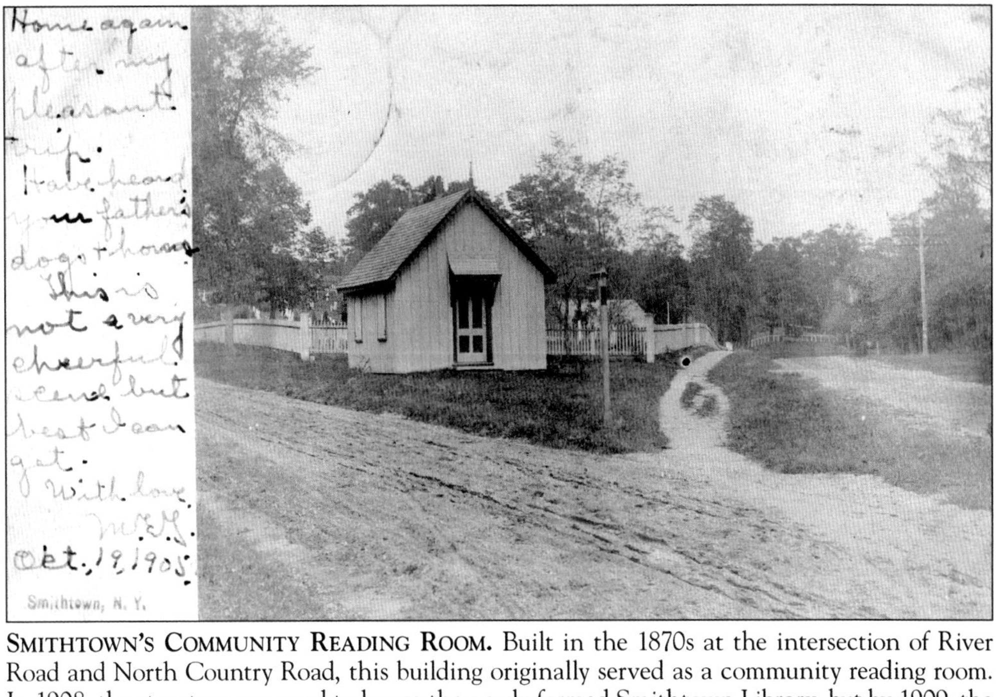

SMITHTOWN'S COMMUNITY READING ROOM. Built in the 1870s at the intersection of River Road and North Country Road, this building originally served as a community reading room. In 1908, the structure was used to house the newly formed Smithtown Library, but by 1909, the library had outgrown the modest space and moved out. In 1912, the building was relocated to the Smithtown Cemetery and converted into a tool shed.

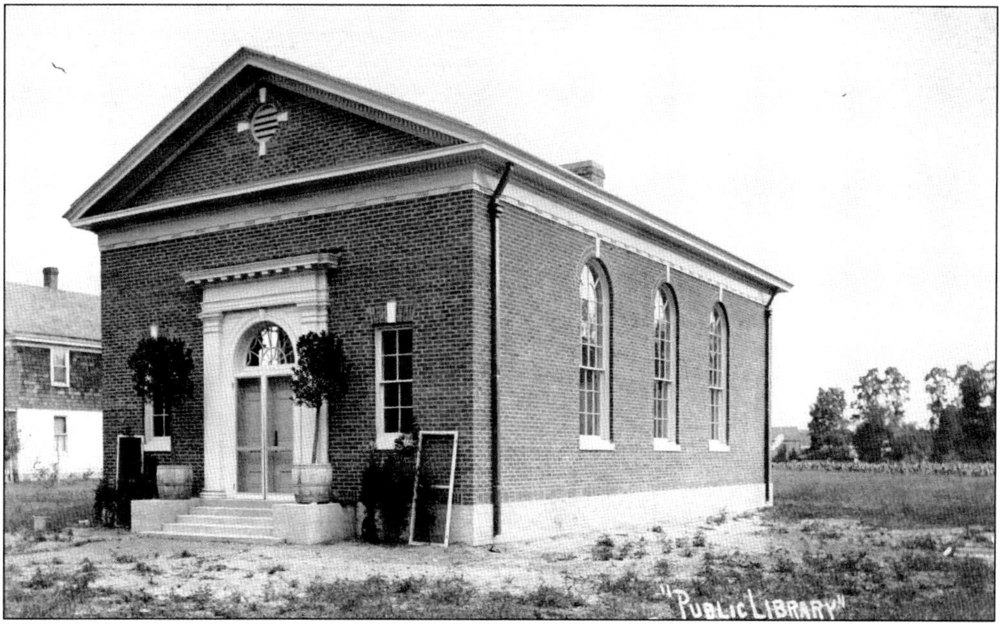

SMITHTOWN LIBRARY'S ORIGINAL BUILDING. Library trustee Cornelia Smith Butler donated a building site, persuaded her son Lawrence Butler to design the library gratis, and then provided funding for its construction. The building was dedicated and opened in the spring of 1912. It remained on this site until November 15, 1950, when it was moved across Middle Country Road to the village green. This original building is the children's wing of today's Smithtown Library.

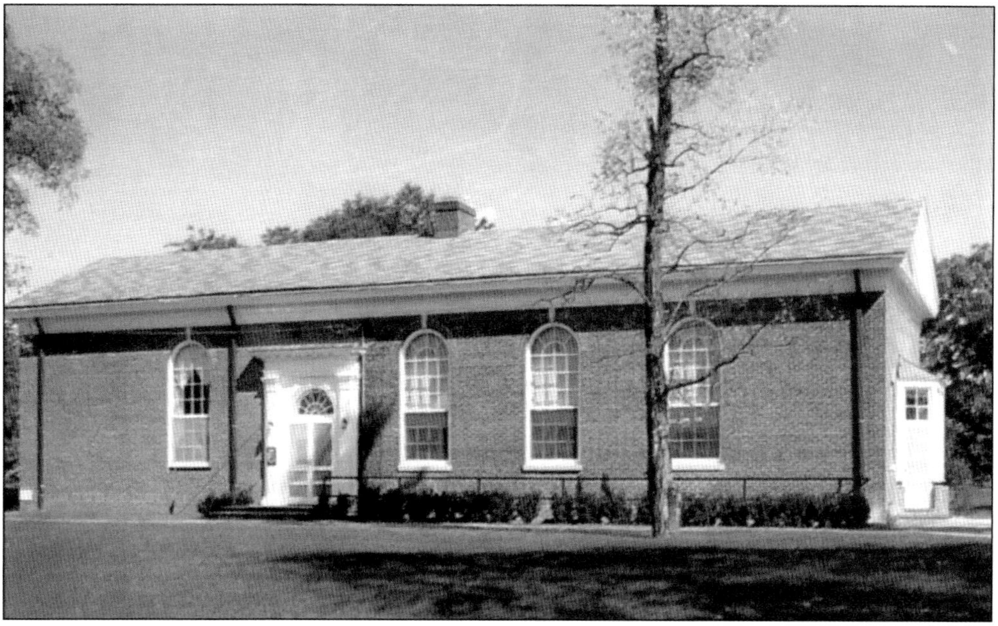

SMITHTOWN LIBRARY. Changes were made to the original library when it was moved to the village green. The front door was replaced by a bay window, and the entrance door was moved to the west side of the building. An extension was built onto the back of the building that housed offices for the librarians.

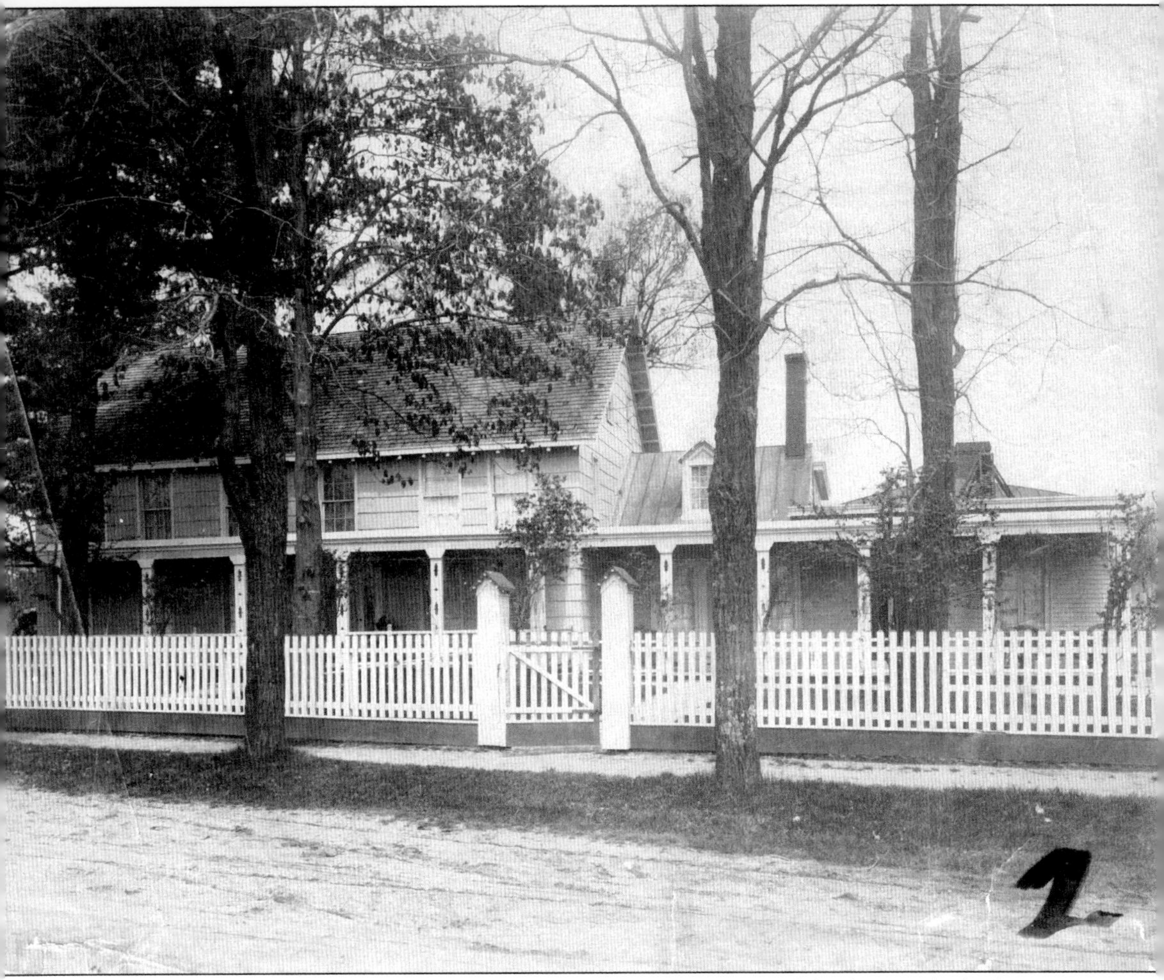

JOHN LAWRENCE SMITH HOMESTEAD, C. 1900. The oldest part of this house, the little wing to the right with the peaked roof, may actually date from 1720. The Blydenburghs built and owned this house until 1845, when John Lawrence Smith acquired the homestead and enlarged it for his family that grew to include two boys and five girls. After Smith's death in 1889, it passed to his son James Clinch Smith, who occupied it until 1912 when he died in the *Titanic* tragedy. Bessie Smith White, the youngest daughter of John Lawrence Smith and widow of Stanford White, then inherited the house. Her grandson Peter White was living in the homestead when the Smithtown Branch Preservation Association bought it in the early 1970s.

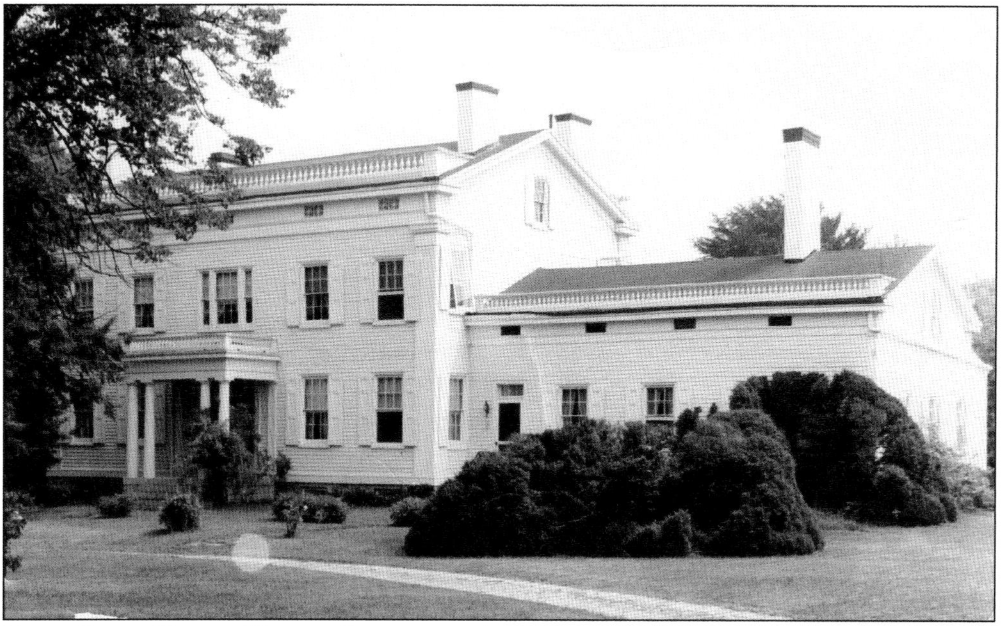

Mills Pond House. The small wing at right is the original house built by Timothy Mills on North Country Road in St. James sometime before 1700. This earlier portion of the home contains a huge brick chimney and fireplace with an attached beehive oven. Although the original house was partially destroyed by fire, William Wickham Mills restored it in 1838 when he added the three-story Greek Revival addition to the structure.

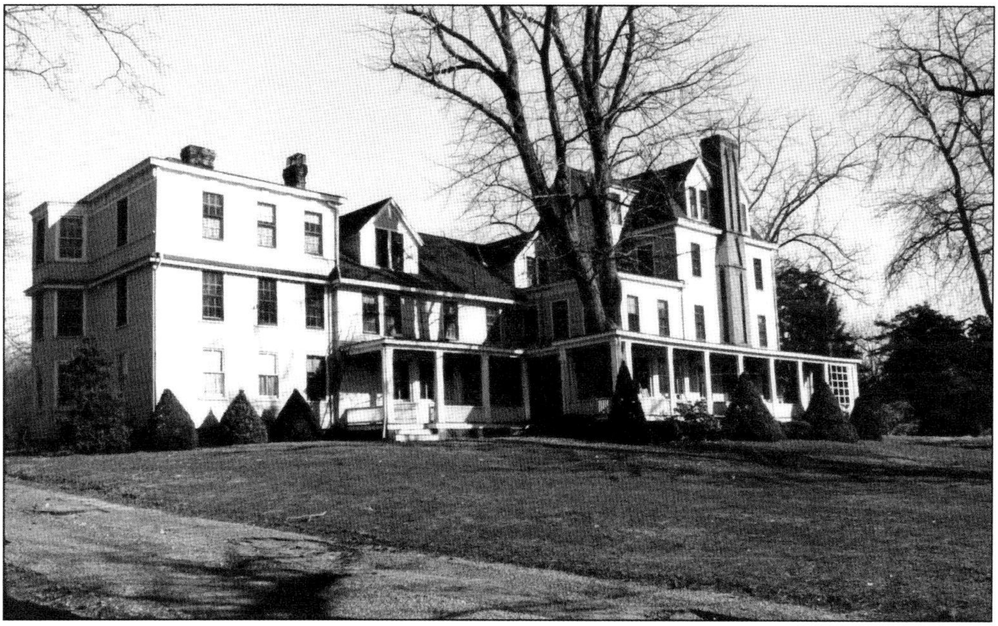

Caleb Smith House. Caleb Smith I, a great-grandson of Richard Smythe, built the core of this building, the small house with the dormer windows, in 1752 and 1753. By the dawn of the 20th century, the house had been renovated and expanded to serve as the clubhouse of the Wyandanch Club, which purchased the site in 1888. Today it plays host to the Caleb Smith House Museum.

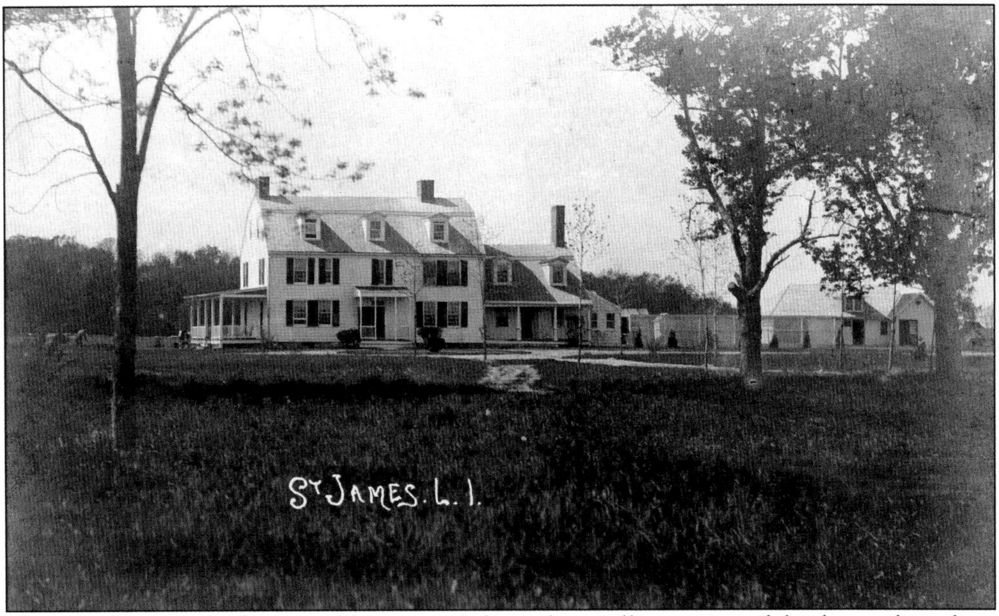

TIMOTHY HOUSE. Architectural historians believe the small east wing of this house dates from approximately 1750, while the larger west wing dates from about 1800. In 1839, the home was purchased by Ebenezer Smith II (1784–1866) and subsequently deeded to his son Timothy Carll Smith (1811–1877). When Lawrence Butler acquired the property in 1903, he moved the house 200 feet back from North Country Road to where it sits today.

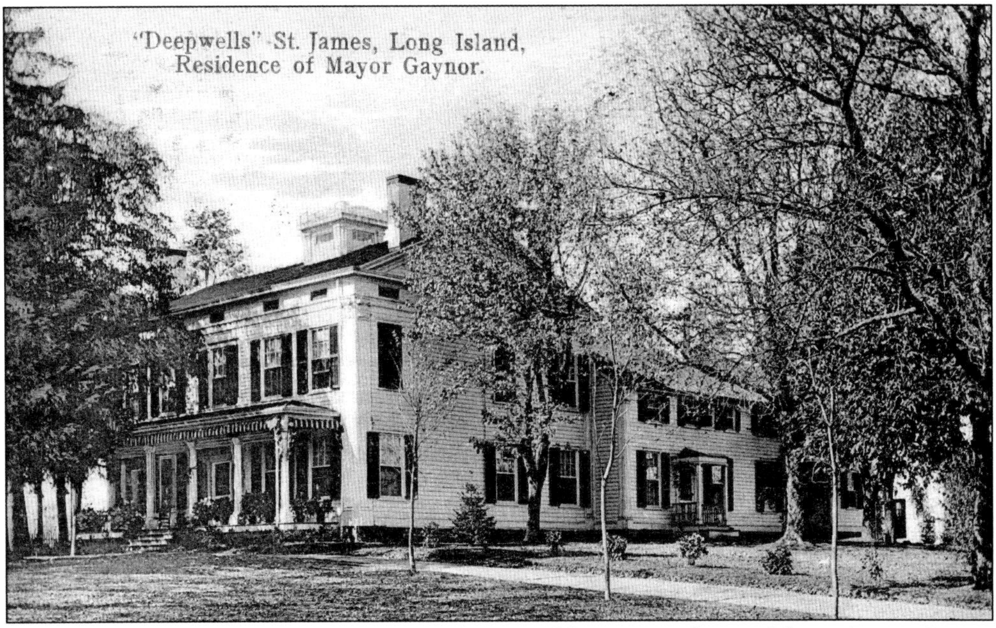

DEEPWELLS. Completed in 1847, this Greek Revival home was designed by architect George Curtis for Joel L. G. Smith. In 1905, New York State Supreme Court justice and future New York City mayor William J. Gaynor purchased the home and the accompanying 10 acres of land to serve as a summer residence for his family. It was Gaynor who had the two deep, hand-dug wells—from which the house takes its name—installed.

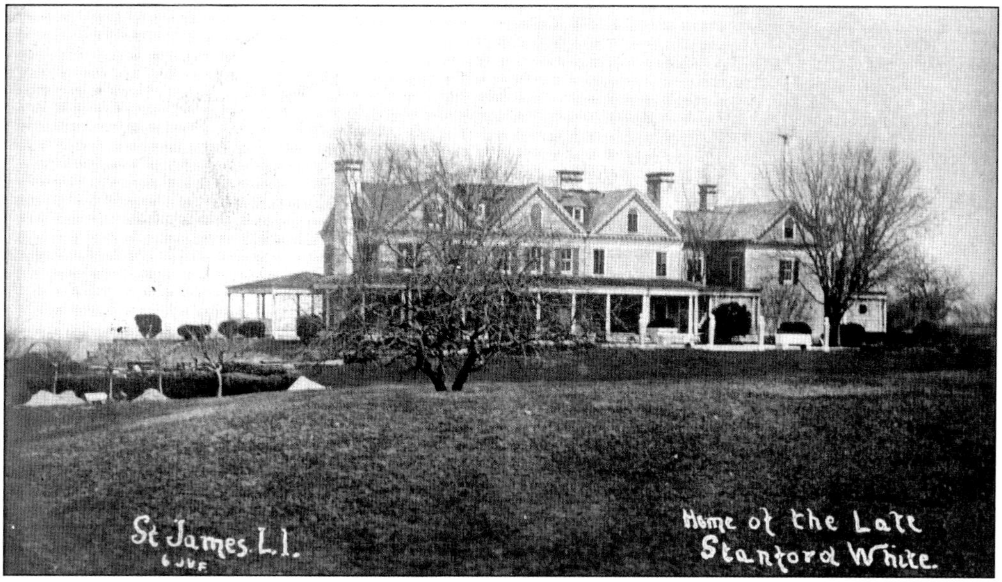

STANFORD WHITE'S BOX HILL. Not long after her marriage to Stanford White in 1884, Bessie Springs Smith convinced her husband to purchase Samuel Carman's farmhouse, which stood on a bluff overlooking St. James Harbor. The original 1850s farmhouse is on the right in the photograph. White remodeled the house several times and created the 15,000-square-foot house known as Box Hill seen in the photograph with its 13 gables and pebble-dashed exterior.

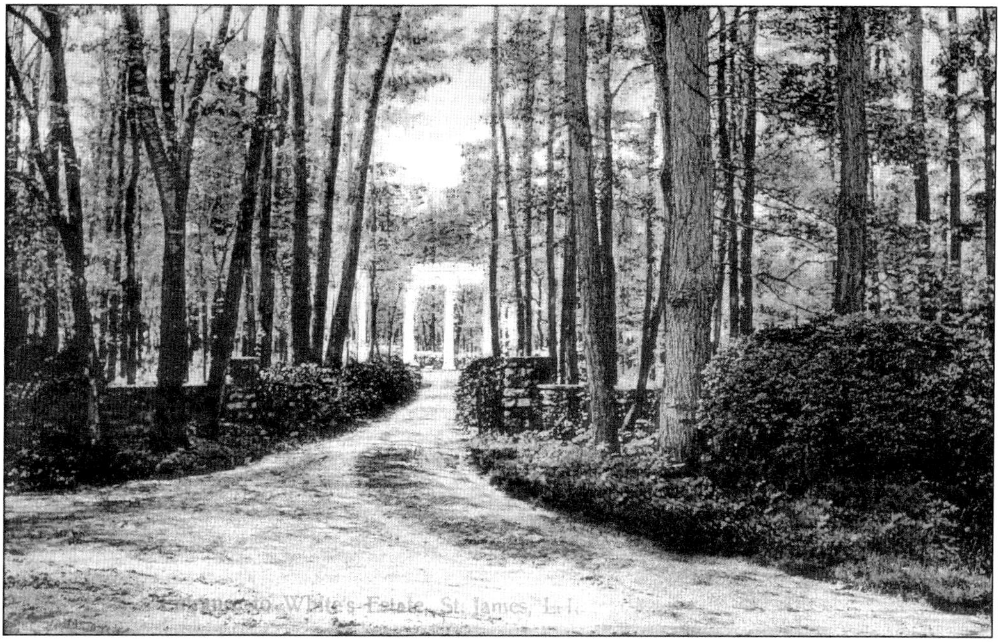

RUINS AT BOX HILL. White was an eclectic collector of historical artifacts from different time periods and cultures. He designed gardens around sculptures, Greek columns, and sarcophagi. This scene captures temple ruins in the distance.

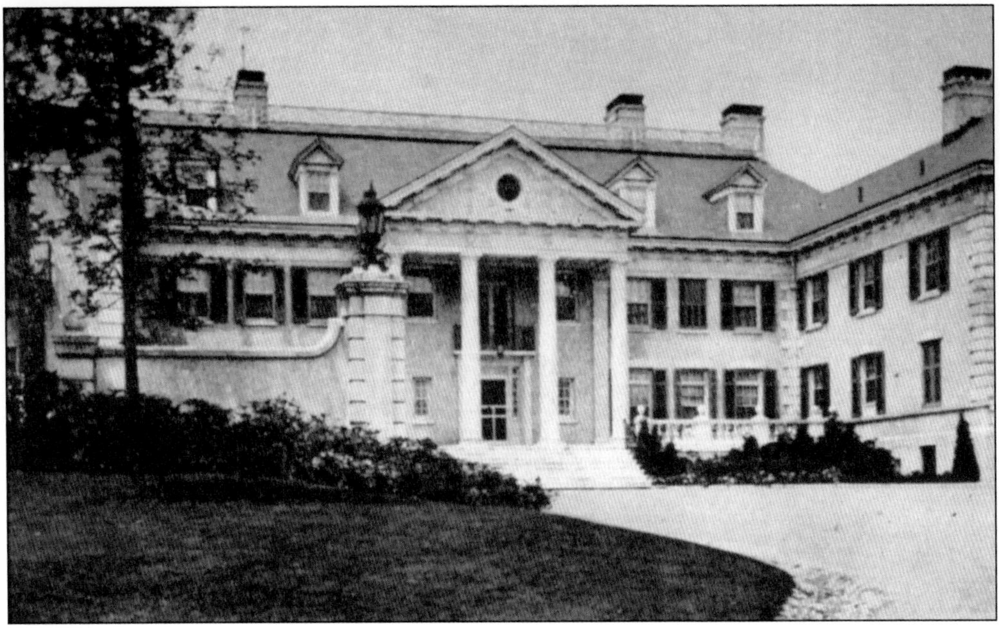

THORNTON ESTATE. In July 1908, Louise Clementine Archer Thornton purchased 52 acres of land in St. James and, in 1909, began construction of this house. The neoclassical mansion containing 74 rooms along with 18 bathrooms was built on a scale that rivaled many Gold Coast structures. In 1914, William Thornton purchased the estate and in 1918 sold it to his two sisters, Lucille T. Thornton and Adelaide T. Corbett, for $1.

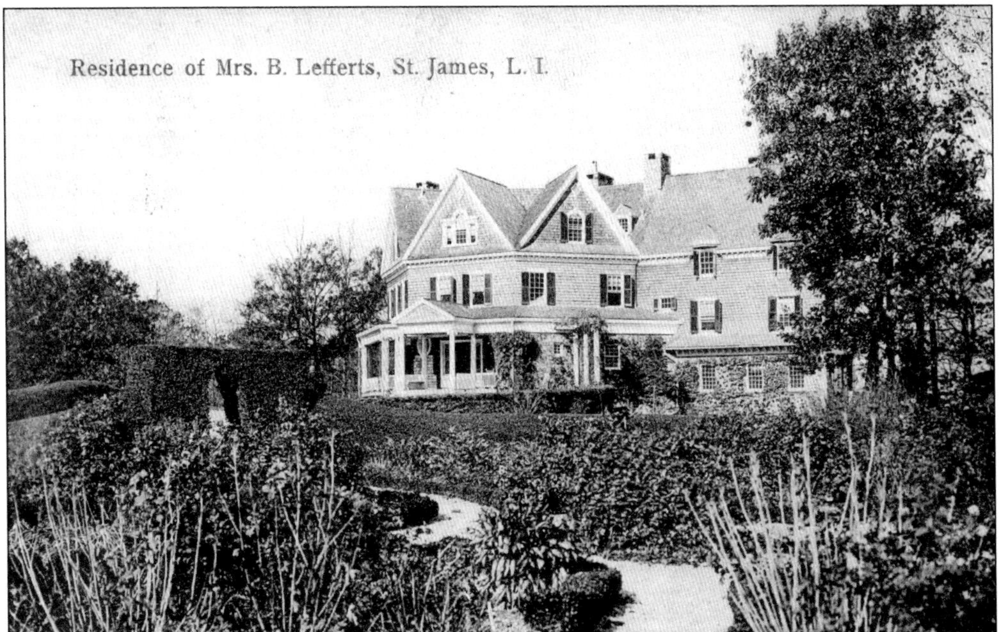

WETHERILL HOUSE. Designed by Stanford White for his sister-in-law Kate Smith Wetherill, Wetherill House remains one of the famed architect's most interesting creations. Combining octagonal floor plans with a gabled roof and a two-and-a-half-story service wing base, White designed the structure in the form of a Maltese cross.

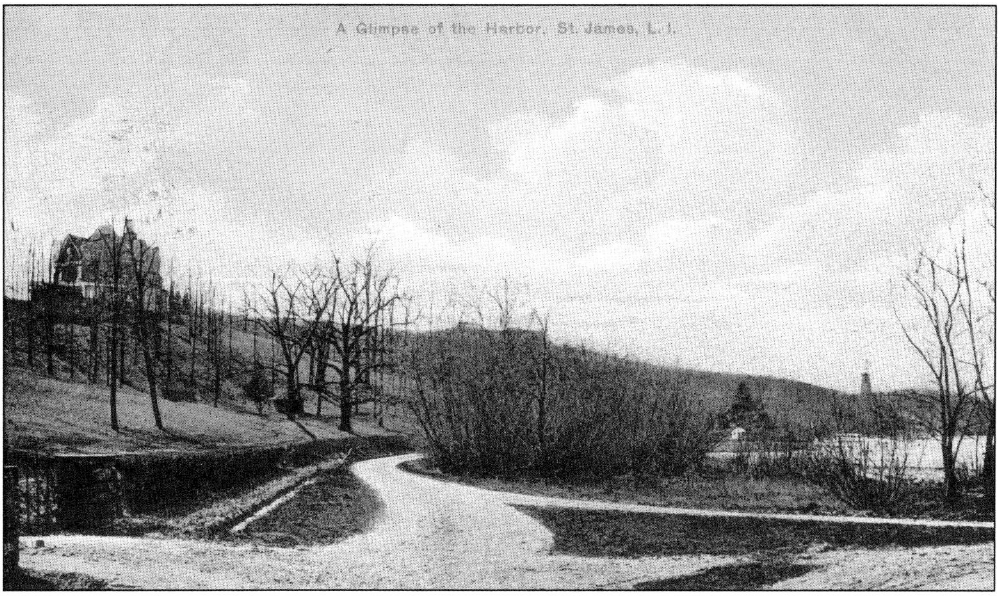

HARBOR IN ST. JAMES. This view of St. James Harbor (also known as Stony Brook Harbor) shows the Wetherill House on the hill to the left, White's home of Box Hill in the center, and the Butler windmill to the far right. The intersection in the foreground of the photograph is that of Harbor Hill Road and Harbor Road in the village of Head of the Harbor. In the early 20th century, daughters of the John Lawrence Smith family began to build elegant country estates that surrounded St. James Harbor.

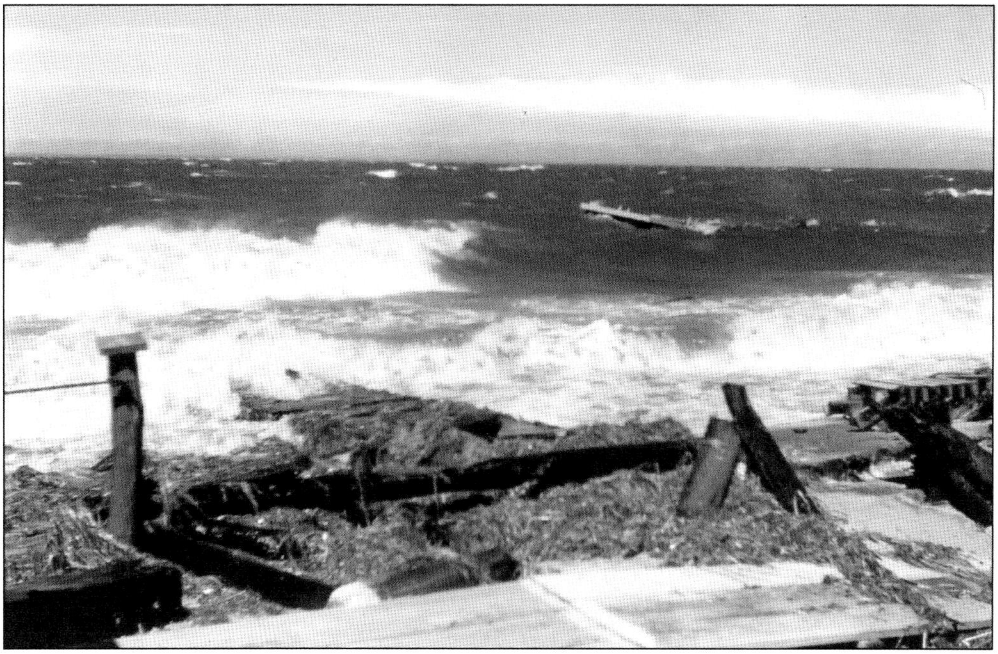

NISSEQUOGUE BEACH CLUB. Boating in the sound can get tricky, especially in stormy weather. Beachfront property owners in Smithtown suffered as well during the Hurricane of 1938, the storm seen here, and others, when the waves washed away sandy beaches and buildings constructed too close to the water's edge were smashed to bits.

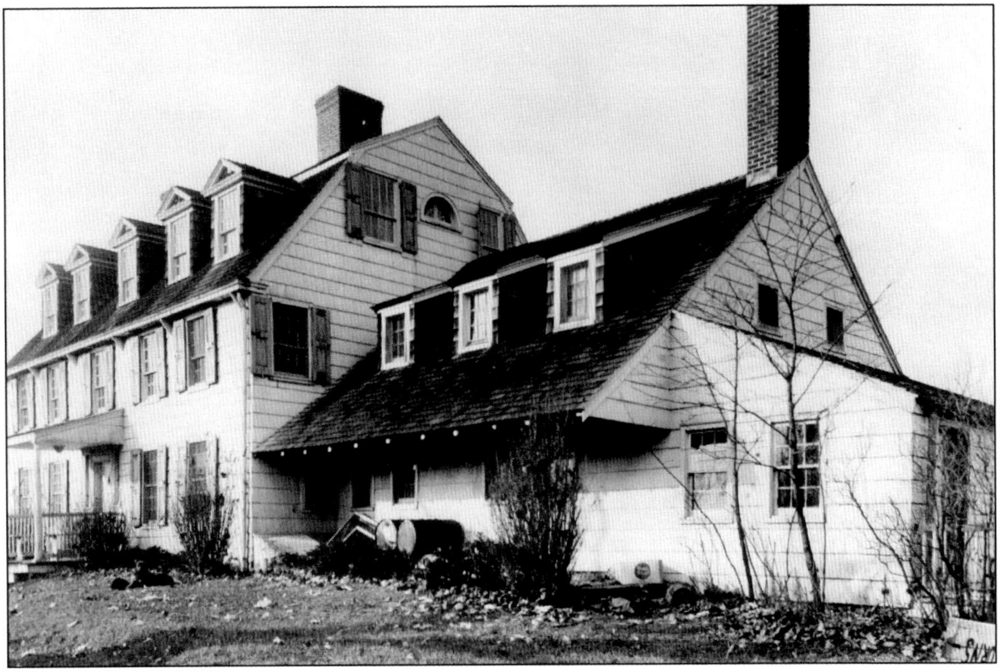

Joshua Smith House in Hauppauge. This house was a fine example of early Long Island architecture, having been originally built as a saltbox around 1760 for Joshua Smith I, a great-grandson of the patentee, Richard Smythe. The house was home to three generations of Joshua Smiths, including Joshua I (1732–1814), Joshua II (1763–1845), and Joshua Brewster III (1801–1860).

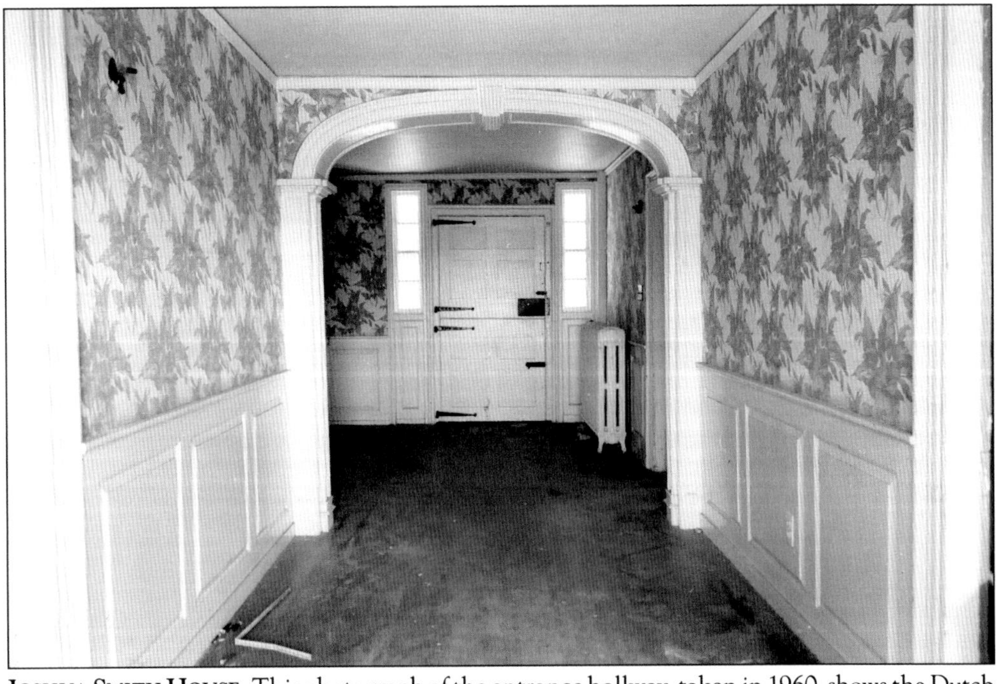

Joshua Smith House. This photograph of the entrance hallway, taken in 1960, shows the Dutch door with its strap hinges and square lock. Henry Francis du Pont acquired the hand-carved arch in the front hall for the Winterthur Museum in Delaware. The house was demolished in 1960.

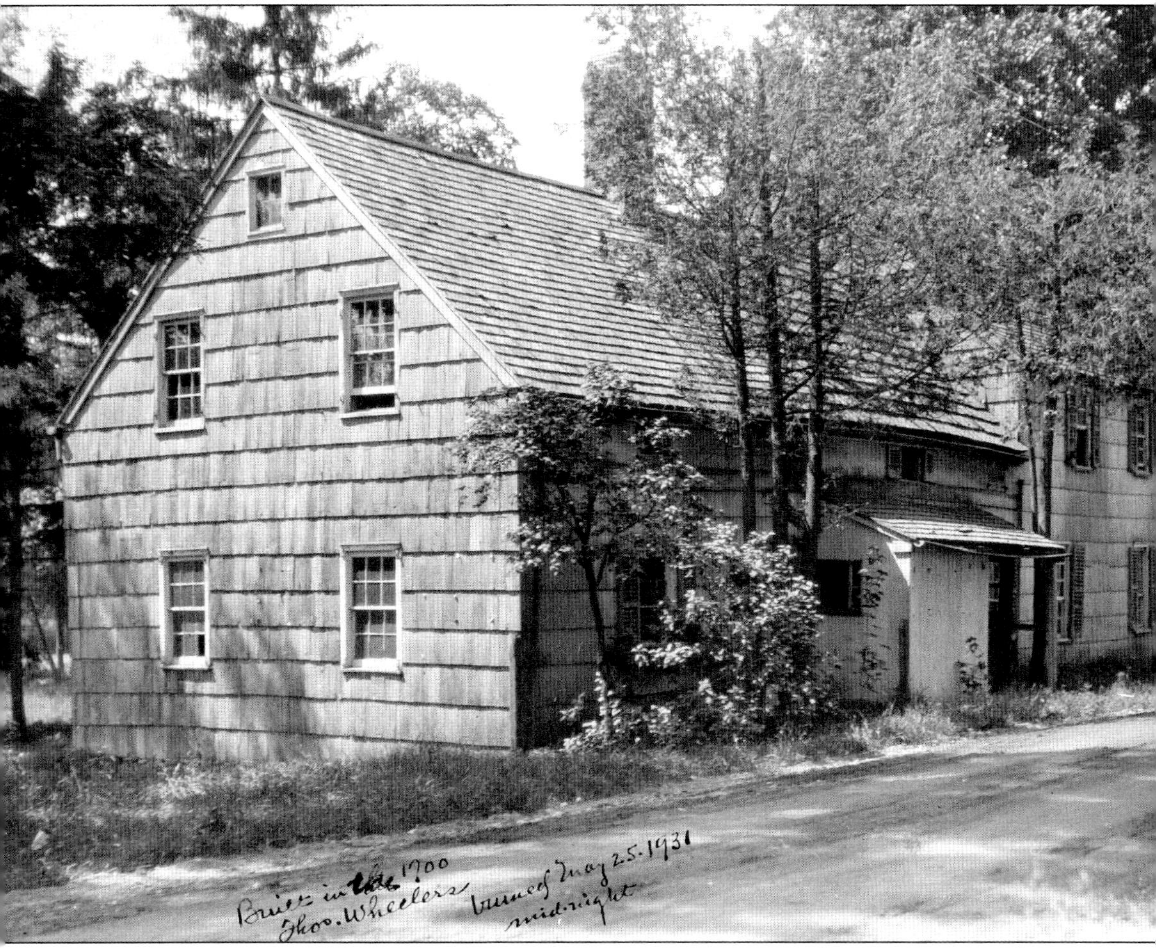

WHEELER HOUSE. Built by Thomas Wheeler sometime before 1753, the house was inherited by his son Timothy Wheeler and then by his grandson Richard Wheeler. The house stood on the triangular plot of land formed by the intersection of Town Line Road and Wheeler Road (now Route 111). The house was destroyed by fire at about midnight on May 25, 1931.

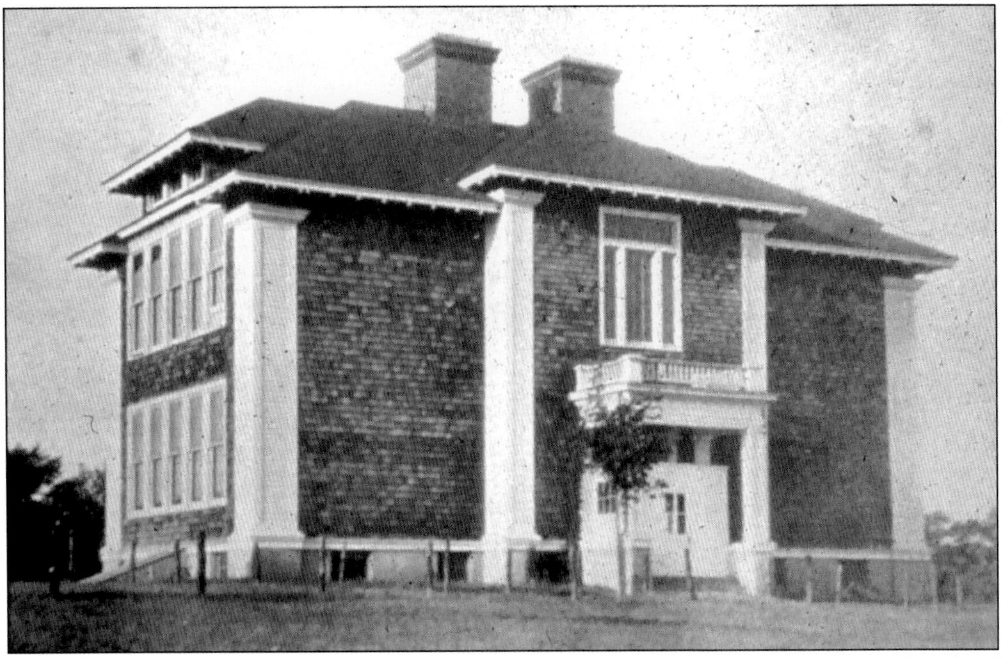

HAUPPAUGE DISTRICT SCHOOL. The landmark school building located on the south side of Townline Road near Schoolhouse Lane housed kindergarten through grade eight. Hauppauge students then attended either Smithtown High School or Islip High School for grades 9 through 12.

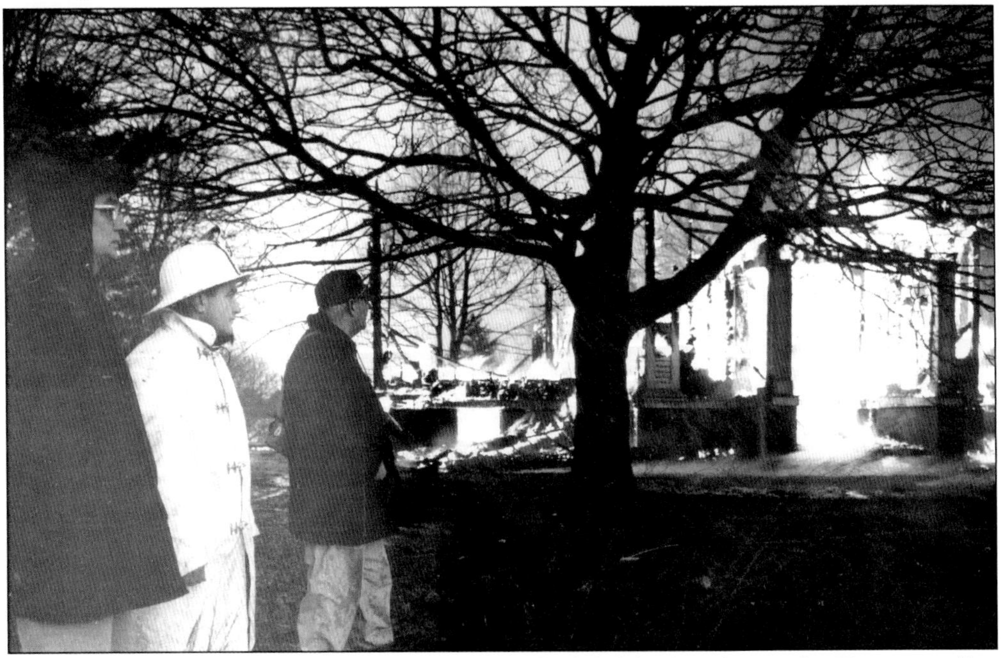

HAUPPAUGE DISTRICT SCHOOL FIRE, C. 1965. Scheduled for demolition, the Hauppauge Fire Department set the former school ablaze as a training exercise for the community volunteer firefighters. With a modern hook and ladder fire truck, the Hauppauge Fire Department kept the fire under control.

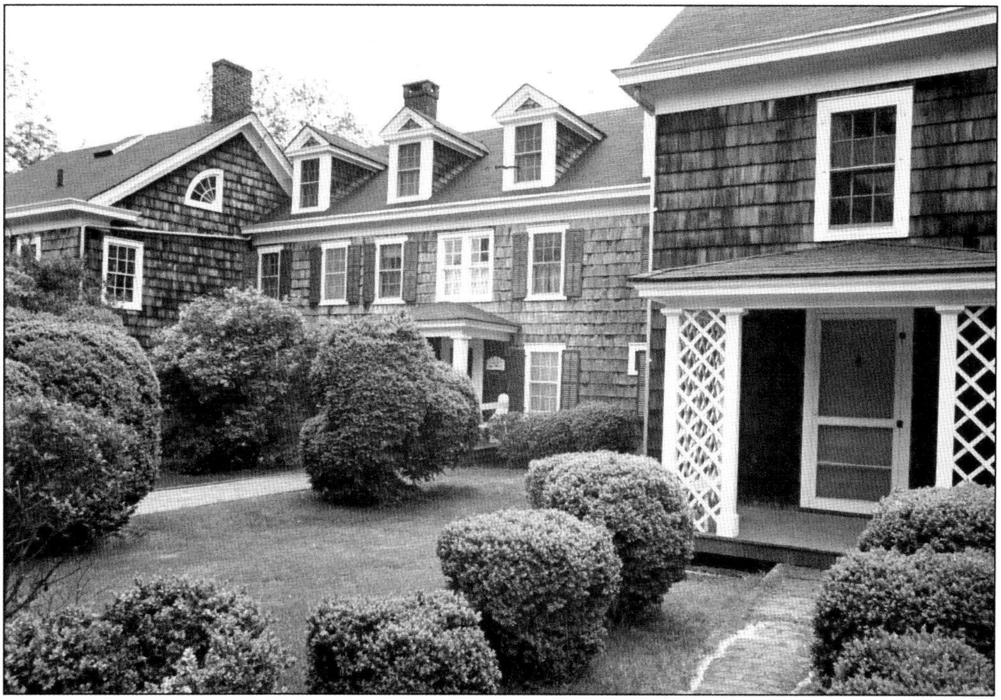

HOYT HOUSE AT HOYT FARM PARK. The central core of this house was built by Elnathan Wickes in 1770. Generations of the Wickes family cultivated the property until 1910 when the farm was sold to Edwin Chase Hoyt and Maria Louisa Moran Hoyt. To accommodate their growing family, the Hoyts expanded the original farmhouse by adding wings to each side as well as two additional stories.

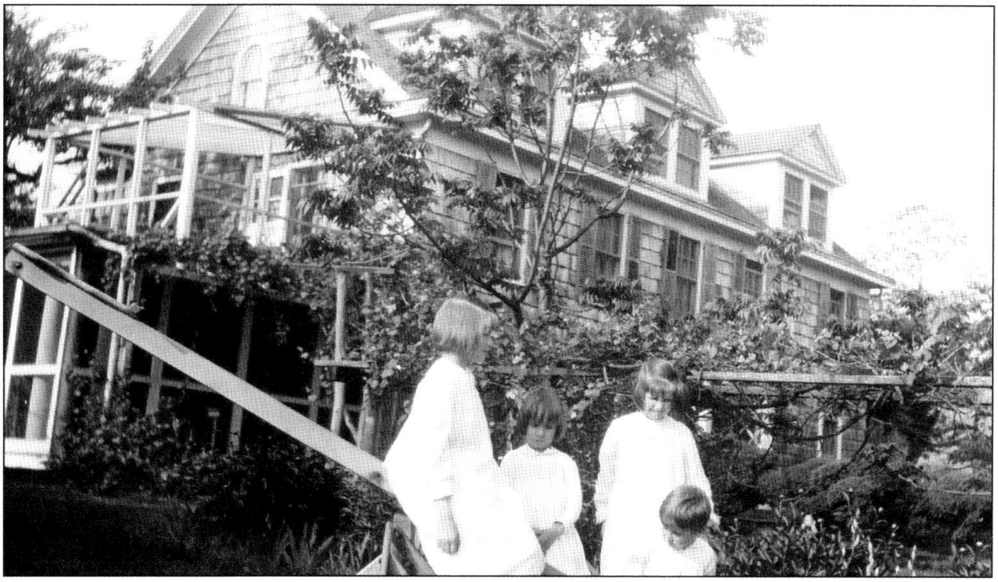

HOYT FAMILY CHILDREN. The Hoyt children are photographed behind their home. Some of the farmland surrounding the house was eventually converted into apple and peach orchards by Edwin Hoyt. In 1966, the Town of Smithtown purchased the Hoyt House and the 133-acre Crooked Hill Farm site and established Hoyt Farm Park.

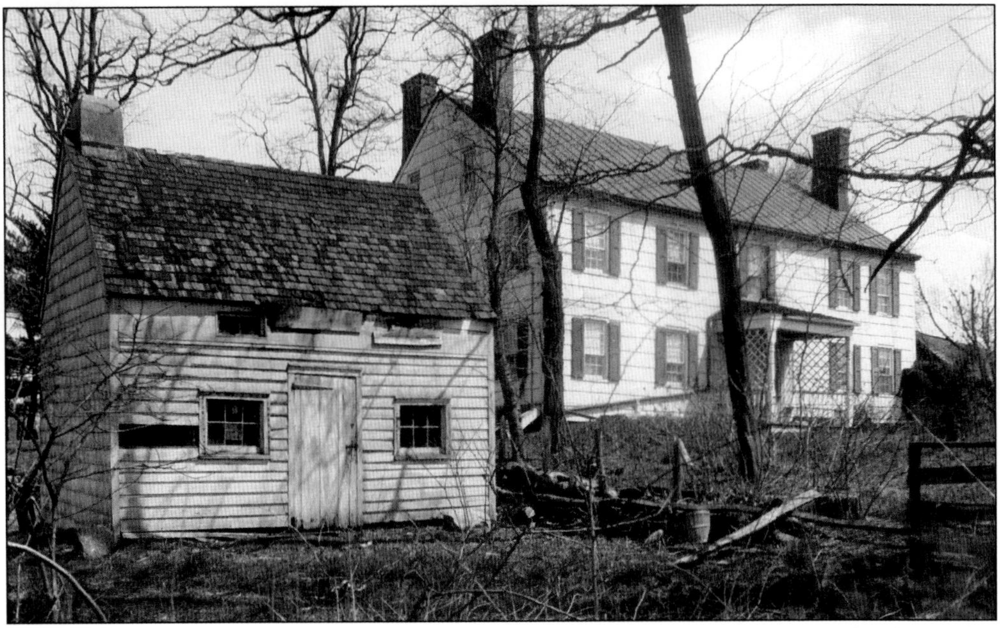

CALEB SMITH II HOUSE. In 1819, Caleb Smith II, a great-great-grandson of Richard Smythe, constructed his new house around a preexisting structure in Commack, its original location. The earlier section may predate the Revolutionary War. In 1955, the structure was relocated to Smithtown and became the Smithtown Historical Society's headquarters. The little house in the foreground, built for Smith's manumitted black slaves, was demolished.

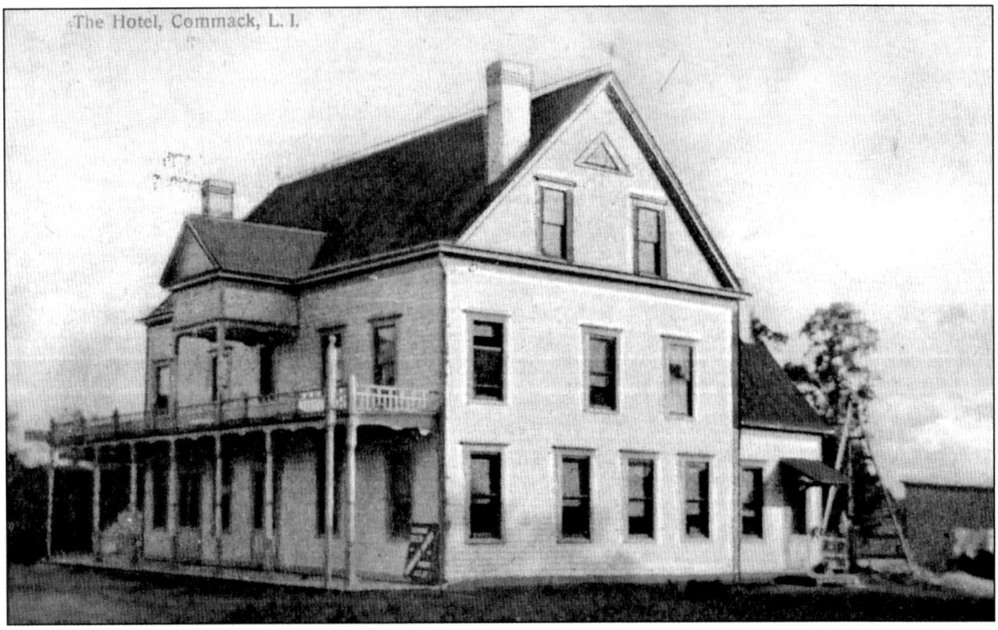

COMMACK HOTEL, C. 1908–1910. The Commack Hotel stood in the heart of Commack on the southwest corner of the intersection of Jericho Turnpike and Commack Road from the 1880s until it was destroyed by fire in 1965. The triangular framework seen here at the rear of the hotel suspended a long pole and bucket that could be lowered into an adjacent well to provide freshwater to the structure.

THE NORTH SCHOOL. Through most of the 19th century, this little one-room schoolhouse was the only one in District No. 18, which served the children living north of Jericho Turnpike in Commack. In addition to the schoolhouse, the district had its own trustee and employed just one schoolteacher. The school, which was in operation until 1899, was located north of the Methodist church.

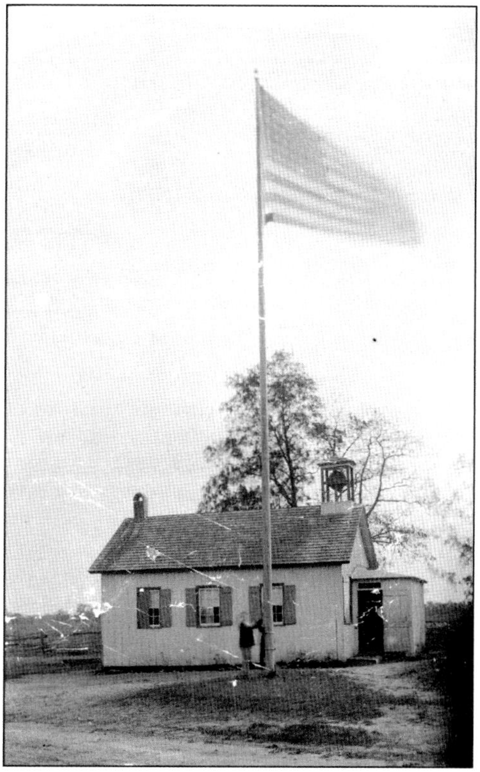

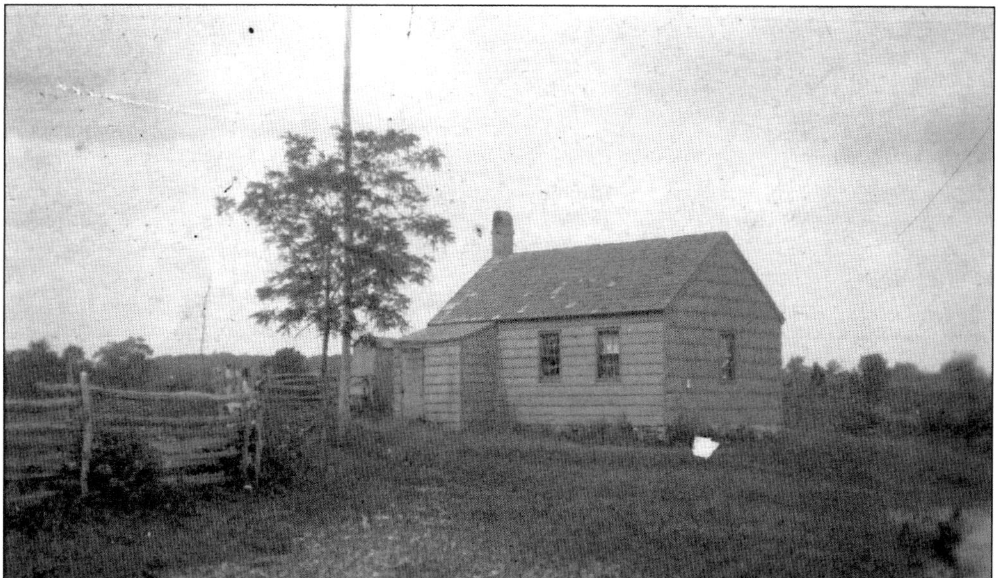

THE SOUTH SCHOOL. This one-room schoolhouse resided in District No. 10 through most of the 19th century. District No. 10 served children south of Jericho Turnpike until 1899, when District No. 18 and District No. 10 were combined to form one large district. The new district provided a much larger schoolhouse for its children. The school seen here stood on the west side of Commack Road just north of the present-day Commack Library.

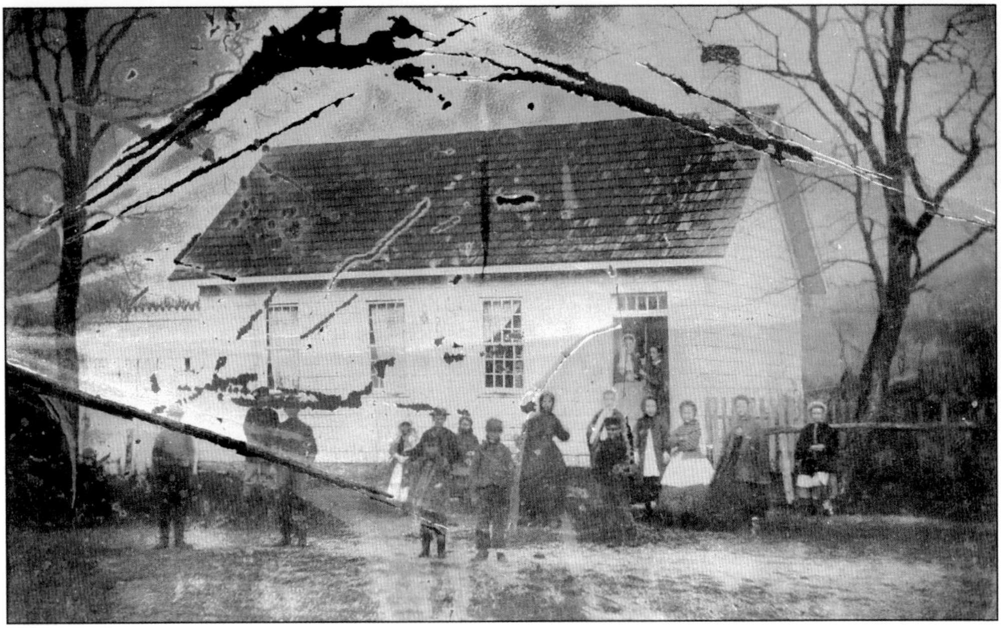

First Schoolhouse in Smithtown, c. 1860. Smithtown's first school, also known as the Whitman School House, is now located on Singer Lane south of Main Street. Built in 1802, it was originally located just west of the Presbyterian church and operated as a private school. In 1816, Smithtown taxpayers purchased it and allowed it to serve as a public school. A young Walt Whitman taught here in the 1837–1838 school year.

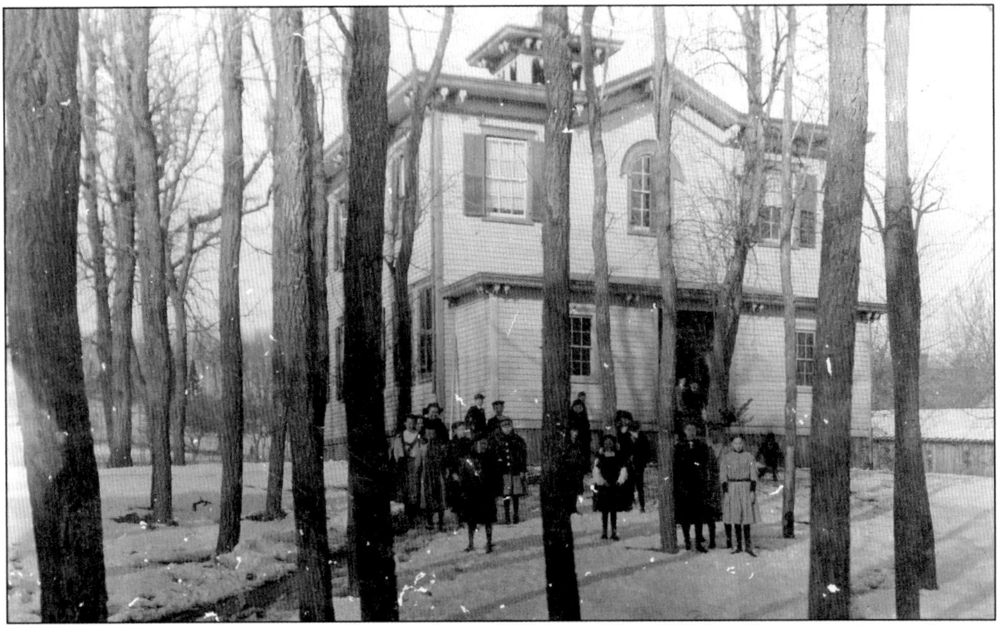

The Academy, c. 1869. This school was built following the formation of the Smithtown Union Free School District No. 1 on April 4, 1868. The new school was built to replace the recently moved original schoolhouse. The academy building served the community until a new one was constructed in 1908. The old building was sold and relocated to Main Street where it became the Weiss and Forman Store.

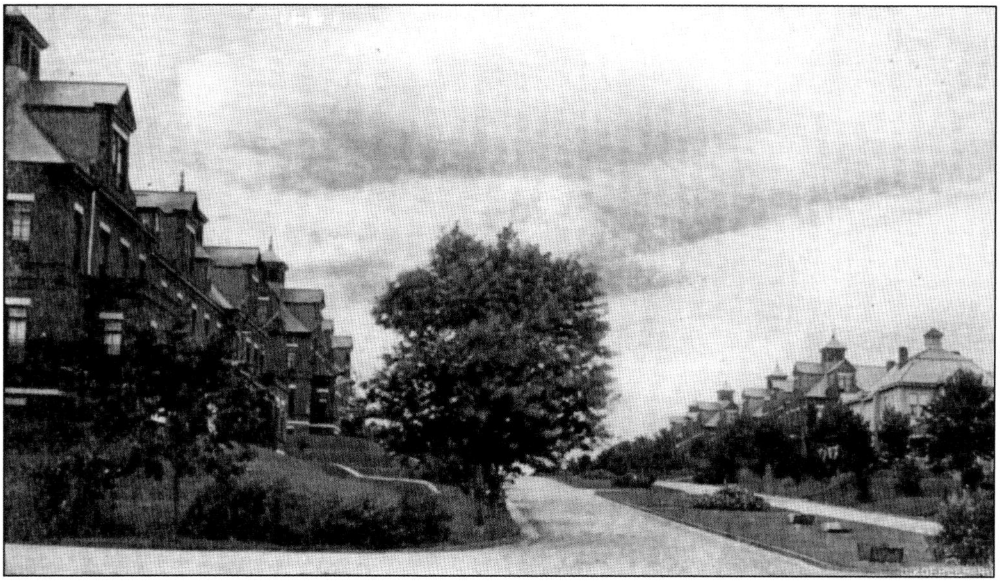

Kings Park State Hospital. The Kings Park State Hospital was an institution run by New York State that was dedicated to research into the causes, diagnosis, and treatment of mental illness. It began in 1885 as a farm where the overcrowded Kings County Asylum sent patients for therapy. Then it became the Long Island State Hospital, and in 1905, the name was changed to the Kings Park State Hospital. Patients and staff were housed in large wooden buildings that were constructed along the boulevard, the main access road into the hospital's parklike grounds.

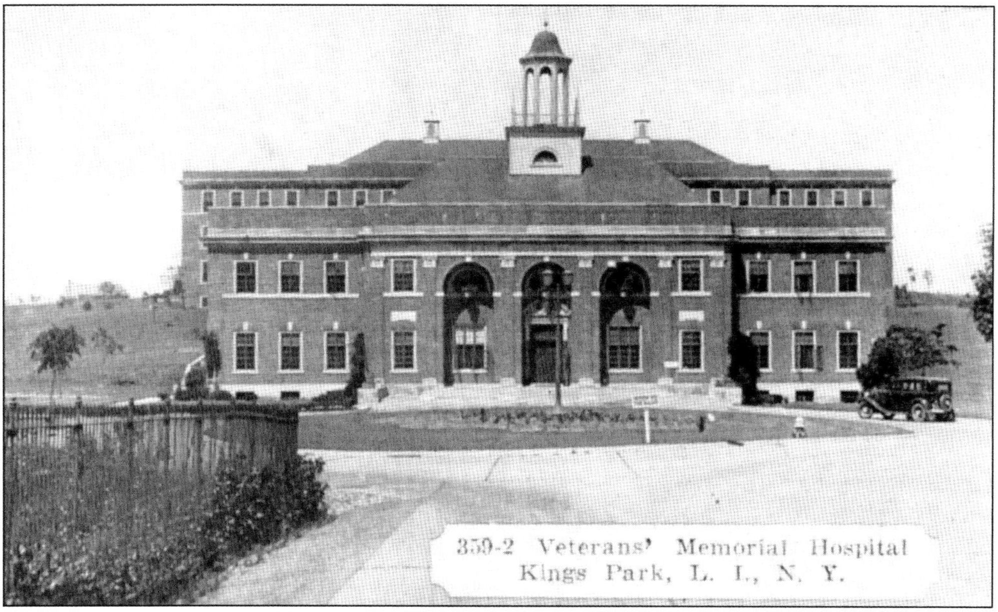

Veteran's Memorial Hospital. The creation of a separate facility for the care and treatment of mentally disabled veterans was a new concept and was heralded as one of the most important events in the history of the state hospital system. In September 1927, the Veteran's Memorial Hospital was formally dedicated and began receiving patients. By 1930, 626 veterans of World War I and the Spanish-American War were being treated and cared for at the Veteran's Memorial Hospital.

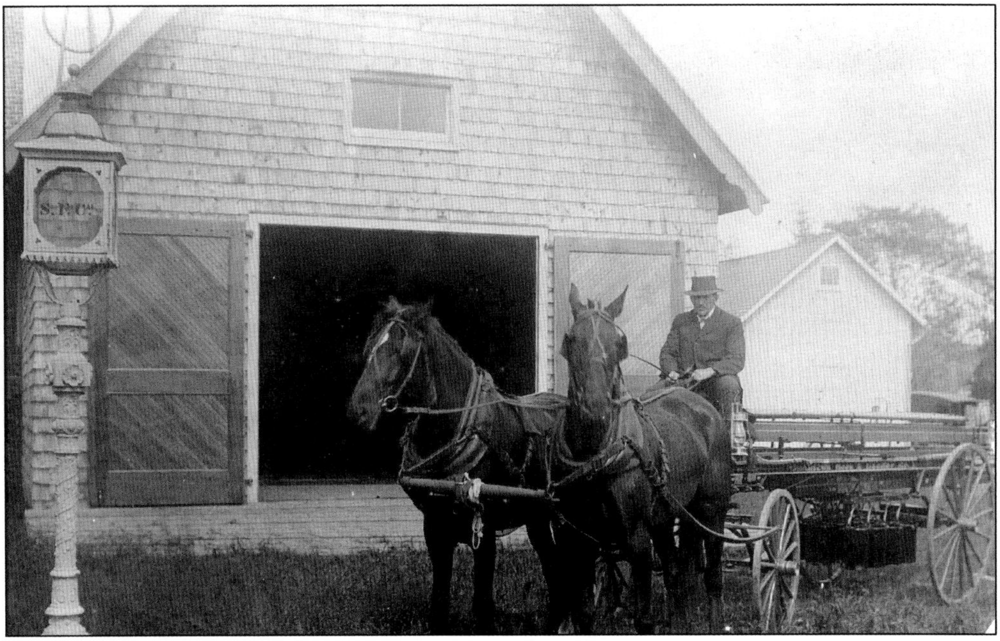

SMITHTOWN FIRE COMPANY. This photograph was taken in front of the newly completed firehouse on Bellemeade Avenue in 1909. Clinton Darling is driving the new hook and ladder wagon that the Smithtown Volunteer Hook and Ladder Company purchased from a manufacturer in Rhode Island for $375. The new wagon made it possible, with the help of the bucket brigade, to fight fires in two-story buildings.

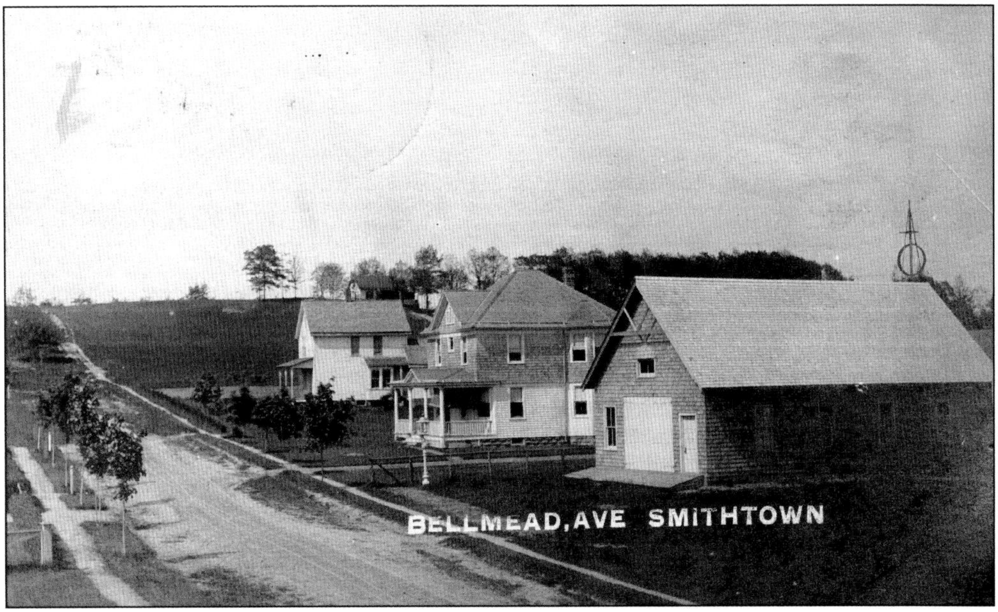

BELLEMEADE AVENUE, C. 1912. This photograph was taken after the firehouse was built in 1909 but before the bell tower was added in 1913. The firehouse, with its steel tower and attached locomotive drive-wheel rim, is to the right in the photograph. To sound the alarm, a fireman had to climb to the platform on the tower, grab a sledgehammer, and wallop the rim.

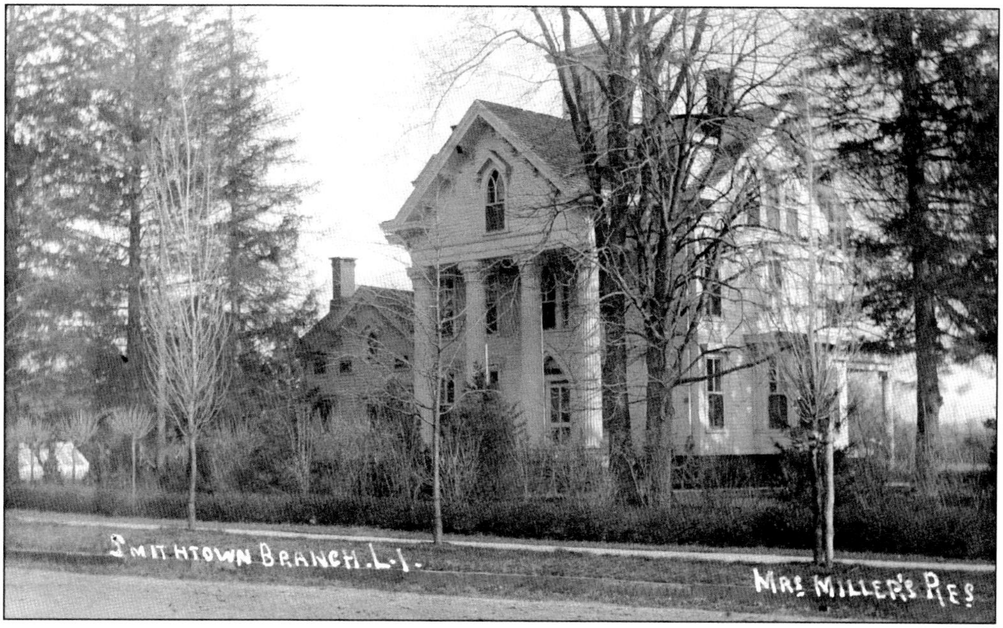

Miller House on Main Street. Mary Ely Miller owned this house when these photographs were taken. The Miller estate of over 100 acres extended from Lawrence Avenue to Singer Lane and south from Main Street to Miller's Pond. The property was actively farmed in the 1940s, and many people remember the stench of rotting cauliflower in the fall. The property was sold to developers in 1953, and the first shopping center in the Village of the Branch was constructed along the Main Street frontage. The Miller House was demolished several years later, and a Howard Johnson was built on the site.

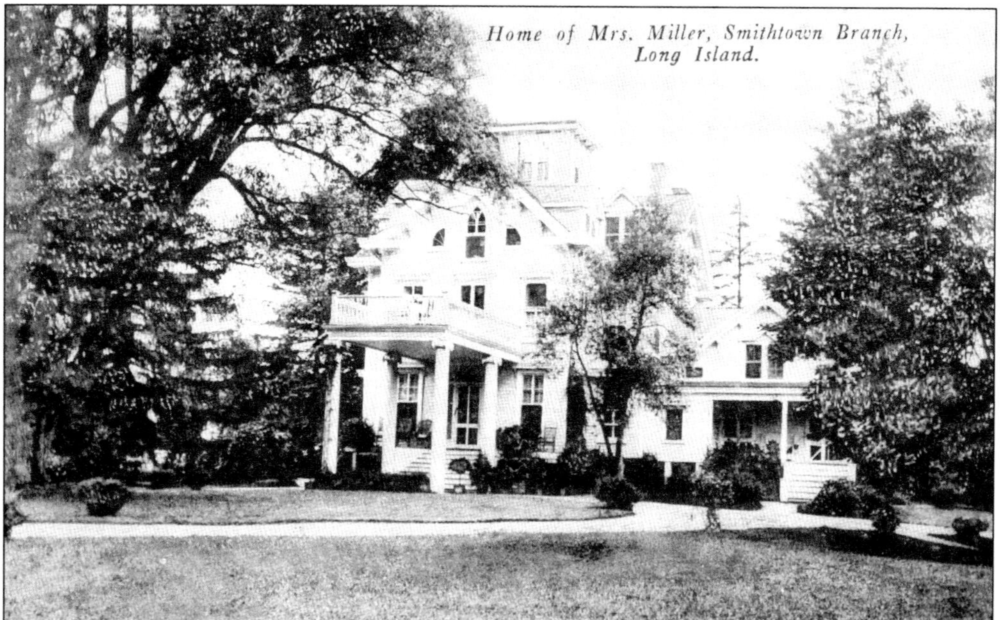

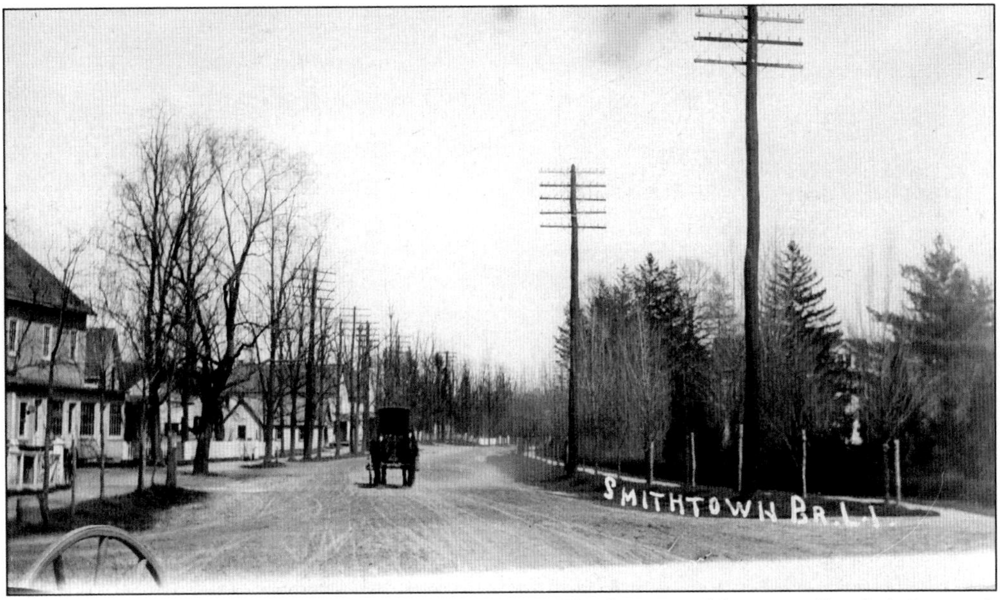

MAIN STREET IN SMITHTOWN BRANCH, c. 1912. The horse and buggy still ruled the road, but modern marvels such as telephones were beginning to appear in Smithtown Branch. This photograph was taken in front of the Miller property looking to the east down Main Street. The little single-story building with its gable end facing Main Street, visible through the trees, is the Smithtown Branch Post Office. The next building is the Royal Arcanum Hall, and farther east is Huntting's General Store.

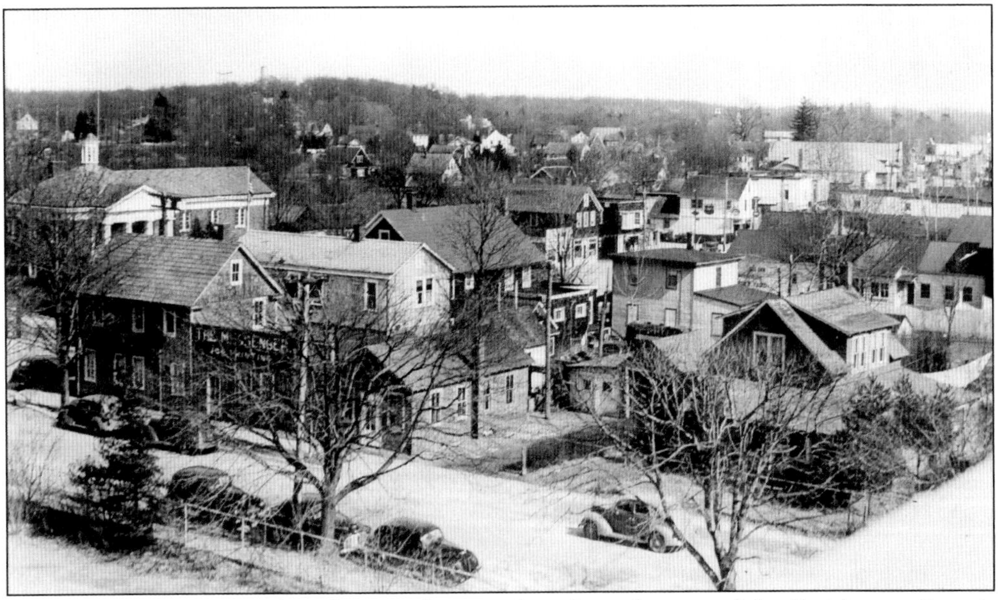

SMITHTOWN BRANCH. This photograph was taken from the top of the Smithtown Branch School on New York Avenue and looks east along Main Street. The wing attached to Smithtown Town Hall was constructed in 1930. This part of the town, Smithtown Branch's business district, was where the heaviest concentration of stores and businesses was found. Change was coming to Smithtown Branch, as evidenced by the stoplight hanging from wires at the intersection of Maple Avenue and Main Street.

Six

Kicking Back

For much of its history, Smithtown has been associated with recreational pursuits. During the mid- to late 1800s, long before the population explosion and mass development created the suburban sprawl of today, Smithtown's streams, fields, and woodlands attracted a number of hunters and outdoorsmen to the area. Equestrian activities including horse shows and races have a long and well-documented tradition in the town. Formal English foxhunting, with all its associated etiquette and decorum, has persevered through the shifting landscape to continue as an organized event to this day. The Nissequogue River, Lake Ronkonkoma, and Long Island Sound have allowed many over the years to indulge in a variety of water sports, and their associated beaches have long welcomed beachgoers in both formal and informal parties. Over the years, residents of Smithtown have also had ample reason for celebration. Major area anniversaries, local weddings, and the ends of wars have each culminated in festive and lively celebrations complete with pageantry, proclamations, and parades that have thrilled numerous generations of the town's residents. Indeed, when it comes to celebration and recreation, the town of Smithtown possesses a rich history of kicking back.

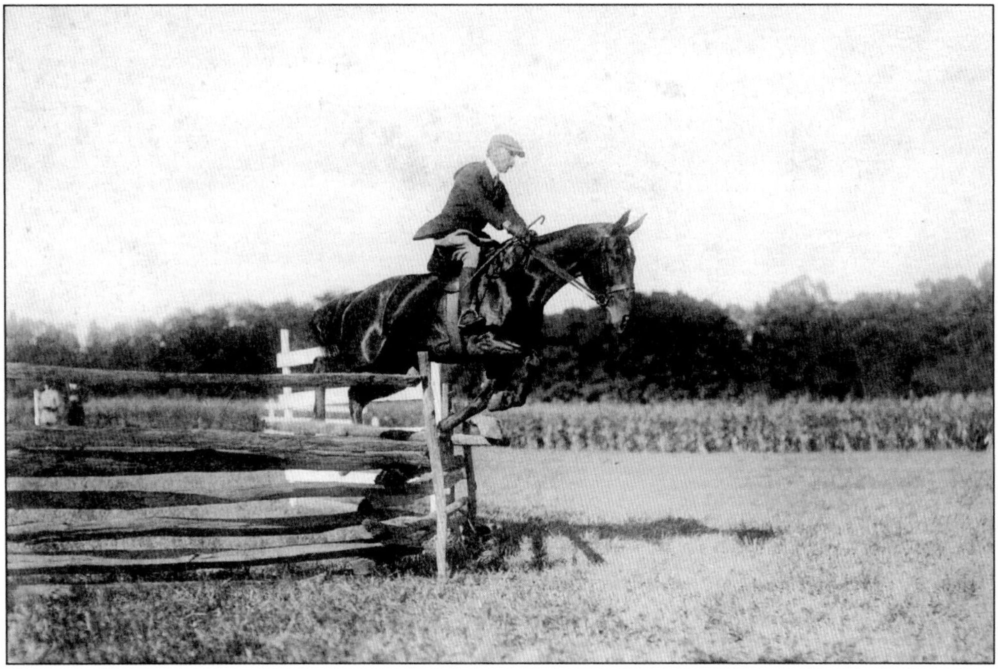

SMITHTOWN HORSE SHOW, C. 1913. Equestrian pursuits were among the most preferred hobbies of Smithtown's elite residents. Founded in 1909, the Smithtown Horse Show was one of the most popular and well attended of its day on Long Island. Horses and riders competed in a wide variety of activities in numerous classes, including saddle, harness, polo, hunting, roadster, and racing. Devereaux Emmet, seen above jumping a hurdle on his horse, was a frequent entrant, attendee, and committeeman of the Smithtown Horse Show Association during its first two decades. Below, Arthur B. Lawrence, another horse show mainstay, leads his horse through an event at the Smithtown Horse Show around 1913.

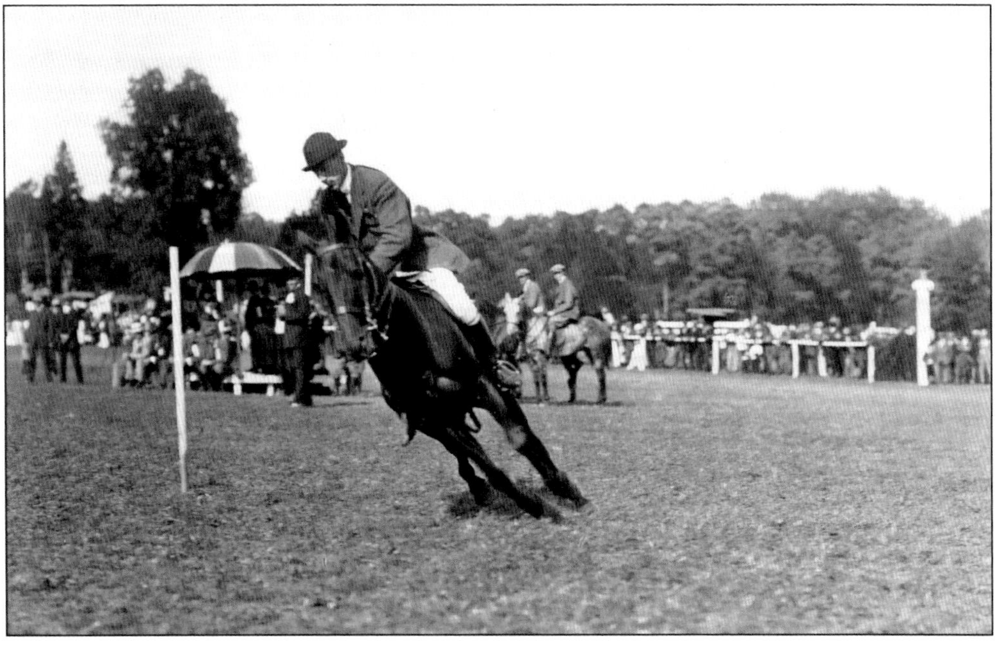

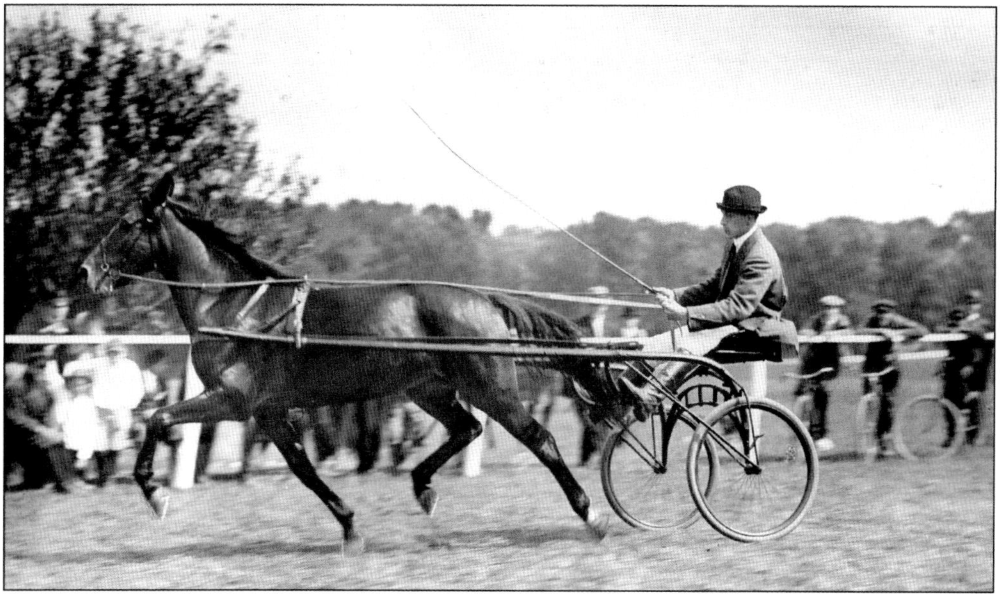

FIFTY ACRE FIELD, C. 1909. Fifty Acre Field, located at what is presently the intersection of Fifty Acre Road and Edgewood Avenue in St. James, played host to a number of equine exhibitions and competitions, including the Smithtown Horse Show. Among the most active participants at the field's competitions was Arthur B. Lawrence, an accomplished horseman, pictured here racing a sulky. In addition to his escapades at horse shows and races, Lawrence also served as one of the Smithtown Hunt Club's first secretaries.

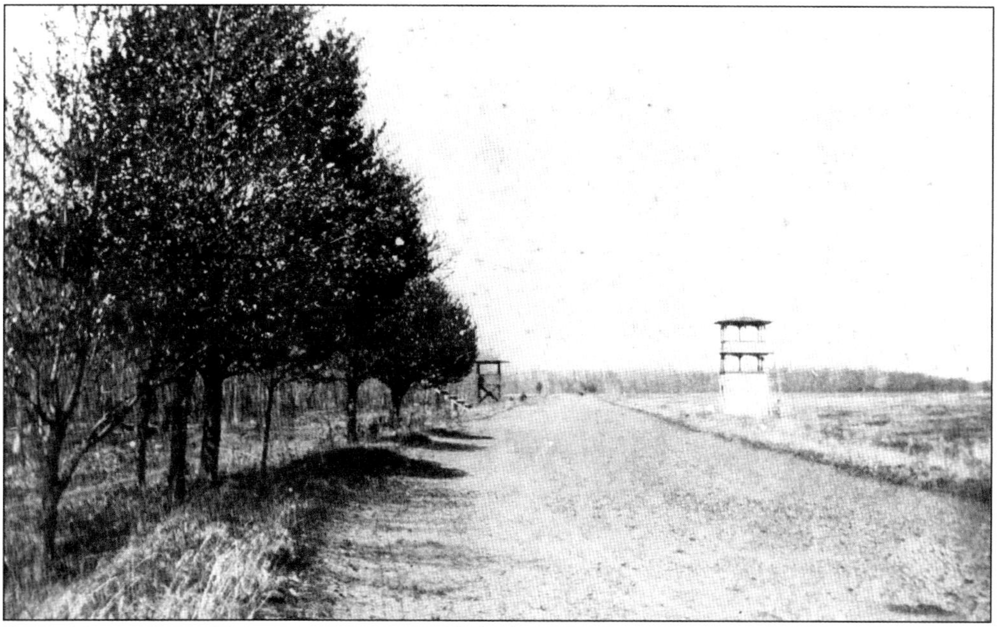

BURR HORSE RACE TRACK, C. 1880. Established in the 1880s, this one-mile oval racetrack was the site of trotting and horse racing in the 19th century, including races featuring the prominent record-breaking mare Lady Suffolk. During the 20th century, bicycle, motorcycle, and car races gradually took the place of horse racing at the track. The site is now part of the Commack High School property.

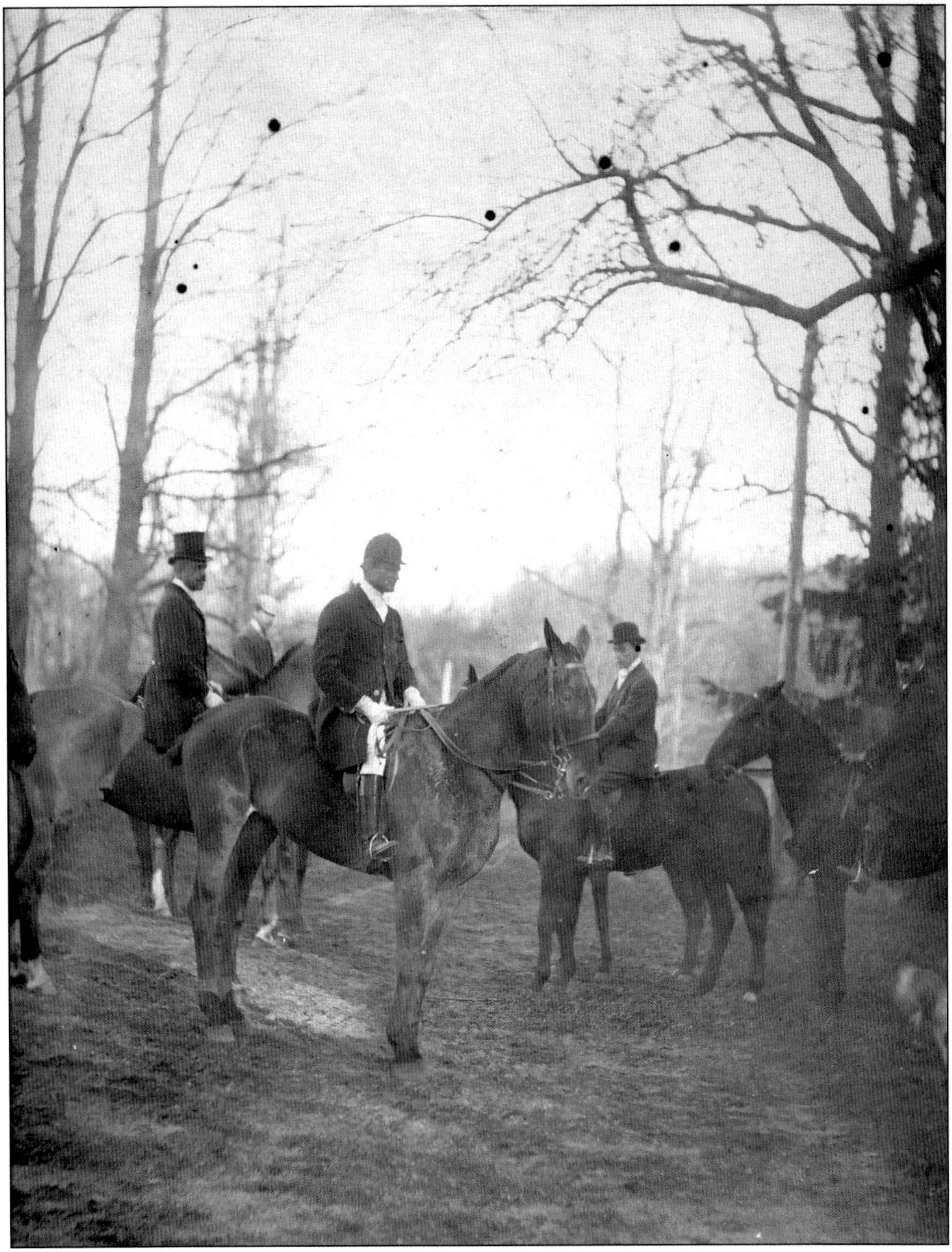

SMITHTOWN HUNT CLUB MEMBERS, C. 1900. Adorned in formal hunting attire, Arthur B. Lawrence (center) and other members of the Smithtown Hunt Club pause briefly from their pursuit of the fox. Founded in 1900, the Smithtown Hunt Club is the only remaining active foxhunting organization on Long Island. While members formerly had free reign to hunt on the many vast estate grounds, development and the accompanying population explosion gradually confined the hunt to state- and county-owned parkland. Due to animal rights issues, the modern Smithtown Hunt Club participates exclusively in exhibitions and the time-honored tradition of "drag hunting" or following a premarked trail of fox scent, rather than hunting an actual fox.

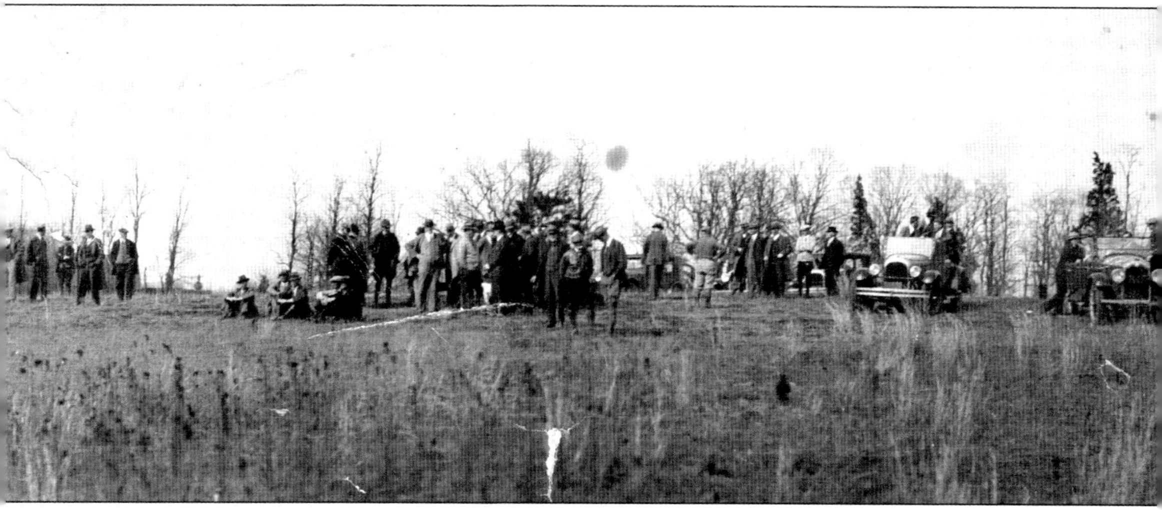

HORSE SHOW TRIALS, C. 1928. Although the Smithtown Horse Show was arguably the most prestigious and glamorous (it was chronicled in the *New York Times* society pages on several occasions), it was by no means the only horse show in Smithtown. In the years following the Smithtown Horse Show Association's founding, the Smithtown Hunt Club offered a rival show and even scheduled the exhibition such that the two shows' dates sometimes overlapped. Despite the rivalries in the various horse shows in Smithtown, or perhaps because of it, fans consistently turned out to take in the affairs.

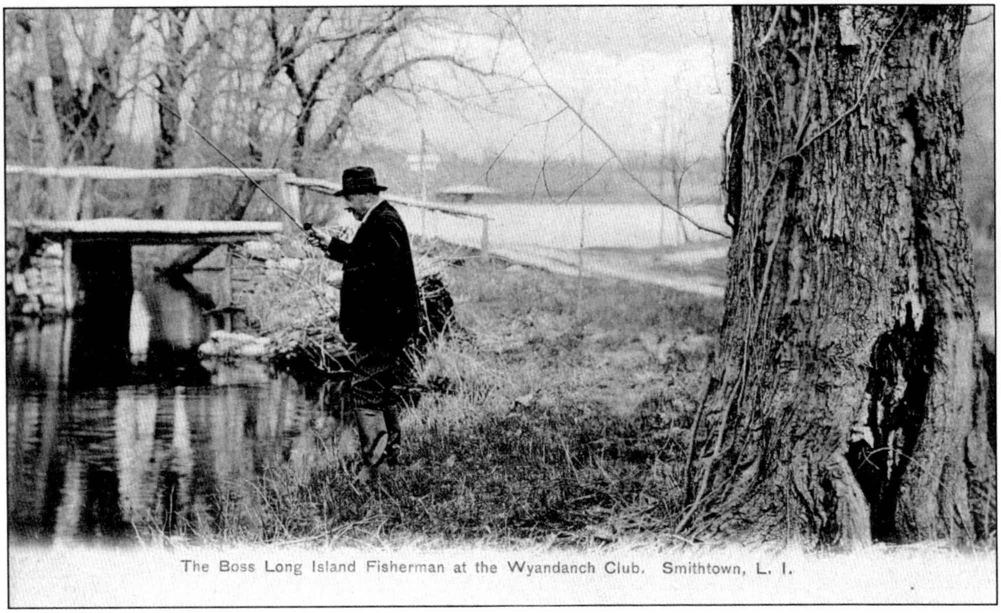

THE WYANDANCH CLUB, c. 1905. In 1888, the Brooklyn Gun Club, later the Wyandanch Club, purchased over 500 acres of land on Jericho Turnpike to serve as a private hunting and fishing retreat. Club members and guests were allowed to enjoy the vast grounds and streams until the club sold its holdings to the State of New York in 1963. The club's former property is now Caleb Smith State Park.

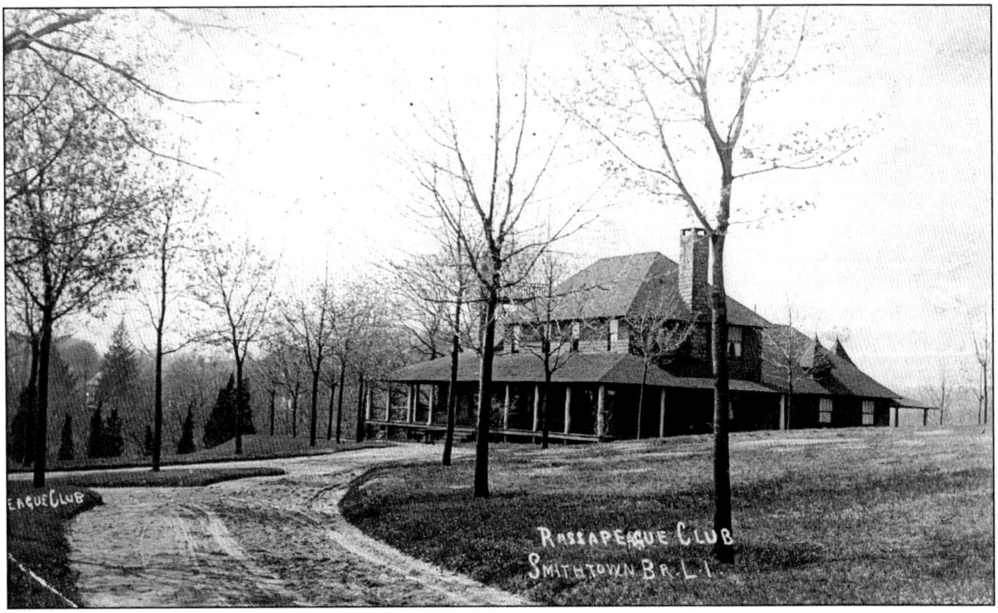

RASSAPEAGUE CLUB, 1908. Nestled on a tract of land north of Edgewood Avenue between River Road and the Nissequogue River was the clubhouse and grounds of the Rassapeague Club. This sportsman's club featured a small and exclusive membership enrollment that included such luminaries as the famed architect Stanford White. By 1920, however, the club had sold its clubhouse and accompanying land to Morgan Jopling, who converted the property to a private residence.

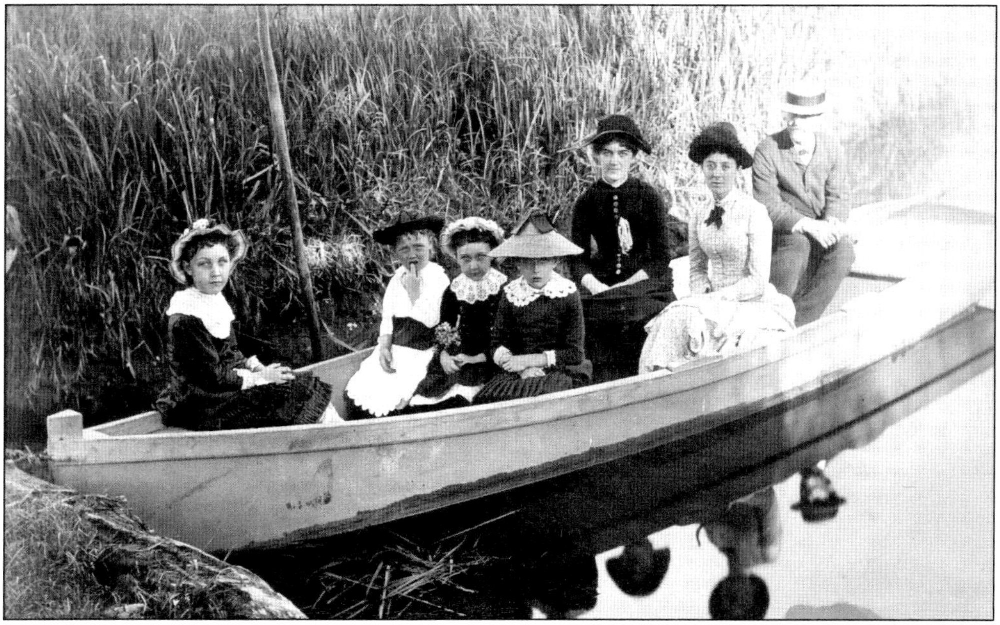

THE MILLS FAMILY OF THE LANDING, C. 1895. The Nissequogue River is a 27-square-mile waterway and home to a complex ecosystem consisting of a diverse population of birds, fish, and plants. Earlier in the 19th century, the river played host to a major shipbuilding industry that produced sloops for pleasure and tasks such as oystering. A much smaller vessel is seen here as the Mills family enjoys a summer outing along the Nissequogue River's pristine shoreline.

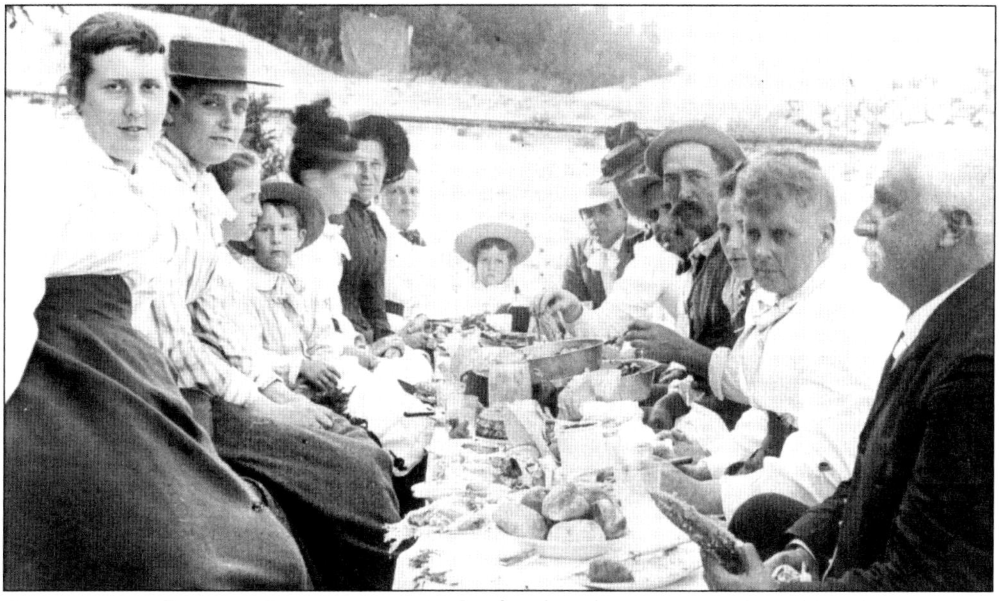

CLAMBAKE AT BECKERS BEACH, C. 1900. Outfitted in the customary formal beachgoing attire of the period, these revelers took to Beckers Beach on the Nissequogue River to participate in a lively clambake. Those pictured here, clockwise from left to right, are Ada Strong, Mary L. Handley, unidentified, Arthur Lawrence, unidentified, Julia Lawrence, unidentified, Charles Lawrence (boy at the head of the table), unidentified, a Mrs. Germond, four unidentified, and Homer Reboul (gentleman with white hair).

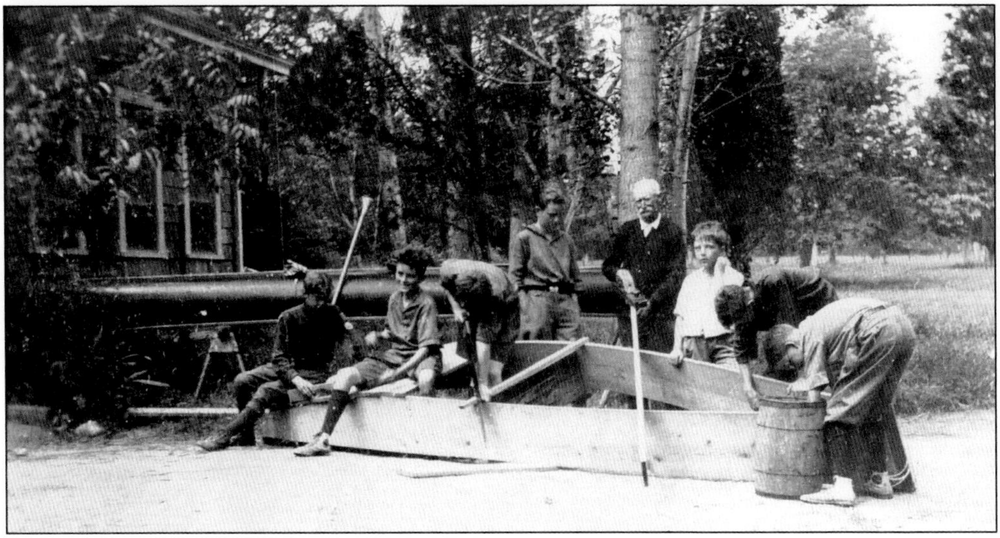

LIFE AT CAMP NISSEQUOGUE, C. 1926. Norman F. Parkes opened Camp Nissequogue (or Camp Nissequogue Harbor, as it was also known) in 1924. Occupying his 100-acre property near Stony Brook Harbor, Parkes boasted of a "camp where every healthy instinct of healthy boys can be gratified under the supervision of wise councillors [*sic*]." The camp ran from July to September and had a limited membership of 100 boys aged seven years or greater. Young men summering at Camp Nissequoge could expect to participate in a number of activities designed to aid their "mental and physical development," including swimming, sailing, boat repair, riding, hiking, and camping. Boys wishing to focus more on their mental development could enroll in the optional St. James Summer School on the camp's grounds. Above, boys work on a small boat undoubtedly under the supervision of "an old ship captain." Below, young boys enjoy a swim and a sail on Stony Brook Harbor's placid waters.

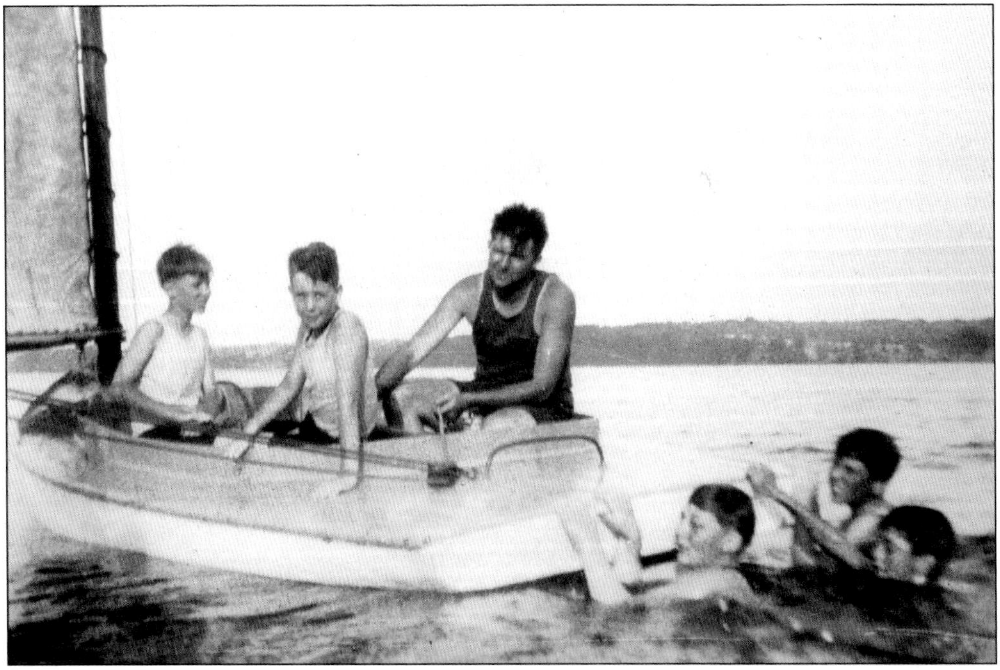

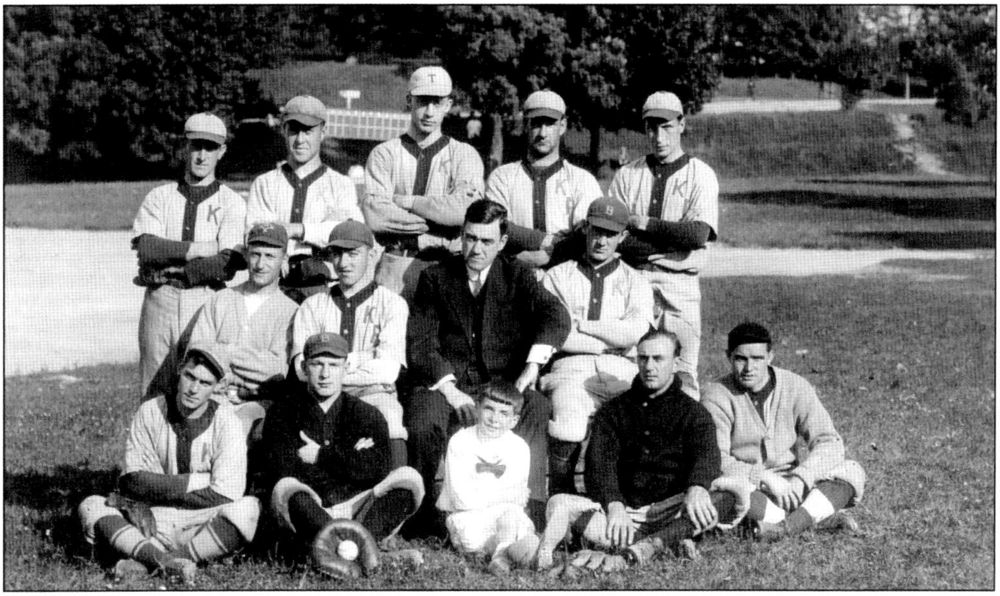

KINGS PARK BASEBALL CLUB, 1913. Comprised of Kings Park State Hospital employees, the Kings Park Baseball Club primarily played other local amateur ball clubs, often at the state hospital's Tiffany Field. Pictured here are members of the 1913 squad.

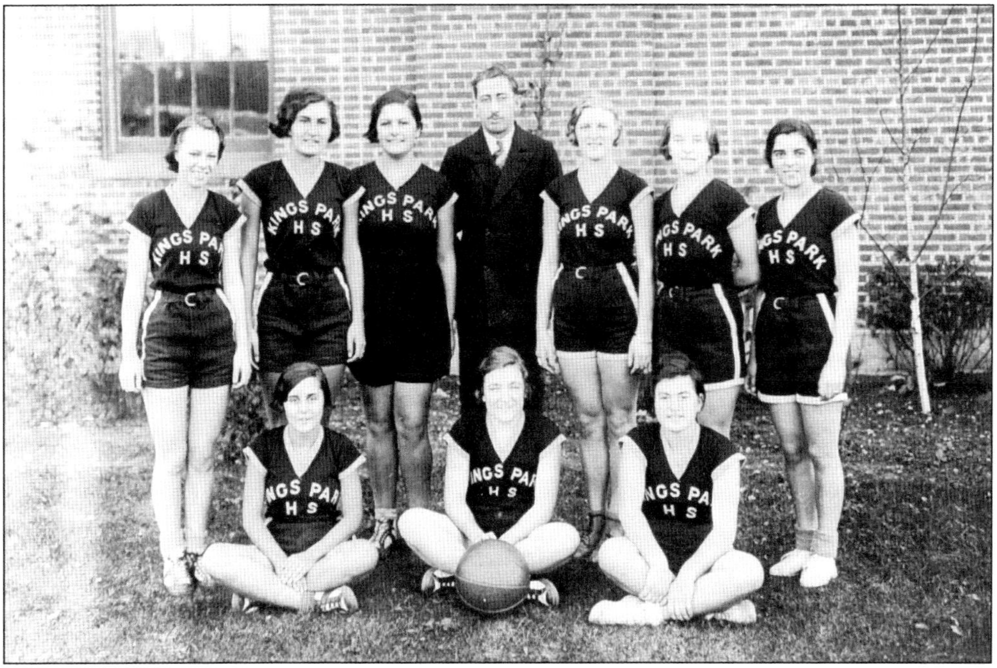

KINGS PARK HIGH SCHOOL WOMEN'S BASKETBALL TEAM, 1932. Smithtown-area high schools have a rich tradition of interscholastic athletic competition that dates from the early 1900s. Here the members of the 1932–1933 Kings Park High School women's basketball team pose for their team photograph. From left to right are (first row) Marie Dolan, Edwina Crowe, and Sarah Stein; (second row) Margaret Nelson, Elizabeth Kiefer, Florence Stattel, coach and future principal Ralph Osgood, Vera Nowick, Jean McErlean, and Catherine Burns.

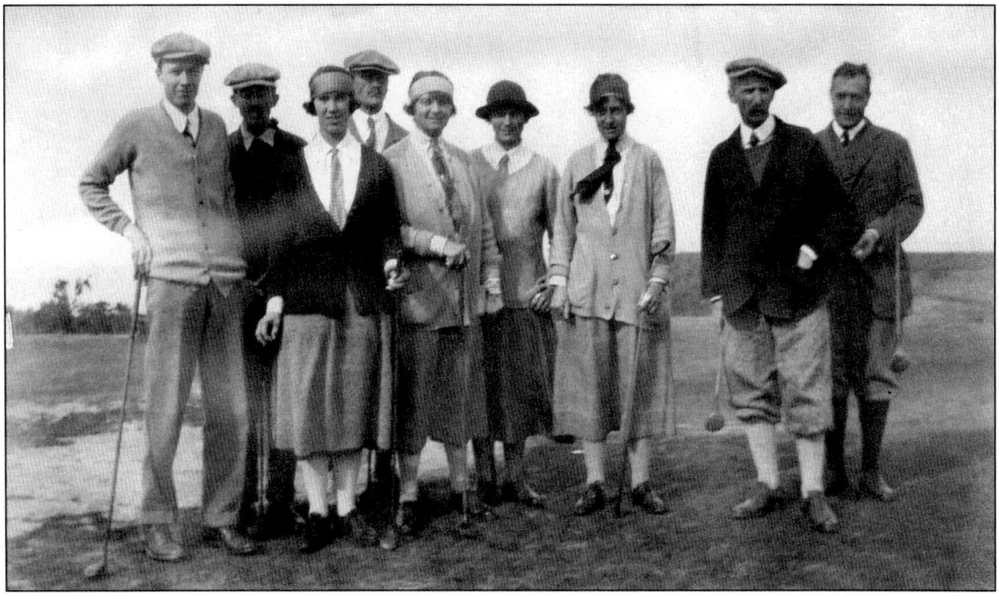

Golf Outing, c. 1920. Golf has a rich tradition on Long Island, dating from the 1890s when Shinnecock Hills Golf Club opened. Closer to Smithtown, Devereaux Emmet (second from right) designed the St. Georges course in Stony Brook in 1917. During the 1960s, Smithtown witnessed a surge in golf course construction, as three local courses, Merrywood (later Smithtown Landing) Country Club, Sunken Meadow Golf Course, and Nissequogue Golf Club, all began operations.

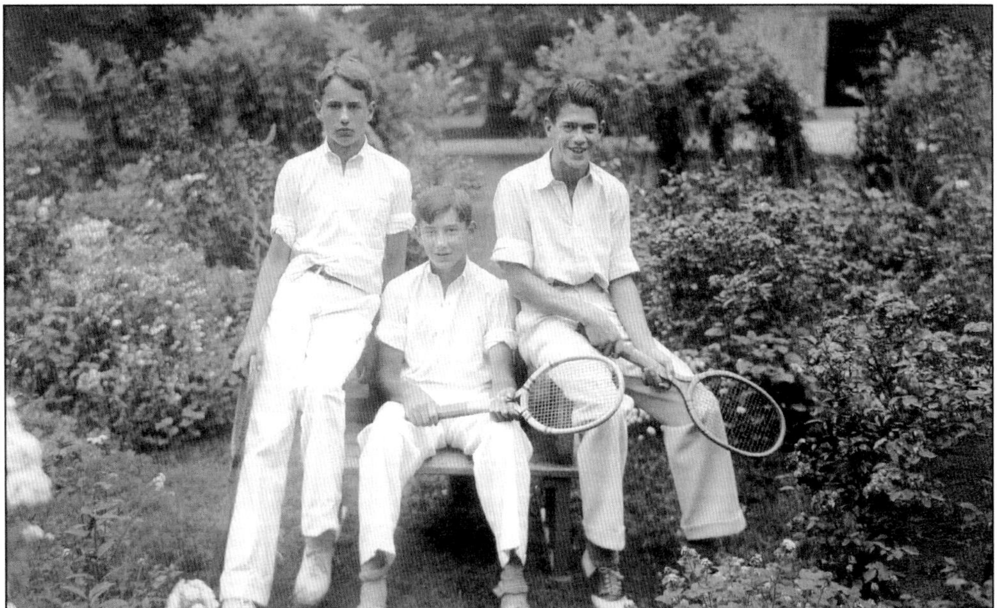

Lawrence and Rockwell Boys, 1930. Tennis was a favorite pastime for the Lawrence and Rockwell boys seen here. Charles Embree Rockwell's daughter Joan Rockwell Gifford recalls that her father and Lawrence "Uncle Larry" Rockwell "played absolutely beautiful tennis together. They were really the team to beat in all the local matches." Pictured here from left to right are Arthur Brewster Lawrence Jr., Lawrence Dudley Rockwell, and Charles Embree Rockwell.

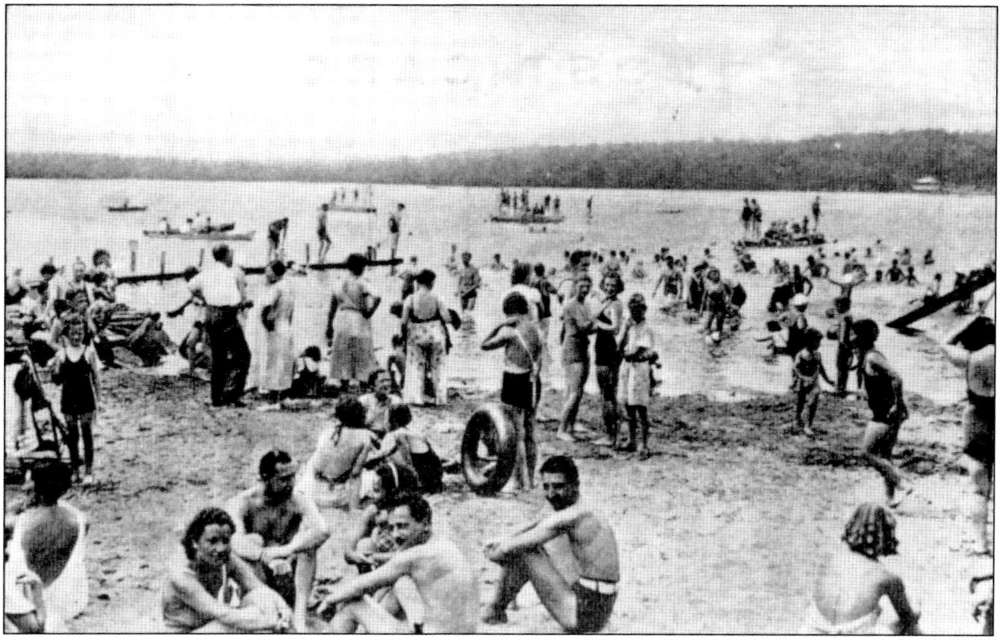

LAKE RONKONKOMA, C. 1940. From the 1930s to the 1950s, Lake Ronkonkoma played host to a thriving tourist industry. Visitors regularly came from as far as New York City to enjoy the lake's many amenities, including several beaches, snack shops, and an amusement park. In more recent years, heavy pollution has at times rendered the lake unsuitable for swimming.

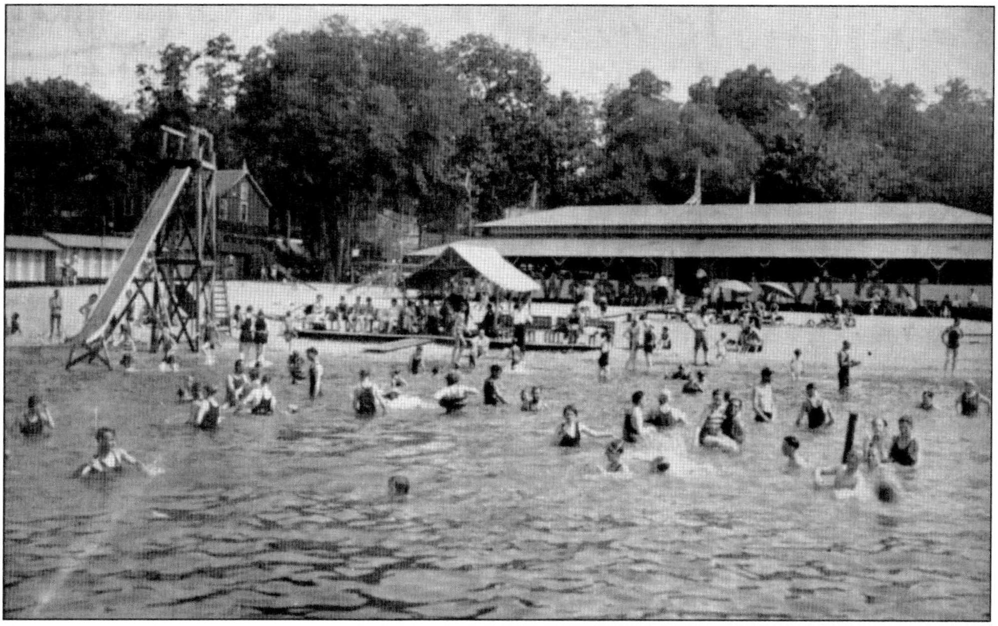

HOLLYWOOD BEACH, 1950. Among the favored spots for local youth to gather during Lake Ronkonkoma's peak years were the beach pavilions. Nesconset native Juliette Kieselstein describes the mid-century scene: "Pavilions surrounded the lake, the lights from them shimmering on the water. Music [filled] the evening air. 'Stardust' was the top hit then and seemed to add to the beauties of the summer nights. Romance was everywhere. It was so beautiful."

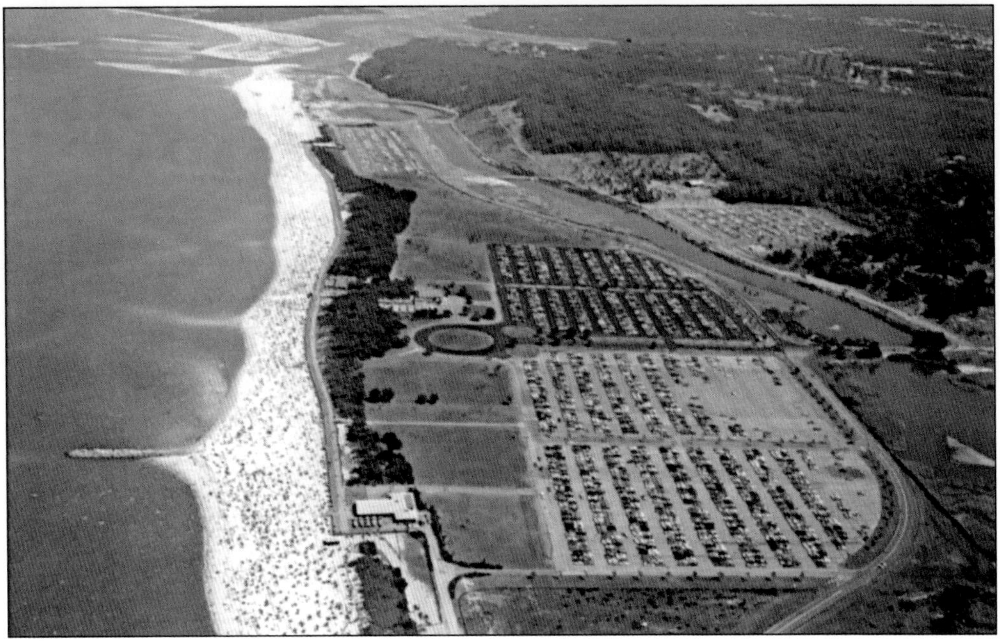

SUNKEN MEADOW STATE PARK, C. 1940. Since it first opened as a state park in 1928, Sunken Meadow State Park has been a popular beach destination not only for residents of Kings Park and Smithtown but also for inhabitants of New York City and Brooklyn seeking fresh air and relief from their otherwise cramped urban existences. Above, an aerial postcard shot shows the massive expanse of the state park's land holdings. Initially comprised of just over 500 acres, the State of New York began an expansion project in the 1950s that resulted in the eventual acquisition of over 1,200 acres for the beachfront park. In the postcard below, beachgoers take in the beautiful sound views from under a sea of umbrellas. Note the distinctive boardwalk at right, a still-popular feature that was constructed just before the state park opened in 1928.

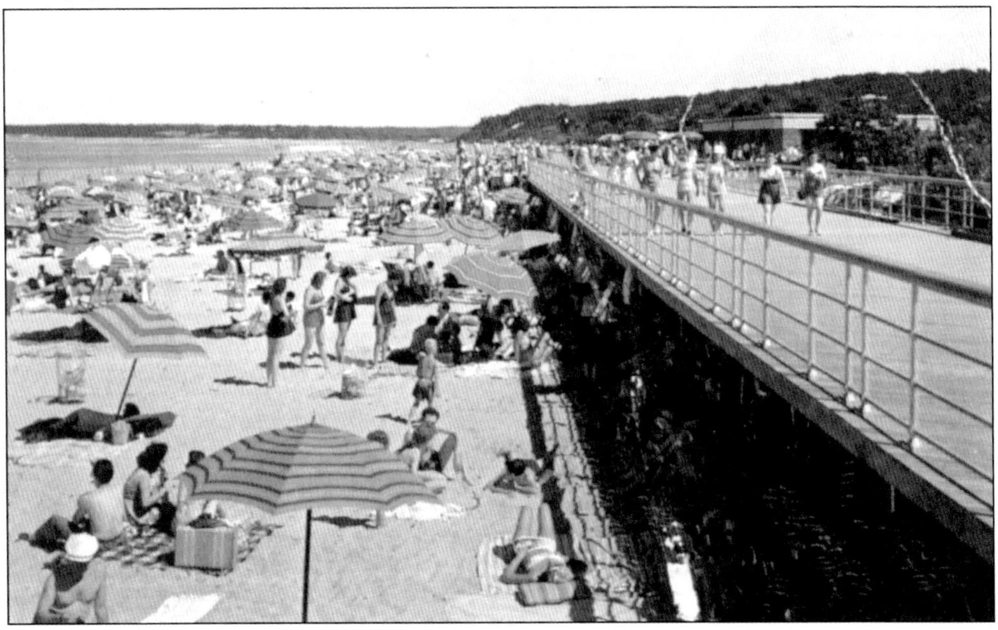

GAY NINETIES PARTY AT THE JOPLING HOUSE, 1937. The Great Depression left many Americans with a sense of longing for the good old days. Smithtown resident Morgan Jopling and friends indulged in their nostalgia with a Gay Nineties party. Gathering at Jopling's residence on River Road, revelers unveiled their take on the 1890s, a happier time free of the current economic tumult. At right, Jopling, outfitted in his 1890s costume consisting of a black dinner jacket, light shorts, and accompanying bicycle, converses with fellow partygoer Albert N. Cournelt. Below, Mrs. Goetschins, Bob Malone, Mr. Moriss, and Larry White enjoy the festivities.

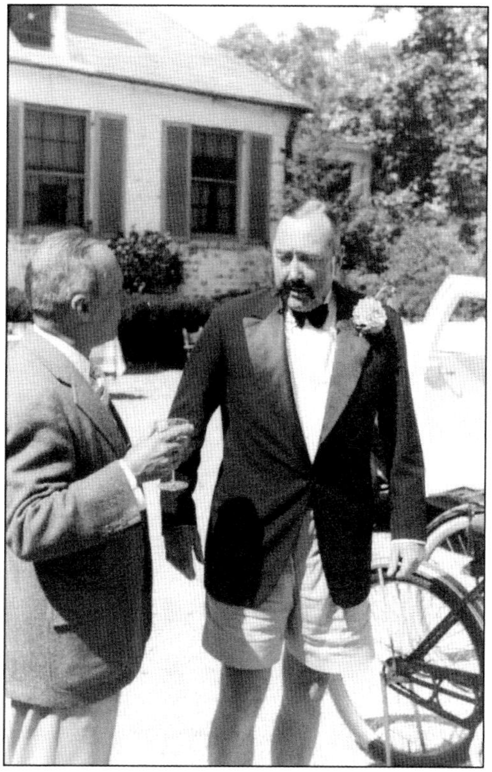

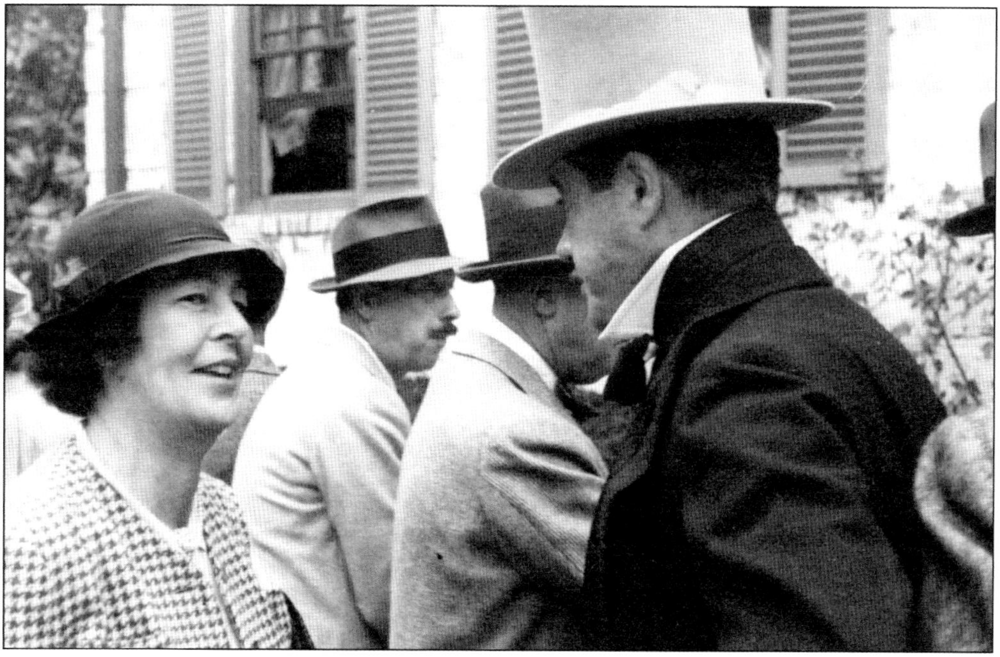

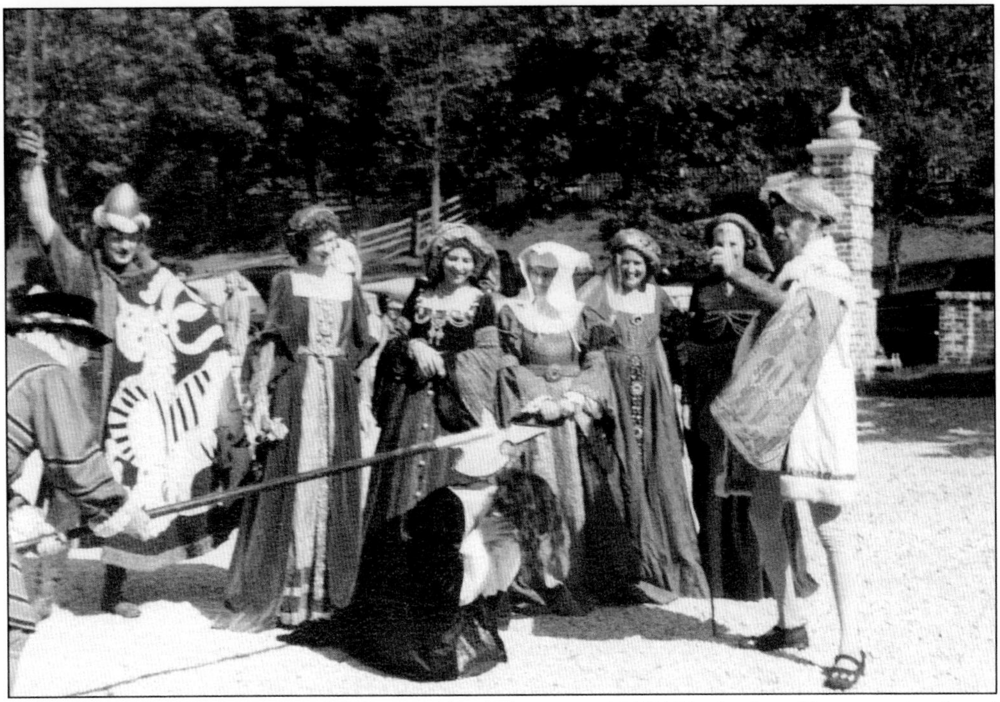

Alden Blodgett as Henry VIII with His Wives, c. 1937. The Jopling House again played host to historical carousing as Alden Blodgett donned a costume of Henry VIII and engaged in a lively reenactment of the life and times of the oft-married monarch. Here Blodgett as Henry prepares to relieve one of his wives of her head.

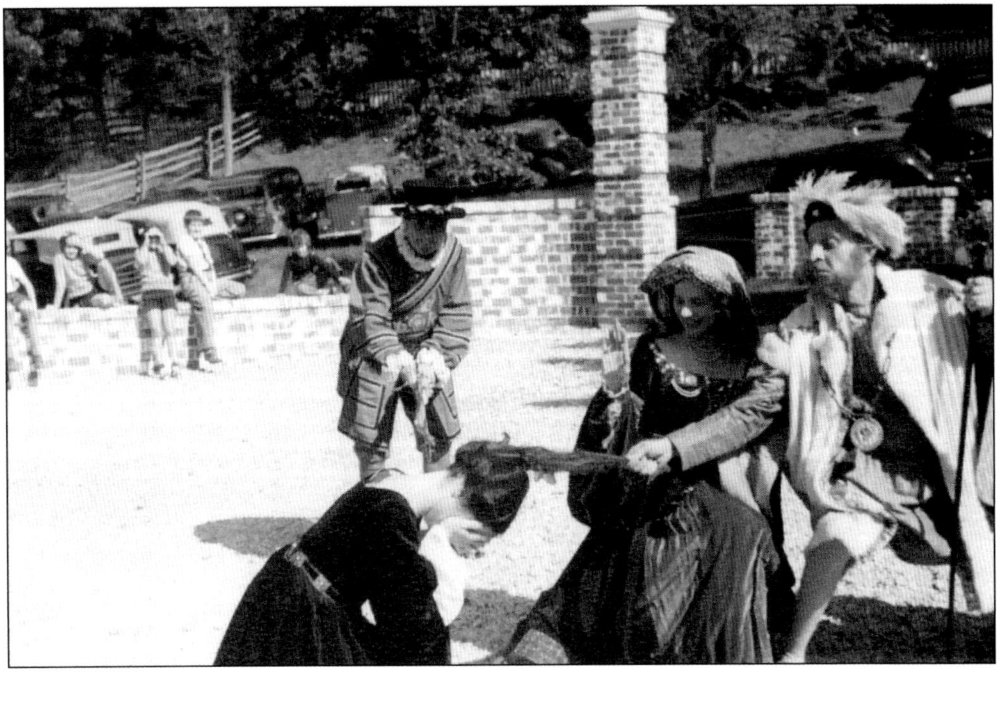

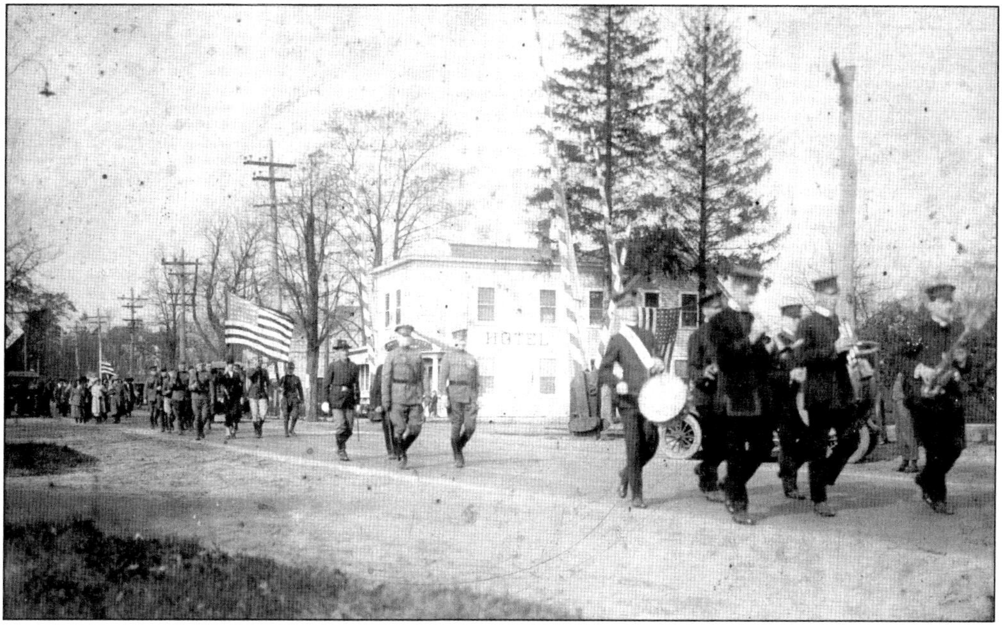

Patriotic Parade on Main Street, c. 1917. Although initially pledged to a doctrine of isolationism at the outset of World War I, by 1917, the United States could no longer avoid entering the fray. Residents of the town of Smithtown did their part to support the war effort by enrolling in the draft and joining the American fighting force. Parades such as this one helped garner support for the troops and keep morale on the homefront at as high a level as possible.

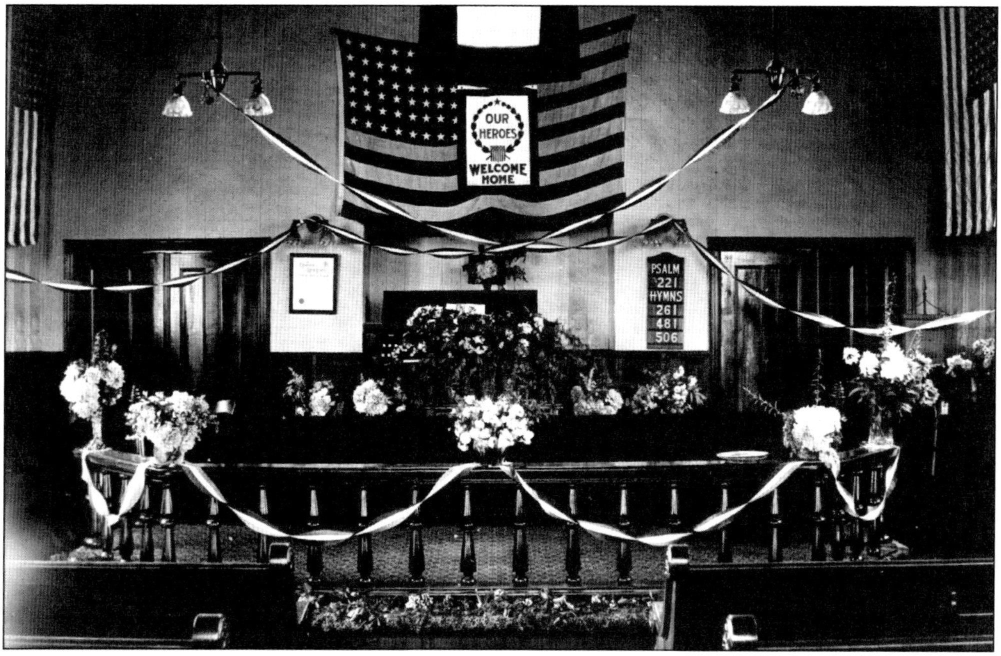

Kings Park Methodist Church, c. 1918. Smithtown offered its fair share of doughboys to the effort. In all, nearly 300 Smithtown men enlisted during World War I. Upon the war's end in 1918, the Kings Park Methodist Church unveiled this elaborate display as a way to welcome back the returning soldiers.

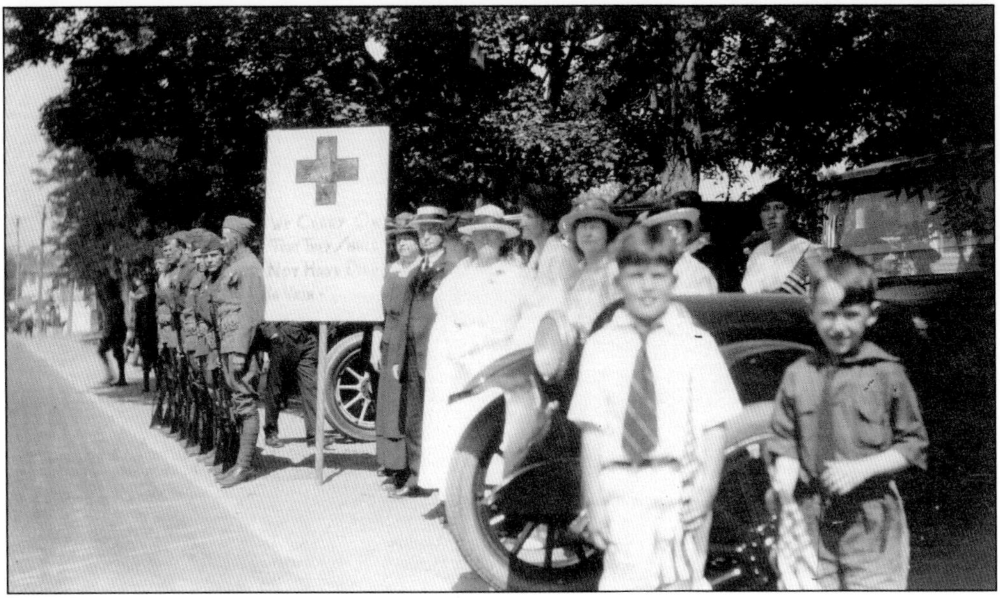

RED CROSS DEDICATION DAY PARADE, C. 1918 During World War I, Dedication Day (now called Memorial Day) took on added significance. Here the Red Cross has organized a parade to honor and remember those who fought for a larger cause during World War I. Founded in June 1917, the Smithtown chapter of the Red Cross did its part to aid the war effort. The organization raised over $24,000, created thousands of hospital and refugee garments, assembled nearly 100,000 surgical kits, and sponsored several successful clothing drives. Above, residents of the town turn out to view the parade and offer their support for United States troops. Below, soldiers line up along the procession's route to honor their fallen comrades.

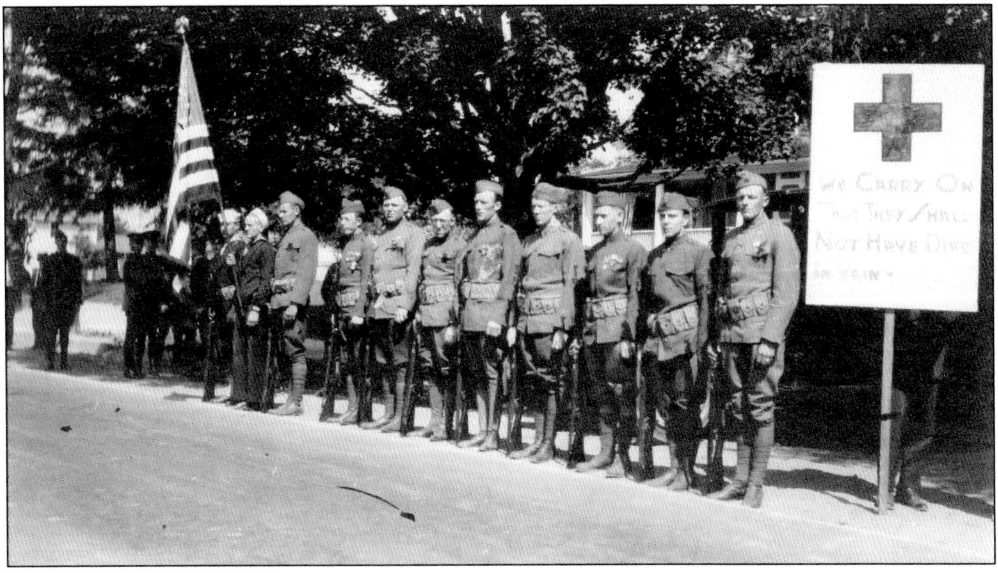

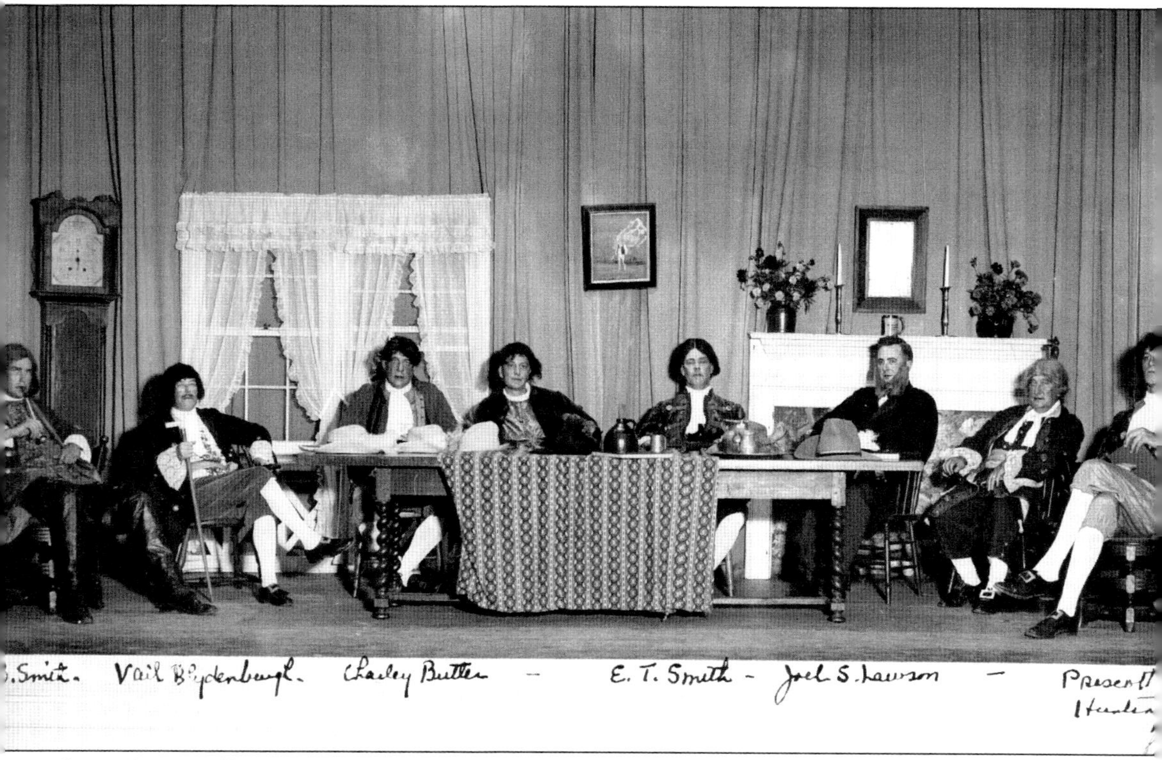

LONG ISLAND TERCENTENARY EVENT, C. 1936. The year 1936 marked the 300th anniversary of the first white settlement on Long Island, an occasion that inspired a wide variety of celebrations throughout the island. Among the highlights of Smithtown's weeklong festivities were artifact exhibits, a Colonial costume dance, and a parade through town led by Gov. Herbert Lehman. Seen here is the cast of the second act of *Smithtown*. According to the play's souvenir program, "Nine public officials of the Town of Smithtown from various periods in its history are discovered seated about a long table. They are convened for a town meeting." Pictured from left to right are Richard Bull Smith (as Richard Smith of 1736), Vail Blydenburgh (as Richard Blydenburgh of 1836), Lawrence Smith Butler (*not* Charley Butler, as identified, but portraying Daniel Smith of 1774–1776), an unidentified participant, Edmund Thomas Smith (as Edmund Smith of 1747), Joel Smith Lawson (as Joel Smith of 1864), an unidentified participant, and Prescott Huntington (as Jonathan Smith of 1727).

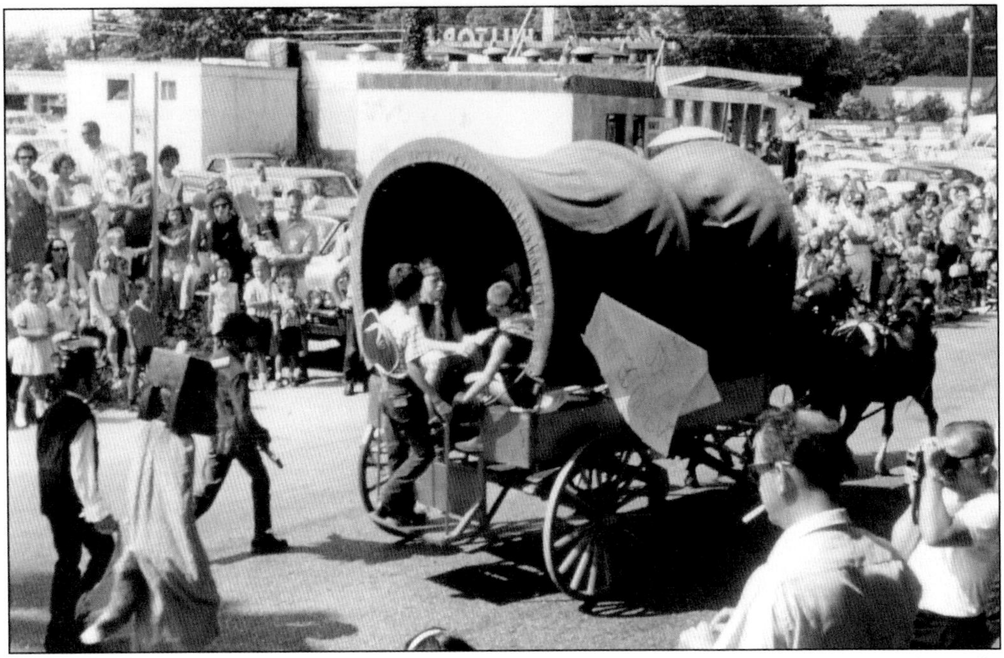

SMITHTOWN TERCENTENARY EVENTS, 1965. In March 1965, residents of Smithtown kicked off a grand celebration to commemorate the 300th anniversary of the town's founding. The festivities featured a full slate of activities for Smithtown's citizenry to get swept up in tercentennial fever. A group of men heralding themselves as the Brothers of the Brush pledged to uphold their civic duty to grow beards, sideburns, or goatees during the entirety of the celebration year. Among the other highlights of the year were pageants, concerts, and special celebration days. Below, revelers, possibly cast members of *Smithtown–the Living Legend* pageant, engage in a historic dance.

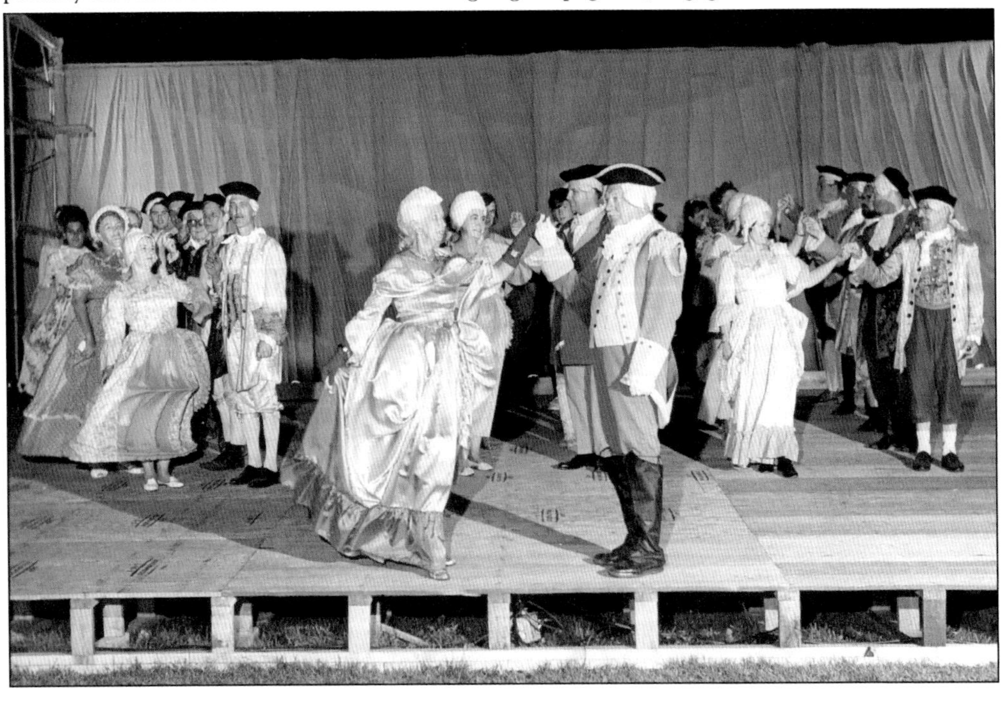

Seven

The Suburban Present

By the dawn of the 1950s, Smithtown had begun the process of suburbanization. Increased accessibility and transportation, the arrival of the automobile and improved roads, and the general westward push of development on Long Island had slowly worked to convert this placid, rural outpost into a burgeoning community. Between 1900 and 1950, the population of Smithtown increased nearly tenfold. The post–World War II housing demand coupled with a general backlash against life in an urban setting and the rise of the real estate development business had conspired by the 1970s to push Smithtown into a fully realized suburb. By 1970, Smithtown was home to nearly 115,000 residents, and with the increased population came the demand for modern conveniences such as supermarkets, bank branches, and shopping centers. By the end of the 1970s, much of Smithtown's pastoral beginnings were relegated to the realms of history and recollection.

That any of the vestiges of Smithtown's past remain to this day is really to the credit of the town's populace. The residents of Smithtown have always been a people concerned with their history. Beginning even in the 1920s, town officials had to overcome immense opposition to improving roadways because some of the town's residents feared the effect that automobiles would have on the town's sleepy demeanor. By the 1950s, concerned citizens had banded together to create organizations such as the Smithtown Historical Society and the Smithtown Branch Preservation Association, institutions charged with the responsibility of ensuring that modernity would not completely eclipse the past. Since the middle of the 20th century, other organizations such as the Deepwells Historical Society, the Kings Park Heritage Museum, and the town's historical advisory board have been formed to help do their part to keep the past present in Smithtown. To this day, when issues pertaining to the saving of a piece of the town's history find their way to the town's docket, one can expect to find the local papers' editorial pages filled with the letters and arguments of passionate Smithtown residents. The result is a town characterized as much by its monuments to modernity as it is by the highlights of heritage dotting the landscape.

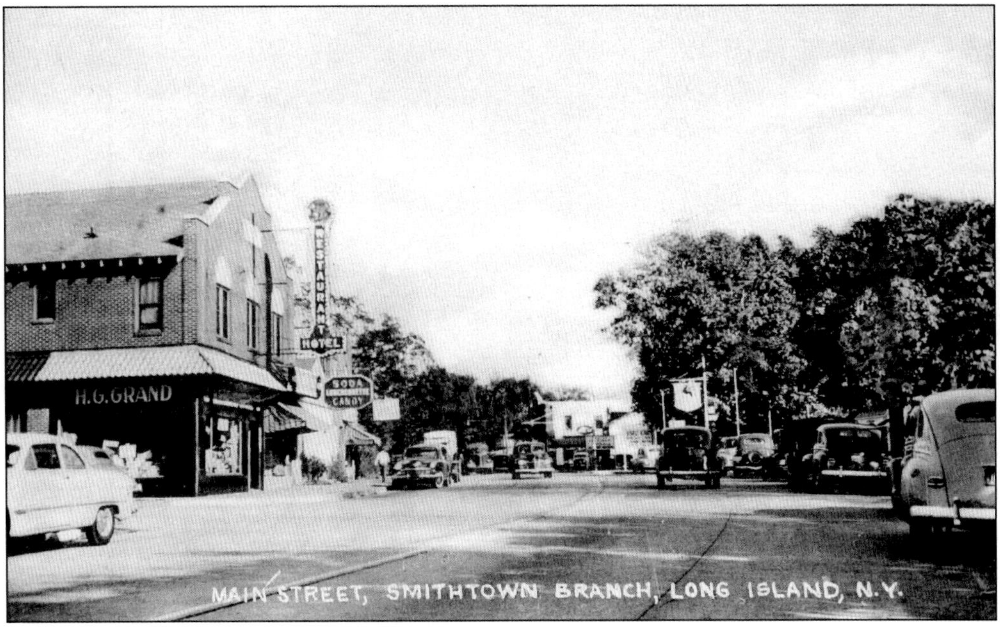

MAIN STREET IN SMITHTOWN BRANCH. By the end of World War II, hints of Smithtown's suburban future began to appear. Above, Main Street plays host to a few businesses and more than a few cars. Below, the trees once present on the south side of the street have made way for an automobile dealership, among other businesses. These photographs of Main Street were taken looking to the east from Karl Avenue. The area is known more today for its typical traffic jams and congestion than for any landscape details.

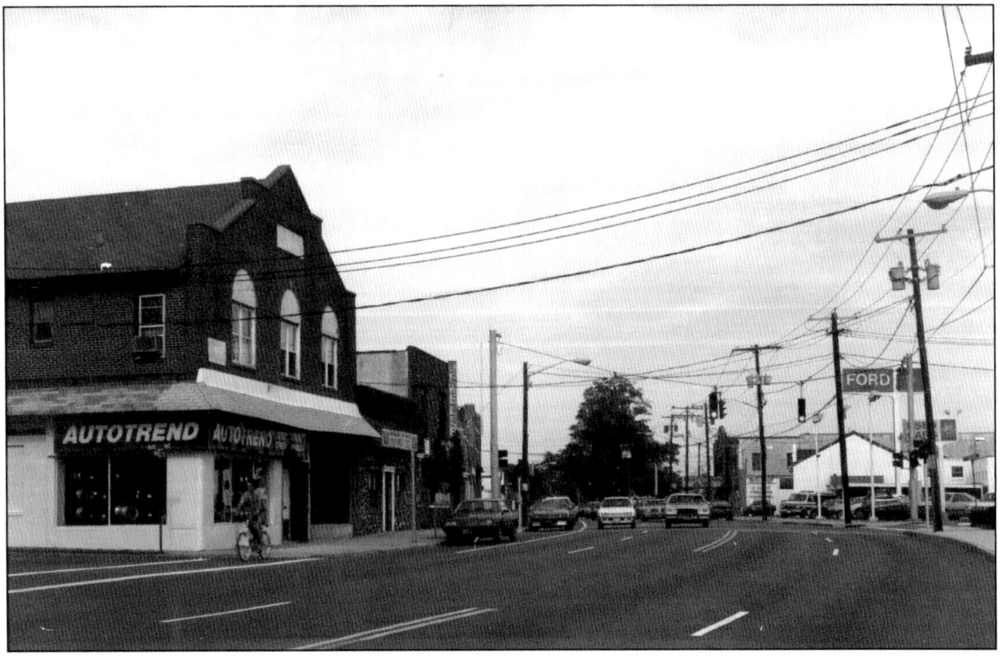

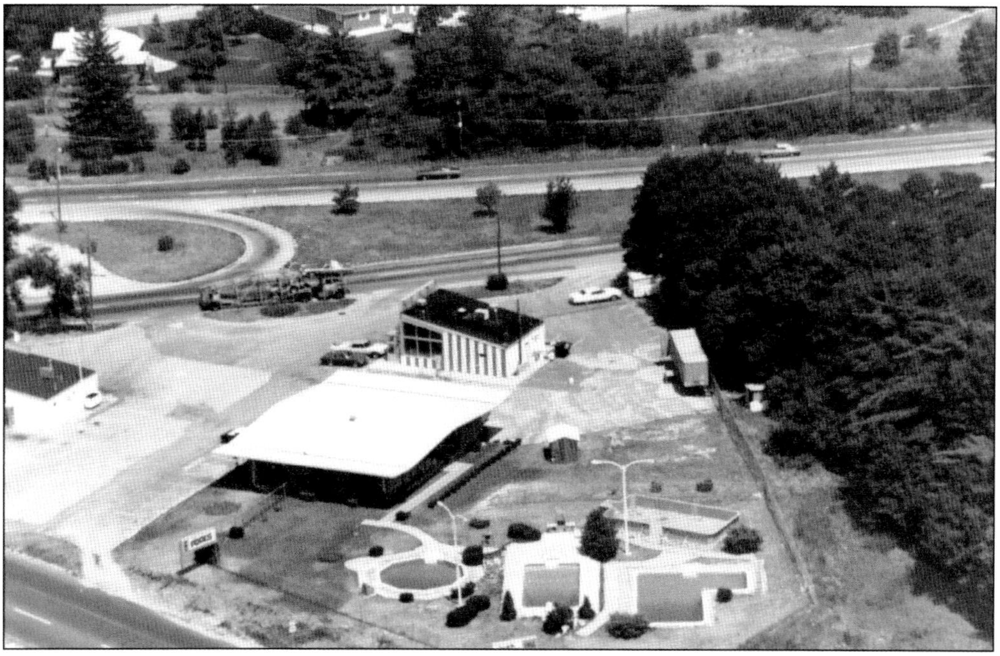

AERIAL VIEW OF HAUPPAUGE, C. 1976. Taken just south of where the sprawling Joshua Smith home site once stood at the intersection of what is now Veterans Highway and Route 347, the area's once-characteristic fields have been largely replaced by housing developments, shopping centers, and other businesses such as the pool supply company and Carvel ice-cream shop seen here.

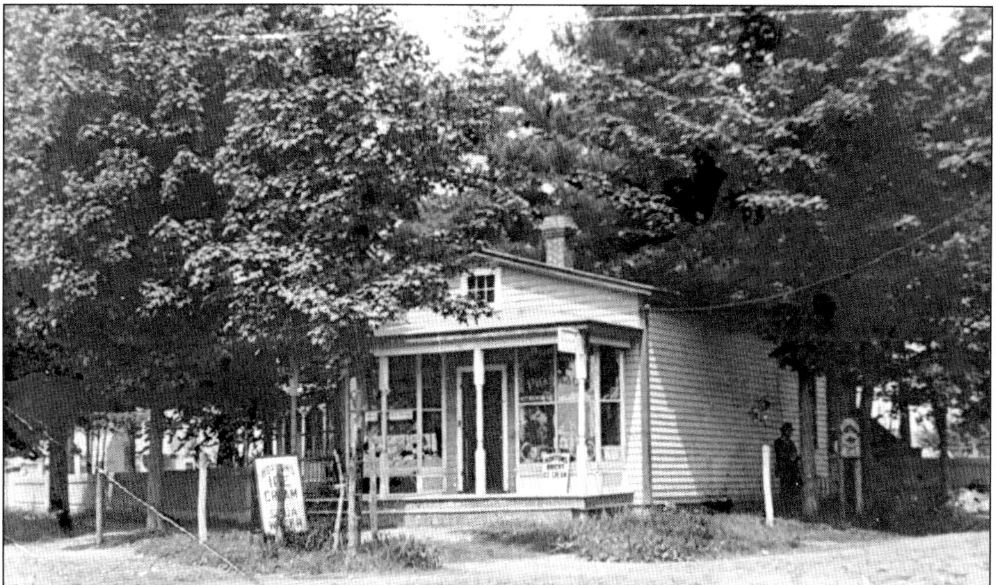

LANDING PHARMACY, C. 1965. This photograph of Landing Pharmacy, located in the heart of Smithtown's business district on the northwest corner of Main Street and Landing Avenue, was taken in 1965. The building's surroundings evoke the area's rural past and offer little hint of the impending development. By the mid-1970s, the open setting surrounding this corner had given way to a cluster of small businesses. (Lee Corbani.)

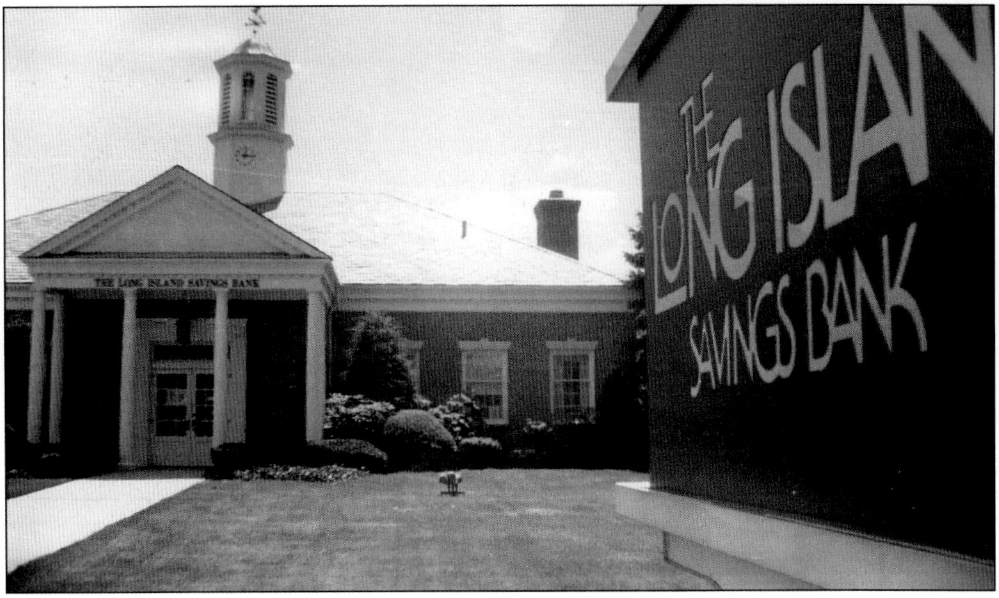

The Long Island Savings Bank, c. 1979. As the population in once-remote areas such as Smithtown began to grow, businesses including supermarkets and banks began to realize the immense lucrative potential of branching out. The Long Island Savings Bank, formerly the Long Island City Savings Bank, first started looking eastward in the 1960s. By the end of the 1970s, the bank's growth had reached Suffolk County, with new branches being opened in West Islip and Hauppauge (seen here).

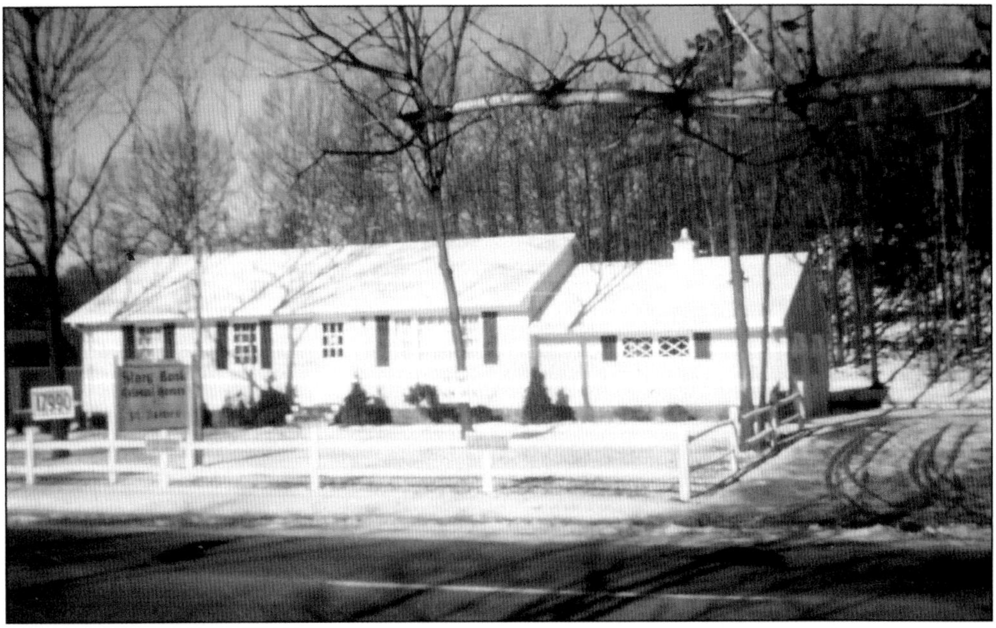

A Story Book Home, c. 1965. Much like the rest of the town of Smithtown, Nesconset's rapid population explosion is partially due to the rise of the real estate development business and the subsequent increase in affordable homes. By the end of the 1960s, Nesconset's population had risen from 3,070 residents to 10,048. Here the Nesconset-based developer Story Book Homes displays a model home at the apparent price of $17,990.

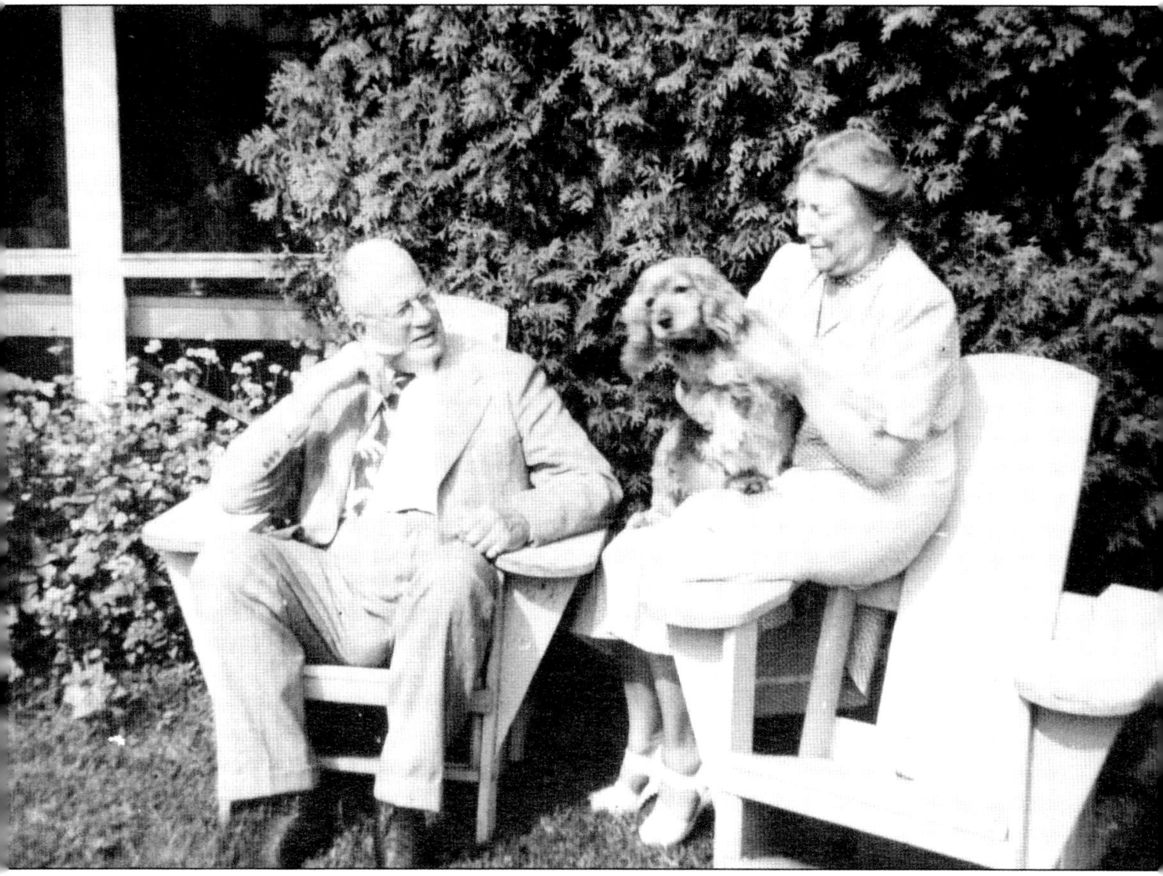

PROGRESS AND PRESERVATION, C. 1953. Both Charles Stewart Butler (left) and Anna Blydenburg (right) had an important impact on the development of Smithtown. During his tenure as town supervisor from 1924 through 1925, Butler implemented sweeping changes, including the paving of the roads, the installation of traffic lights at key intersections, and the acquisition of motorized machinery for the town's highway department. While many of these changes were not popular at the time, the improvement of the area's infrastructure spurred the town's development. Blydenburg, on the other hand, was instrumental in the town's push for preservation. A founding member of the Smithtown Historical Society, Blydenburgh's financing of the relocation of the Caleb Smith II House provided a home and headquarters for the fledgling society while saving the 18th-century structure from demolition. Butler did, however, leave his mark on the town's heritage. His collection of scrapbooks remains a valuable research tool for those interested in Smithtown's past. The books, dating from the 1880s to the 1940s, are now in the collection of the Smithtown Historical Society.

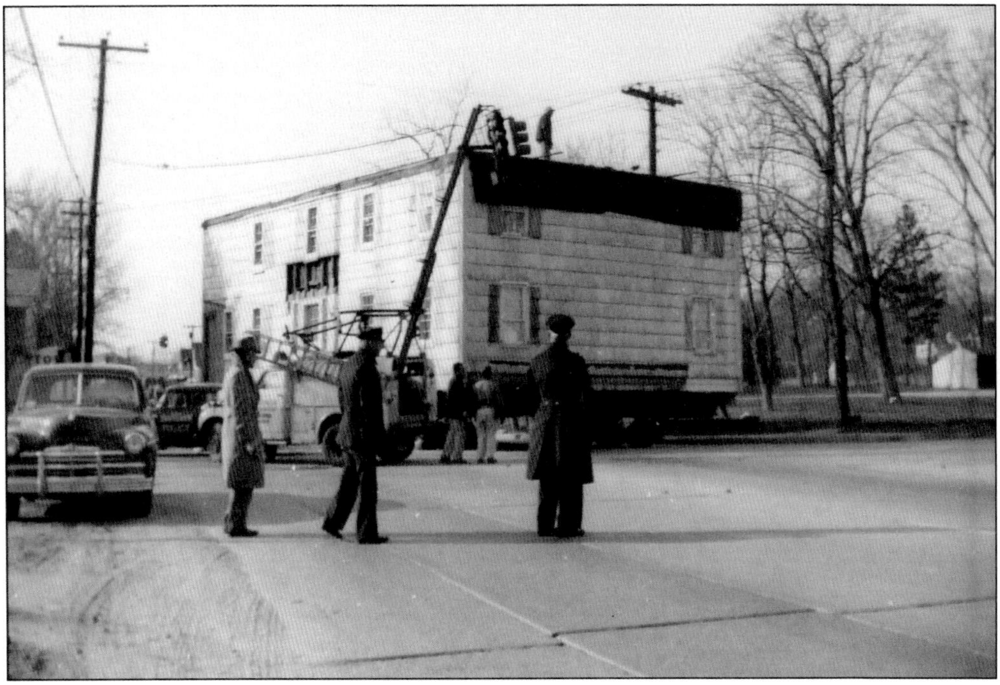

Caleb Smith II House, c. 1955. Saving the Caleb Smith II House from the effects of real estate development was no easy task. After clearing the initial hurdles of finding a new location for the structure and financing for the move, all that was left was the monumental task of physically relocating the house. Anna Blydenburg, the move's chief financier, enlisted the services of David Brothers House Movers and contractor Richard Brush. In order to reduce both the height and considerable weight of the house, the chimneys and roof were removed and shipped via truck to the new location. The movers began the four-hour journey under police escort at 8:00 a.m. on November 22, 1955. Above, the Long Island Lighting Company helped facilitate the move by using "ladder poles, ropes, and very efficient men" to lift obstructive wiring and allow the massive structure to pass unimpeded. Below, the Caleb Smith II House nears its final location on the village green adjacent to the Smithtown Public Library.

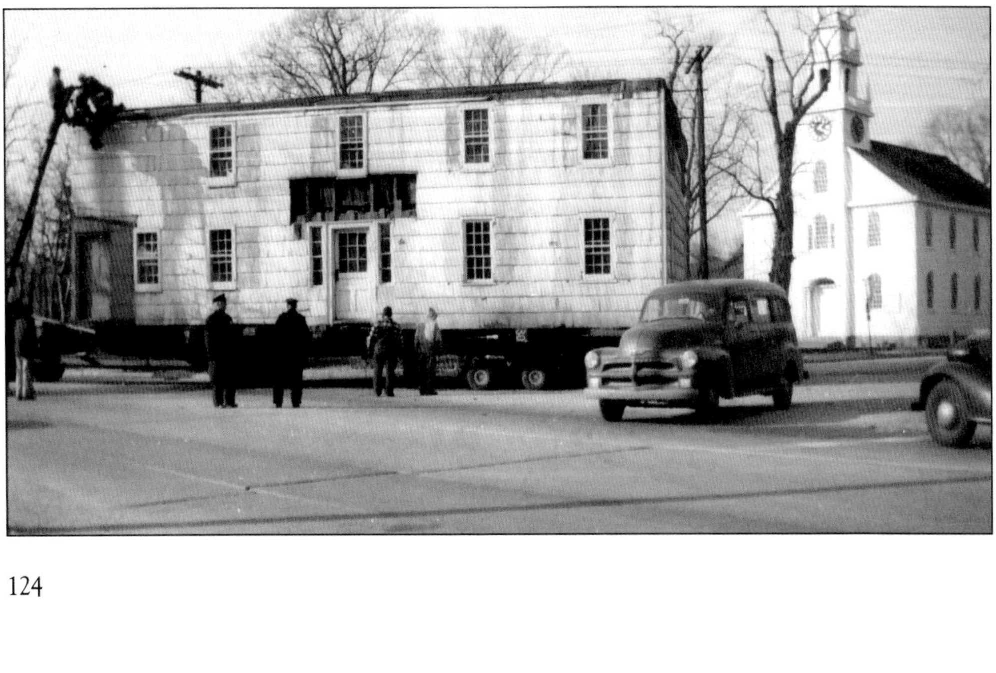

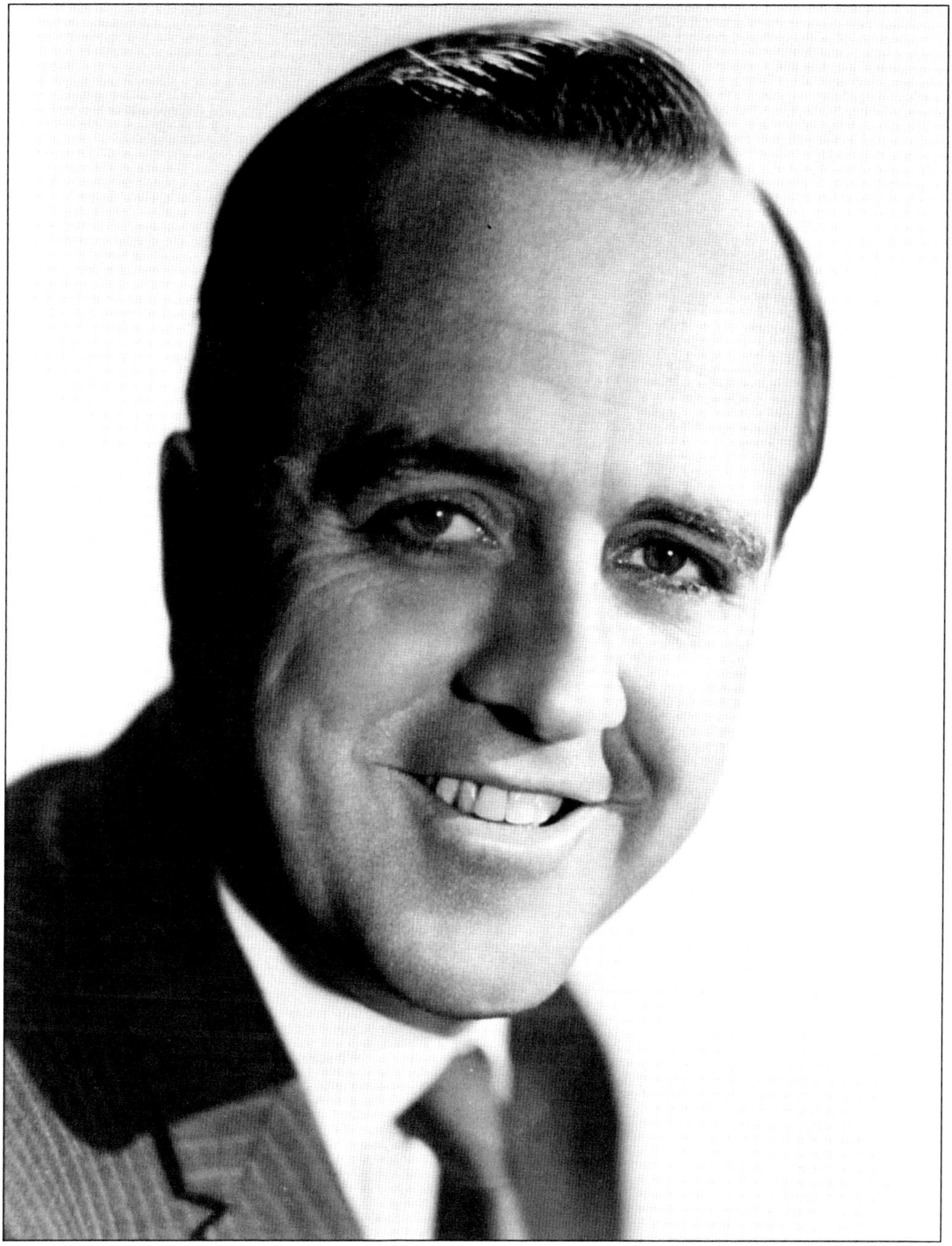

JOHN V. N. KLEIN, C. 1965. John V. N. Klein rose through the ranks of local Republican Party politics to become Smithtown town supervisor in 1964, a position he held until 1969. Under Klein's leadership in the 1960s, the Hauppauge Industrial Park became an important local economic engine, creating hundreds of jobs and enormous revenues. Shortly after becoming Suffolk County executive in 1972, Klein put farmland preservation near the top of his agenda and developed a groundbreaking strategy to maintain family farms. "I grew up in Smithtown," he later told a reporter. "I had seen prime farmland disappear."

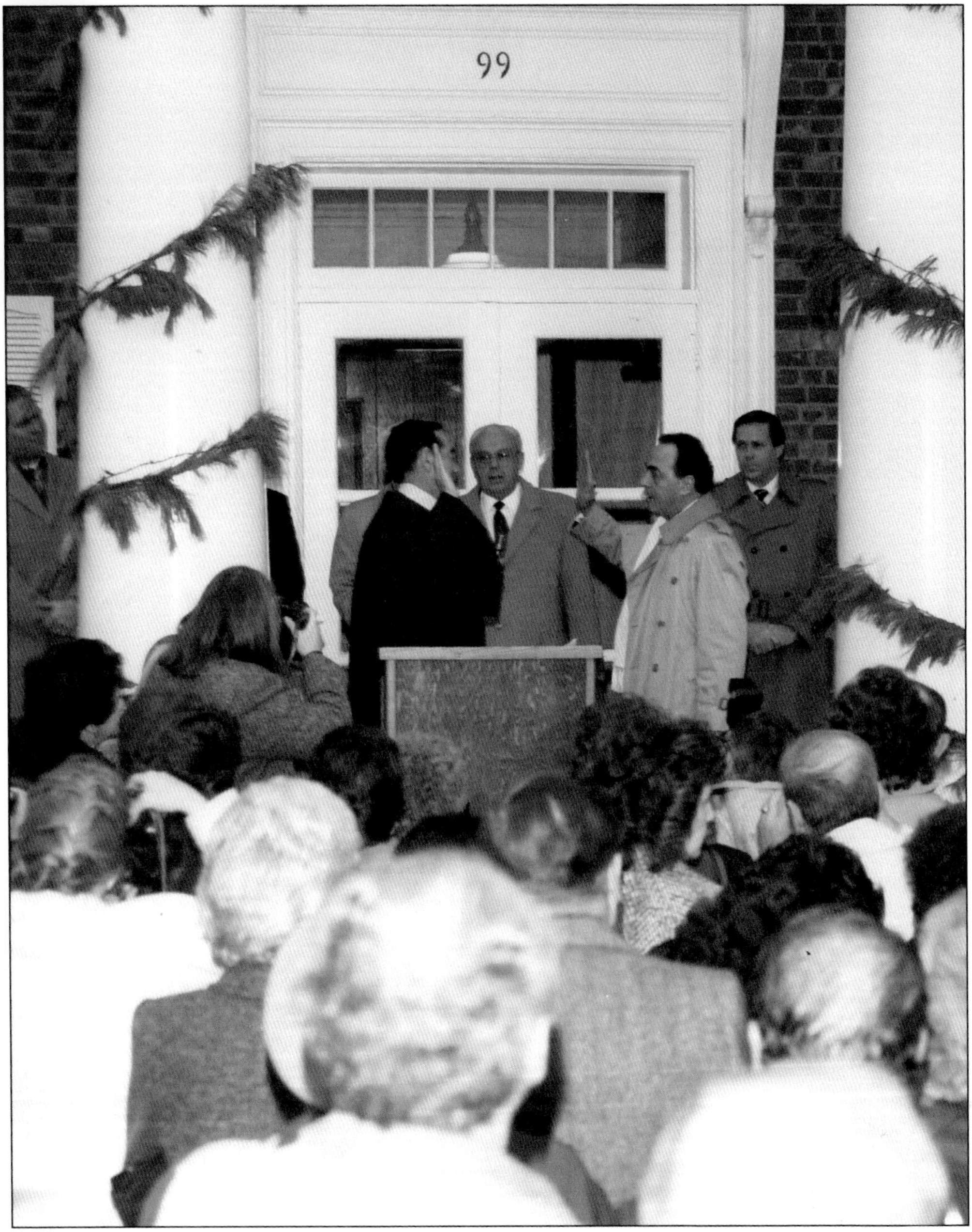

SWEARING-IN CEREMONY, C. 1988. First elected in 1978, Patrick Vecchio has been the supervisor of the Town of Smithtown for the past 30 years (as of the writing of this book). Vecchio's tenure has wrought a mixture of both preservation and progress to the town. During his time in office, Vecchio created and encouraged the town's historical advisory board to deal with issues pertaining to the town's array of historic buildings. His tenure as supervisor has also been marked by such progressive initiatives as purchasing vehicles that are fueled by alternative energy sources for the town. Here Vecchio is sworn into office to begin another term as supervisor on January 3, 1988. The gentleman at far right facing the camera is former town councilman and coauthor of this book Brad Harris. (Town of Smithtown.)

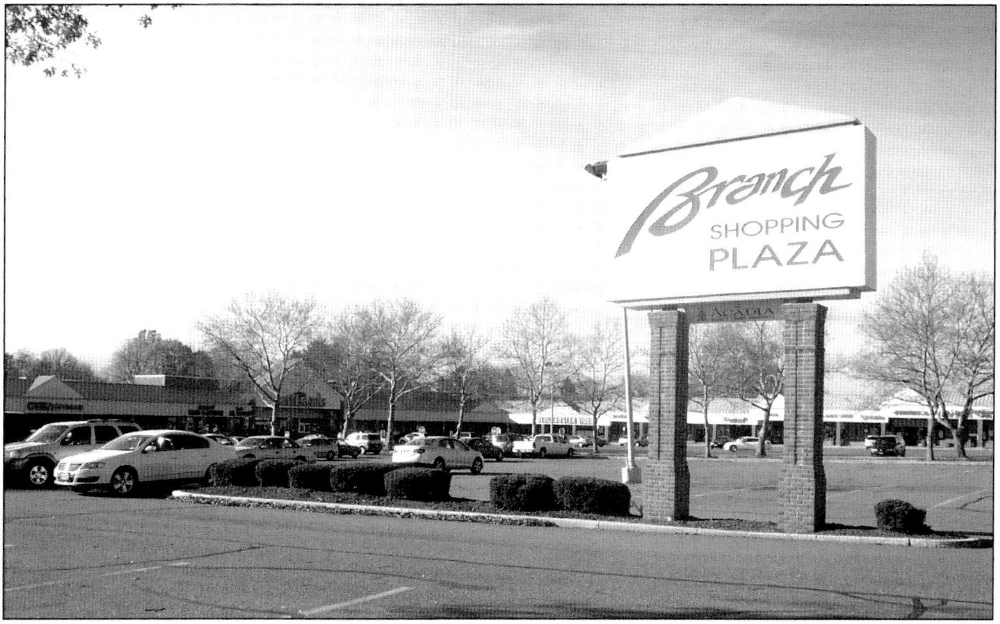

BRANCH SHOPPING PLAZA, 2008. Having evolved far from its rural roots, the Smithtown of the 21st century is a fully realized suburb, complete with a wide array of modern conveniences, including supermarkets, fast-food eateries, and a number of shopping centers. Built during the 1960s, the Branch Shopping Plaza, seen here, resides on what were once the open fields of the sprawling Miller estate just west of the intersection of Routes 25 and 111 in Smithtown.

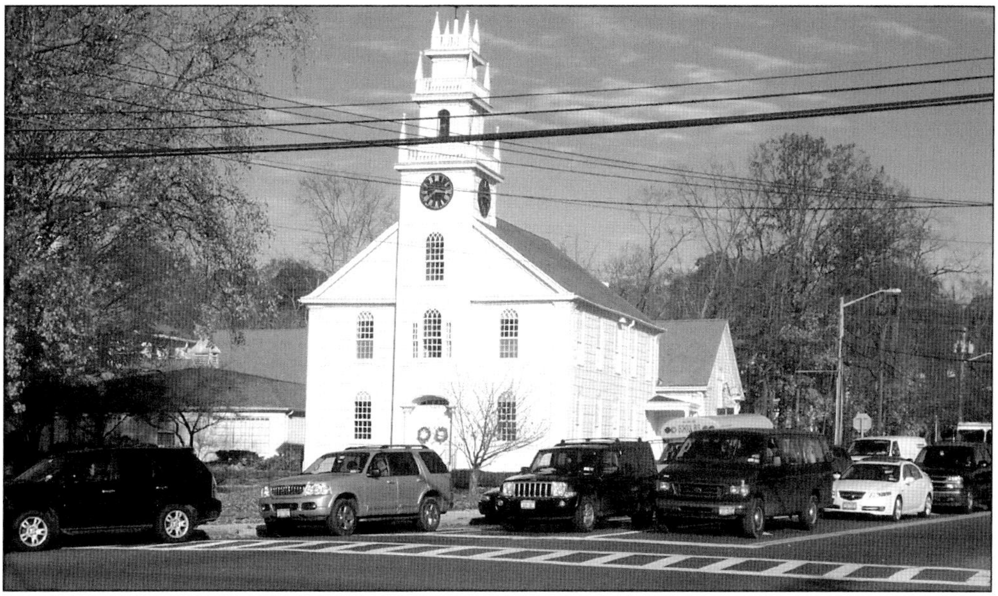

ROUTE 25 AND NORTH COUNTRY ROAD, 2008. Although suburban, Smithtown is strongly in touch with its history and heritage. The result is a singular community with an interestingly blended character of past meets present. Traffic begins to pile up during the morning rush hour at Route 25 and North Country Road (Route 25A), one of Smithtown's busiest intersections. Quietly towering over this mass of modernity is the historic First Presbyterian Church of Smithtown, built in 1827.